HERMENEUTICS AND TRADITION IN THE *Saṃdhinirmocana-sūtra*

BUDDHIST TRADITION SERIES

Edited by

ALEX WAYMAN

VOLUME 53

HERMENEUTICS AND TRADITION
IN THE
Saṃdhinirmocana-sūtra

JOHN POWERS

MOTILAL BANARSIDASS PUBLISHERS
PRIVATE LIMITED • DELHI

First Indian Edition: Delhi, 2004

ISBN: 81-208-1926-8

Also available at:

MOTILAL BANARSIDASS

41 U.A. Bungalow Road, Jawahar Nagar, Delhi 110 007
8 Mahalaxmi Chamber, 22 Bhulabhai Desai Road, Mumbai 400 026
236, 9th Main III Block, Jayanagar, Bangalore 560 011
120 Royapettah High Road, Mylapore, Chennai 600 004
Sanas Plaza, 1302 Baji Rao Road, Pune 411 002
8 Camac Street, Kolkata 700 017
Ashok Rajpath, Patna 800 004
Chowk, Varanasi 221 001

Printed in India
BY JAINENDRA PRAKASH JAIN AT SHRI JAINENDRA PRESS,
A-45 NARAINA, PHASE-I, NEW DELHI 110 028
AND PUBLISHED BY NARENDRA PRAKASH JAIN FOR
MOTILAL BANARSIDASS PUBLISHERS PRIVATE LIMITED,
BUNGALOW ROAD, DELHI 110 007

To Jeffrey Hopkins

My advisor and mentor.

CONTENTS

FOREWORD

This is a wonderful book for presenting different, probably complete possibilities for understanding the hermeneutics in the *Saṃdhinirmocana* scripture. And we need not agree with certain ones of his conclusions to appreciate these excellent and clear presentations of the Buddhist positions. So I sincerely recommend the inclusion of this book in the Buddhist Tradition Series.

ALEX WAYMAN

PREFACE

This book is the result of a process of study and reflection that began with a desire to translate the *Saṃdhinirmocana-sūtra* and eventually precipitated a number of related projects. During the years I have spent thinking about the ramifications of this seminal work, I have become increasingly interested in the social and political dimensions of Buddhist texts, and these considerations are reflected in the present volume. Every text exists within a particular socio-political context, and many authors are specifically concerned with influencing their communities, altering power relations in their favor, and advancing the cause of their particular reference group(s). It is my belief that the *Saṃdhinirmocana-sūtra*, like many other Buddhist texts, is not simply the result of the mystical experiences of an enlightened sage, but is a conscious attempt to influence power relations in the Buddhist communities which studied and debated its teachings.

The focus of this study is the hermeneutical thought of the sūtra, considered in light of the socio-political milieu in which it was written. Of particular interest is the philosophical worldview of Indian Mahāyāna Buddhism, the assumptions of which underlie every part of this text. Without understanding where the *Saṃdhinirmocana* stands in relation to this context, many of the ideas of this text could be opaque to a modern reader. The present study is an attempt to outline important aspects of the context in which the sūtra was composed in order to highlight some of the possible reasons behind its composition.

Since this is the result of years of critical reflection, I feel indebted to a number of people whose insights shaped my own thinking and forced me to reexamine initial assumptions about the text and sharpen my own focus and ideas. The most important of these influences is my graduate advisor, Dr. Jeffrey Hopkins, whose critical insights forced me to defend every contention I made about the sūtra. Although many of the ideas of the present volume differ from those of Dr. Hopkins, his penetrating criticisms were crucial in the process of finding my own approach and voice.

Thanks are also due to Geshe Yeshe Thabkhe of the Central Institute of Higher Tibetan Studies in Sarnath for his help in exploring the mysteries of the *Saṃdhinirmocana* and the commentaries of Asaṅga and Jñānagarbha. Geshe Palden Dragpa of Tibet House spent many long hours reading the commentary of Wonch'uk and helping me work through Tsong kha pa's *Essence of the Good Explanations* (*Legs bshad snying po*). Khamtrul Rinpoche generously made time to explain the philosophy of the sūtra in light of the meditation theory of the Rnying ma school, and Geshe Jampel Thando patiently answered innumerable questions on terminology and grammar. The late Kensur Yeshe Thubten introduced me to many subtle points of controversy that have arisen from this text, and I am particularly grateful to H.H. the Dalai Lama for taking time from his busy schedule to answer my questions on problems of scriptural interpretation raised by the *Saṃdhinirmocana*.

In addition to these Tibetan scholars, several Western scholars have been of great help in this project. In particular, Dr. Christian Lindtner read a draft version of my translation of the sūtra and made a number of helpful suggestions. Dr. Ernst Steinkellner generously shared his vast expertise in Buddhist studies, particularly in regard to the commentarial tradition on the sūtra, and Dr. Helmut Eimer helped to clarify the relations between the various recensions of the text. Finally, a special thanks to my wife Cindy, whose help in discussing philosophical problems and insights has been invaluable. More importantly, without her constant encouragement and understanding this work might never have been completed.

Grinnell College
Grinnell, Iowa, December, 1992

ABBREVIATIONS

BCLS	*Bulletin de la Classe des Lettres et des Sciences Morales et Politiques, Académie Royale de Belgique.*
BEFEO	*Bulletin de l'École Française d'Extrème-Orient.*
Bhāṣya	Asaṅga's *Ārya-saṃdhinirmocana-bhāṣya.* Tohoku #3981.
BSOAS	*Bulletin of the School of Oriental and African Studies.*
D	Sde dge edition of the *Saṃdhinirmocana-sūtra*, vol. *mdo sde ca.*
EB	*The Eastern Buddhist.*
HJAS	*Harvard Journal of Asiatic Studies.*
IBK	*Indogaku Bukkyō-gaku Kenkyū.*
IHQ	*Indian Historical Quarterly.*
JA	*Journal Asiatique.*
JAAR	*Journal of the American Academy of Religion.*
JAOS	*Journal of the American Oriental Society.*
JIABS	*Journal of the International Association of Buddhist Studies.*
JIP	*Journal of Indian Philosophy.*
JRAS	*Journal of the Royal Asiatic Society.*
KDBK	*Komazawa Daigaku Bukkyō-gakubu Kenkyūkiyō.*
KDBR	*Komazawa Daigaku Bukkyō-gaku Ronshū.*
Lamotte	Étienne Lamotte. *Saṃdhinirmocana-sūtra: L'explication des Mystères* (Louvain and Paris, 1935).
LC	Library of Congress.
MCB	*Mélanges Chinoises et Bouddhiques.*
P	Peking edition of the *Saṃdhinirmocana-sūtra* (#774, vol. 29).
PEW	*Philosophy East and West.*
Stog	Stog Palace edition of the *Saṃdhinirmocana-sūtra*. Leh, Ladakh: Shesrig Dpemzod, 1975-1980, vol. *ja.*
SUNY	State University of New York.
T	Taishō edition of the Buddhist canon.

TBS *Tibetan and Buddhist Studies Commemorating the 200th Anniversary of the Birth of Alexander Csoma de Körös*. Budapest: Akadémai Kiadó.

Wonch'uk Wonch'uk's commentary on the *Saṃdhinirmocana-sūtra*, entitled *Commentary on the Superior Sūtra Explaining the Thought* (*'Phags pa dgongs pa nges par 'grel pa'i mdo'i rgya cher 'grel pa*, *Ārya-saṃdhinirmocana-sūtra-ṭīkā*. Tohoku 4016, #5517, vol. 106.

WZKSOA *Wiener Zeitschrift für die Kunde Süd- und Ostasiens*.

CHAPTER ONE

INTRODUCTION

The *Sūtra Explaining the Thought* (*Saṃdhinirmocana-sūtra*) is a seminal work of Mahāyāna Buddhism and is one of the main scriptural sources for the Yogic Practice (Yogācāra school) of Indian Buddhism.[1] The Yogācāra school is one of the two main philosophical schools of Indian Mahāyāna Buddhism (the other being Madhyamaka), and the *Sūtra Explaining the Thought* figures prominently in the philosophical analyses both of people associated with Yogācāra and people associated with other schools and movements. The sūtra's discussions of hermeneutics, meditation, soteriology, and epistemology have been influential throughout Mahāyāna Buddhist literature and are cited and discussed in treatises from India, Tibet, Mongolia, China, and Japan. However, although it holds an important place in Mahāyāna Buddhist literature, it has received surprisingly little attention from Western scholars. Étienne Lamotte's 1935 French translation has been the only extensive study of the sūtra in any Western language, and my forthcoming translation will be the first in English.[2]

The present study is mainly devoted to an examination of the sūtra's discussion of Buddhist hermeneutics, which has had a major

---

1 See A.K. Warder, *Indian Buddhism* (Delhi: Motilal Banarsidass, 1970), pp. 430-31. When I refer to "the Yogācāra school" or "the Yogācāras" in this study, I primarily refer to Asaṅga and Vasubandhu and their commentators Sthiramati and Sumatiśīla.

2 See Étienne Lamotte, *Saṃdhinirmocana-sūtra, L'explication des Mystères* (Louvain and Paris: Université de Louvain & Adrien Maisonneuve, 1935). My translation, along with a critical edition of the Tibetan texts, has been accepted for publication by Dharma Publishing, Berkeley, CA.

The bibliography for the present study lists all of the articles on the *Saṃdhinirmocana-sūtra* that I have been able to locate. For a more complete listing of works on Yogācāra, see John Powers, *The Yogācāra School of Buddhism: A Bibliography* (Metuchen, NJ: Scarecrow Press, 1991).

influence in every country to which Mahāyāna Buddhism traveled. The goal will be not simply to report what the sūtra says, however, but rather to analyze the reasons behind what it says, what it implies but does not explicitly state, and how the sūtra's theories influenced subsequent Buddhist thought. One of the conclusions of the study is that the concern of the author(s) of the sūtra was not simply to create new exegetical models and innovative vocabulary and that an underlying aim (and result) of the thought of the sūtra was to alter power relations within the Buddhist community. As we will see, the sūtra presents a hierarchical model in terms of which Buddhist exegetes are to interpret Buddha's intention, and this model gives people following the *Saṃdhinirmocana* a measure of control over the interpretation of texts that were normative for groups whose ideas conflicted with the sūtra and the Yogācāra tradition. By creating a hierarchical exegetical schema, the *Saṃdhinirmocana* influenced the subsequent course of debate in Buddhist hermeneutics and forced rival groups to debate (to a greater or lesser degree) on its terms and using its terms.

The sources for this study will be the sūtra itself (in both its Tibetan and Chinese recensions), commentarial literature from India, Tibet, and China that discusses the hermeneutical thought of the sūtra, and contemporary models in terms of which the thought of the sūtra will be framed and analyzed.

The present section will discuss current scholarly opinion on the sūtra and some of the issues that have caught the interest of contemporary scholars. This will be followed by a short description of the commentaries that are used in this study and an overview of the sūtra. The second section will discuss the title of the sūtra. In this section I argue that the title implies a hermeneutical concern and orientation and that this is reflected in the various Tibetan and Chinese translations, as well as in commentarial literature that discusses the range of possible meanings of the words of the title.

The third section is primarily concerned with the concept of the "ultimate" (*don dam pa, paramārtha*) in the sūtra, which has important implications for its presentation of hermeneutics.[3] In this section, I first present the sūtra's discussions of the nature of the ultimate and how these have been interpreted in commentarial literature and then compare the sūtra's analysis with the presentations of some contemporary scholars. A central concern of this section is to demonstrate that the sūtra's discussion of the "ultimate" is noticeably at odds with how it has been understood and explained by several scholars.

The fourth section will discuss the presentation of hermeneutics in the *Saṃdhinirmocana*, focusing on the seventh chapter. This is the central concern of the present study. The analysis of the sūtra's hermeneutical models draws from a wide range of literature and approaches the sūtra from a number of quite different perspectives, which include philological analyses of the Tibetan and Chinese titles of the sūtra and comparison of the sūtra's exegetical models and relevant interpretations of commentaries on the sūtra. I will also examine some of the debates the *Saṃdhinirmocana* inspired among traditional Buddhist thinkers and will analyze the sūtra in terms of cognitive dissonance theory and contemporary hermeneutics. These discussions form the preliminary material for an analysis of the political dimensions of the sūtra's ideas; this speculates on some of the underlying motives and concerns of the author(s) of the text. The fifth section summarizes the concerns, problems, and conclusions of the previous sections.

---

3 In this study I have chosen to indicate technical terms first in Tibetan and then where appropriate to give the probable Sanskrit equivalents. The reason for this procedure is that there is no extant Sanskrit manuscript of the sūtra and my reading of the sūtra is based on eleven Tibetan texts (as well as Hsüan-tsang's Chinese translation). Thus, all Sanskrit terms are speculative to some extent, and it seemed appropriate to first indicate the actual technical terms found in the texts from which I am working and then speculate on what I consider to be the most probable Sanskrit equivalents.

THE SAṂDHINIRMOCANA-SŪTRA AND ITS PLACE IN BUDDHIST LITERATURE

With respect to origin of the text, we have very little reliable information. As Lamotte remarks, it represents an important stage in the development of Mahāyāna doctrine and serves as a transition between the Perfection of Wisdom Sūtras and the Yogācāra school of Asaṅga and Vasubandhu.[4] Since it refers to and discusses doctrines of the Perfection of Wisdom Sūtras, it must have been written sometime after at least the earliest of these, that is to say, after the first or second century A.D.[5] It is quoted in several works by Asaṅga and Vasubandhu, and most of the sūtra (except for the introduction and the colophons that conclude chapters) is quoted in the *Compendium of Ascertainments* (*Viniścaya-saṃgrahaṇī*), which is traditionally attributed to Asaṅga.[6] I agree with Lambert Schmithausen's assessment that the *Saṃdhinirmocana-sūtra* could not have existed in its present form prior to the end of the third century A.D., since it refers to Perfection of Wisdom Sūtras and it is recognized as a sūtra and quoted as such by Asaṅga and Vasubandhu, who probably lived in the fourth or fifth centuries A.D.[7]

---

[4] Lamotte, p. 14.

[5] With respect to the development of early Mahāyāna, see Lewis Lancaster, "The Oldest Mahāyāna Sūtra", *EB* #8.1, 1975, pp. 30-41 and A.K. Warder, *Indian Buddhism*, pp. 373-5.

[6] The *Viniścaya*'s citation of the sūtra is in Peking vol. 111, and ranges from page 83b to 107d. It includes brief comments that preface the citation of each chapter. Lambert Schmithausen argues that the *Viniścaya* is actually a composite work made up of materials from different periods, but he adds that it could have been compiled or at least redacted in its final form by Asaṅga (see his *Ālayavijñāna*; Tokyo: International Institute for Buddhist Studies, 1987). See also Schmithausen's "Spiritual Practice and Philosophical Theory in Buddhism", in *German Scholars on India* (Bombay, 1976), in which he argues that the section which quotes the *Saṃdhinirmocana* is a comparatively later portion of the *Viniścaya*. He contends that the sūtra was probably written prior to the final redaction of the *Viniścaya*.

[7] For discussions of Asaṅga's dates, see: (1) A.K. Warder, *Indian Buddhism*, pp. 435-7; (2) NAKAMURA Hajime, *Indian Buddhism: A Survey With Bibliographical Notes* (Hirakata: Kufs Publications, 1980), p. 264, where he places Asaṅga at 310-390 A.D.; (3) Alex Wayman, *Analysis of the Śrāvakabhūmi Manuscript* (Berkeley, 1961), pp. 19-46; and (4) Sylvain Lévi, *Mahāyāna-sūtrālaṃkāra* (Paris, 1911), pp. 1-7, where he provides a biography of Asaṅga that is drawn from the biographies of Paramārtha, Hsüan-tsang, and Tāranātha.

The dates of his brother Vasubandhu have been the subject of much scholarly speculation. For a short bibliography of these, see John Powers, *Two Commentaries on the Saṃdhinirmocana-sūtra by Asaṅga and Jñānagarbha* (Lewiston and Queenston: The Edwin Mellen Press,

The *Saṃdhinirmocana* was originally written in Sanskrit, but at the present time no Sanskrit manuscripts of the text have been found.[8] It exists in Tibetan and Chinese versions, and Lamotte's study of the *Saṃdhinirmocana* includes a French translation, along with portions of a commentary attributed to Asaṅga.[9] In addition, there are four commentaries on the sūtra in the Tibetan *Translations of Treatises* (*Bstan 'gyur*; these will be discussed below), a treatise that discusses the reasoning processes outlined in the tenth chapter of the sūtra (entitled *Summary of the Sūtra [Explaining the Thought] by Way of Valid Cognition of Correct Words*),[10] and a number of indigenous Tibetan texts that discuss it in the Dge lugs pa school.[11]

The earliest Chinese translation of the sūtra is the one by Guṇabhadra (求那跋陀羅) in 443-45 (T 678), but this translation is only a portion (the ninth and tenth chapters) of the text as it exists today.[12] The first Chinese translation of the sūtra that corresponds

---

1992), pp. 22-23. Other references on this and related subjects may be found in John Powers, *The Yogācāra School of Buddhism: A Bibliography.*

8 See *Buddhist Text Information* #2, pp. 5-7, which provides a bibliography of extant materials on the sūtra, and John Powers, "The Tibetan Translations of the *Saṃdhinirmocana-sūtra* and *Bka' 'gyur* Research" (forthcoming in *Central Asiatic Journal*), which discusses the Tibetan recensions of the sūtra.

9 Lamotte's Tibetan version ranges from pp. 31-166, and his excerpts from Asaṅga's commentary are scattered throughout the text.

10 *Bka' yang dag pa'i tshad ma las mdo'i btus pa*, attributed to Khri srong lde brtsan (Peking #5839; Sde dge #4352).

11 The *Saṃdhinirmocana* is one of the main bases of Tsong kha pa's seminal treatise on Buddhist hermeneutics, *The Essence of the Good Explanations* (*Legs bshad snying po*: Peking vol. 153; translated by Robert Thurman as *The Essence of True Eloquence*; Princeton: Princeton University Press, 1984). This work has spawned a number of sub-commentaries in the Dge lugs pa school, and several examples are listed in the bibliography.

In addition to these, there are five commentaries which are now lost that are listed by Ernst Steinkellner in his article, "Who Is Byaṅ chub rdzu 'phrul?" (*Berliner Indologische Studien*, 1989, pp. 229-252).

12 According to Seng-yu (*Ch'u san tsang chi chi*; T 2145, pp. 55.12, 105), Guṇabhadra translated the last two chapters of the sūtra into Chinese under the title *Hsiang hsü chieh tou ching* in two chapters (*chüan*). These are listed in the Taishō as two separate sūtras, entitled *Hsiang hsü chieh tou ti p'o lo mi liao i ching* (T 678) and *Hsiang hsü chieh tou ju lai so tso sui shun liao i ching* (T 679). Guṇabhadra also translated a work entitled *Ti i i wu hsiang lüeh*, which has been lost. Fragments that survive in the *Fa hua hsüan lun* (T 1720) by Chi-tsang (549-623) indicate that this work may have been a translation of the first four chapters of the sūtra.

to its present form is by Bodhiruci (菩提流支) in 514 (T 675).[13] In addition, there is a translation by Paramārtha (眞諦) in 557 (T 677) that contains an introduction (which does not correspond to the introductions in the extant Tibetan texts) and the first four chapters, and there is a translation of the complete text by Hsüan-tsang (玄奘) in 647 (T 676).[14] There is also an anonymous translation of chapter ten (T 679) later attributed to Guṇaprabha.[15]

While the Tibetan versions in the New Translation style (*skad gsar bcad*) all contain ten chapters and agree on the arrangement of chapters and sections, the Chinese versions differ widely. Bodhiruci's translation is divided into eleven chapters: the preface and the first four dialogues discussing the ultimate comprise one chapter, and the remainder of the book is divided into ten separate chapters. The translations of Hsüan-tsang and Guṇabhadra consist of eight chapters: the preface is treated as a separate chapter, the discussion of the ultimate is another, and the rest of the text is divided into six chapters, which correspond to the divisions in the Tibetan texts.[16]

The fact that three of the early Chinese translations only contain portions of the final version of the *Saṃdhinirmocana* indicates to Lamotte that the text as it exists today is not a unitary work, but instead is a composite of shorter texts brought together by an anonymous redactor. He contends that

> in spite of the efforts of B [Bodhiruci's Chinese translation] and T [a Tibetan translation] to present this work as a unitary and homogeneous work,

---

[13] This is listed in the *Li tai san pao chi* (T 2034. pp. 49.45, 85), a catalogue of Buddhist literature. The text is divided into ten chapters and an introduction. For a biography of Bodhiruci, see the *Hsü kao seng chuan* (T 2060, p. 50.428a).

[14] See Lewis Lancaster, *The Korean Buddhist Canon* (Berkeley: University of California Press, 1979), pp. 67-8.

[15] See Lamotte, *Saṃdhinirmocana-sūtra*, p. 9.

[16] In the Tibetan versions, each chapter is named after the Bodhisattva who acts as the main interlocuter, but in the translations of Hsüan-tsang and Paramārtha each chapter is named for the main theme that it discusses.

> a mere glance eliminates this picture; when we compare these versions, we see a collection of portions having different origins and dates.[17]

This is a plausible hypothesis, and it fits what we know of the sūtra, but it could also be the case that the sūtra was brought to China piecemeal and new portions were translated as they arrived. The Buddhist texts that came to China were brought there haphazardly, mostly carried by pilgrims who visited India and returned with texts that were of interest to an individual pilgrim or that were simply available. The spread of Buddhist literature to China was not an orderly one, and the mere fact that different portions of a text were translated at different times does not necessarily mean that that text is a composite, although it does constitute a piece of evidence in support of that hypothesis.

Because of the haphazard nature of the transmission and translation of Buddhist texts into China, however, it is problematic to use differences among Chinese translations as the primary argument for the theory that the *Sūtra Explaining the Thought* is a text whose present form evolved over time. As Peter N. Gregory notes,

> The hermeneutical problem with which Chinese Buddhists were faced was exacerbated by the fact that Buddhism did not come to China as a complete and coherently wrought system. The transmission of Buddhism to China took place over a period of centuries—centuries in which it continued to grow and change in profound ways. The process of transmission, moreover, occurred in a fragmented and haphazard manner. The order in which texts were translated into Chinese, for instance, bore no relation to the chronology of their composition. Later texts were often made available before the earlier texts upon which they were based, or to which they were a reaction. This meant that teachings were introduced divorced from both their historical and doctrinal context, making it even more difficult for the Chinese to arrive at an accurate understanding of them. Furthermore, the Indian and Central Asian missionaries who served as the vital link in this process of transmission, and to whom, perforce, the Chinese turned for authority, hailed from different Buddhist traditions and were themselves

---

17 Lamotte, p. 17. See also UI Hakuju, *Indo Tetsugakushi* (Tokyo: Iwanami Shoten, 1930; reprint 1965), p. 323, where he contends that the presence of concluding verses at the end of chapters seven through ten indicates that chapters one through seven constituted the original text and that chapters eight through ten were composed later and added to this original text. He contends that the Introduction was added last.

often at odds with one another in their interpretation of the various teachings which the Chinese were struggling to comprehend.[18]

Given this situation, it is not possible to use the differences between Chinese recensions of the *Saṃdhinirmocana* as a conclusive source for either establishing or falsifying Lamotte's claims. In a review article discussing Lamotte's translation, Paul Demiéville argues that Lamotte's contentions concerning the supposedly composite nature of the text go beyond what can be supported by the available evidence. He contends that the mere fact that the *Saṃdhinirmocana* does not exist in its present form in the earliest Chinese version does not prove that it is a composite work.[19] A particularly persuasive piece of evidence adduced by Demiéville against Lamotte's hypothesis is his mention of Wonch'uk's statement that when Paramārtha decided to translate the sūtra he only translated the first four chapters because he just wanted to translate that portion of the text which focused on the ultimate (*don dam pa, paramārtha*). Because of this self-imposed limitation he left the rest of the text for later translators.[20]

It should be noted that this situation has a possible corollary in contemporary Buddhist studies. A number of Buddhist texts have been translated piecemeal into Western languages, and many of these are commonly accepted by scholars as works by a single author.[21] Thus, the fact that a text was translated partially in an early

---

18 Peter N. Gregory, "Chinese Buddhist Hermeneutics: The Case of Hua-yen", *JAAR* #I.1.2, pp. 232-3. See also Kenneth Ch'en, *Buddhism in China* (Princeton: Princeton University Press, 1964), pp. 365-386.

19 In an untitled review article, *JA* #228, 1936, p. 646.

20 Ibid., pp. 647-8. See also the *Li tai san pao chi* (T 2034. pp. 49.87.c), which contains a listing for this translation (*Chieh chieh ching*). It states that the translation consists of one chapter, although it originally consisted of eighteen chapters, but "now this scroll is only the fourth chapter." There is no indication of how this text in eighteen chapters compares to present versions of the sūtra.

21 Some examples are: (1) Mervyn Sprung's translation of portions of Candrakīrti's *Prasannapadā* (entitled *Lucid Exposition of the Middle Way*; London: Routledge & Kegan Paul, 1979); (2) Janice Dean Willis's translation of the "Reality" (*tattvārtha*) chapter of the *Bodhisattvabhūmi* (entitled *On Knowing Reality*; New York: Columbia University Press, 1979); and (3) the translation of the *Samādhirāja-sūtra* by K. Régamy (Warsaw, 1938), which only contains a translation of three chapters.

Chinese edition does not necessarily indicate that the text is a composite. The fact that only certain chapters of a work were translated in some recensions might indicate that it was not yet completed, but could also indicate that either the translator did not have access to the complete text or that he only chose to translate a certain portion of it. It would not be surprising if some texts were copied in sections and brought to China, since before the advent of copying machines, typewriters, and computers each copy of a text was laboriously written by hand or, in the case of the Tibetan canon, printed from carved wood blocks. The technology of the time made the copying of texts a time-consuming enterprise, and before the advent of mass transportation many pilgrims may have opted to bring only what they considered to be the most important parts of texts on the arduous journey from India to China.

It should be noted that these considerations are as speculative as Lamotte's and that they do not disprove his thesis. Rather, they are an attempt to posit an alternative explanation for the discrepancies in the Chinese translations. Given the present state of our knowledge of the development of Mahāyāna Buddhism and the textual sources at our disposal, it is doubtful that these issues can be conclusively settled in favor of either hypothesis. Since the *Saṃdhinirmocana-sūtra* was originally written in Sanskrit and no Sanskrit manuscripts of the text have been found, our only clues about its original form come from the Chinese and Tibetan translations and from fragments in other texts. The Chinese translations are notoriously unreliable and vary greatly in quality, and although the Tibetan versions are generally more reliably translated than the Chinese ones, even these are of questionable use in determining whether or not a particular text is or is not a composite work. Both Chinese and Tibetan translations were often prepared by teams of scholars and later edited and redacted, and so the final version of a particular translation is often the work of many hands. Thus, discrepancies within texts and between translations may only represent personal idiosyncrasies in translation style or the work of editors and redactors.

Given these problems, it does not seem possible to settle Lamotte's claims conclusively using philological or textual analysis. In this study, however, my analysis is primarily philosophical, doctrinal, and literary, and in each of these areas the *Saṃdhinirmocana* exhibits a high degree of internal consistency. In terms of thought and structure it is possible to find a great deal of coherence in this text, and the format and style are very consistent, particularly in the Tibetan translations and Hsüan-tsang's version.

Throughout the study I treat it as a unitary work and focus on the philosophical and doctrinal correspondence between the various chapters. My conclusion after studying and translating this text is that it is the work of a single author and that in the sūtra this author outlines a coherent and internally consistent worldview in terms of which Buddhist meditators are to reorient their understanding of reality. The first four chapters focus on the "ultimate", which is crucial for understanding the ontological and epistemological assumptions of the sūtra. Chapter five discusses the nature of consciousness, which in turn is the foundation for the presentation of meditation theory and practice in the eighth and ninth chapters. Chapter seven indicates how Buddha's teachings are to be understood and interpreted. This is crucial to the system outlined in the sūtra, since correctly understanding which of Buddha's teachings are of definitive meaning (*nges pa'i don, nitārtha*) and which are of interpretable meaning (*drang ba'i don, neyārtha*) is said to be essential in order to be able to attain enlightenment. The tenth chapter focuses on the nature and attributes of Buddhahood and indicates the end result of successfully completing the program of practice outlined in the sūtra.

The main concern of this study will not, however, be with questions of authorship, philological issues, or problems concerning the composition and transmission of the text. My primary aim is to explore the thought of the text and how this has been interpreted by Buddhist thinkers, with particular emphasis on the discussions of the ultimate and hermeneutics.

An exploration of philological questions concerned with the background of the text (for instance whether or not there are different strata of authorship and redactions and their relative historical positions) could yield valuable insights into the development of the text, but will not be the focus of the present work. There are two reasons why I have chosen to leave aside philological questions concerned with the development of the text: firstly, the purpose of this study is to look at the thought of the text and its commentaries. It may be the product of more than one author and may have been redacted and translated by a number of people before it reached its present form, and each one may have left an imprint on the text, as Lamotte suggests. However, even if we determine that certain portions were composed at different times and adduce evidence that different redactors had a hand in determining the present versions of the sūtra, this does not entail that we have understood the meaning of the text. Indeed, such investigations would probably lead us progressively farther away from the meaning of the sūtra. Even if we do not know the identities of the creators of the present form of the sūtra, the text as it exists today in its Tibetan recensions is the result of an attempt to present meaningful statements about Buddhist philosophy and religious practice. Since the *Saṃdhinirmocana* has been the focus of numerous commentaries and is a major scriptural source for the Yogācāra school, we know that Buddhist thinkers have perceived it as an important presentation of religious meanings. The author(s), redactor(s), and translator(s) may be anonymous, but the final product of their work is a document that presents a collection of meanings, and these meanings can in principle be understood and explicated.[22] Taking this as a

---

22 This approach is often taken in Biblical hermeneutics, in which the identity of the author of a text may be uncertain, and there may be a number of people (usually anonymous) who had a hand in altering the text before it reached its final form. In both Biblical hermeneutics and Buddhist hermeneutics, however, the final text represents the attempts of one or more people to present a coherent and understandable statement of religious meanings, and the task of later

goal, the purpose of the second and third chapters of this study will be to examine the *Saṃdhinirmocana* in terms of some of the important topics presented in the text and to compare the words of the sūtra with the explanations of the commentators in an attempt to draw out the thought of the text and to see how this compares to the interpretations found in the commentaries.

The commentators whose ideas are considered in relation to the sūtra's presentations uniformly assume that the sūtra is the product of one author, Śākyamuni Buddha, and this basic premise underlies all their explanations.[23] For the sake of understanding their interpretations of the sūtra, it is necessary to realize that for these commentators the *Saṃdhinirmocana* contains the pronouncements of a fully enlightened and omniscient being who is preaching a sūtra of definitive meaning and who is definitively clarifying the thought behind his earlier teachings of interpretable meaning.[24] Thus, for the sake of elucidating the principles of interpretation that formed part of the worldview of the commentators and understanding the conclusions they draw from the sūtra, this study will

---

exegetes (including contemporary scholars) is to determine what these meanings are, or at least to present plausible theories about what the author intended and how the audience to whom it was addressed understood it. In the case of Buddhist texts like the *Saṃdhinirmocana*, there is a living oral tradition of commentary on them that has been preserved in Tibet and that can be of great help to modern students of Buddhism seeking to understand what these texts have meant for those belonging to this tradition. A good statement of how Biblical hermeneutics seeks to understand the meaning of a text even if more than one person may have had a hand in its development can be found in Robert Morgan's *Biblical Interpretation* (Oxford, 1988), chapters 2 and 3 and Claus Westermann, ed., *Essays on Old Testament Hermeneutics* (Richmond, VA: John Knox Press, 1963), pp. 134-199. For a further discussion of meaning and reference, see John Powers, "On Being Wrong: Saul Kripke's Causal Theory of Reference" in *International Philosophical Quarterly*, December, 1992.

23 This idea is discussed by Lamotte, *Saṃdhinirmocana-sūtra*, p. 17, and can be seen in the works of both Yogācāra writers and their opponents. The Yogācāra writers, of course, take it to be a sūtra of definitive meaning, while their opponents (for instance Candrakīrti in his *Madhyamakāvatāra* and Bhavya in his *Tarkajvālā*) contend that it requires interpretation, although they accept it as the word of Buddha.

24 This idea is discussed by Tsong kha pa in his *Essence of the Good Explanations* (*Legs bshad snying po*) in the introductory section of the "Mind-Only" (*sems tsam*) chapters (Sarnath: Pleasure of Elegant Sayings Printing Press, 1973), pp. 1-3. See also Lamotte, *Saṃdhinirmocana-sūtra*, p. 17.

focus on the text in light of their perceptions of it and will relate their interpretations to the present versions of the sūtra.

After discussing the sūtra's ideas and comparing these to the interpretations of various commentators, this study will step back from the text a bit in order to look at the underlying presuppositions and worldview assumed by the sūtra. The goal of this part of the study is to explore how Buddhist notions of tradition and authority are operative in the background of the sūtra's presentations. A core assumption of this analysis is that all rationality functions within rules, norms, and procedures accepted by a particular tradition. This is true for a Buddhist text from ancient India and for contemporary scientists, anthropologists, sociologists, etc.: all either implicitly or explicitly accept certain rules and procedures, as well as certain types of rational argument and criteria of evidence. In my discussion of hermeneutics, an important focus will be making clear the context, rules, and presuppositions concerning authority and tradition that the sūtra assumes, along with how these are used as part of the sūtra's discussion of Buddhist hermeneutics.

This study draws on a wide range of sources. My translation and critical edition of the Tibetan texts of the sūtra utilize twelve different versions, which were also compared with Hsüan-tsang's text and the canonical commentaries. In addition, my exploration of the sūtra's philosophy was informed by a number of provocative interpretations in the Mind-Only (*sems tsam*) section of Tsong kha pa's *Essence of the Good Explanations* (*Legs bshad snying po*) and Dpal 'byor lhun grub's *Commentary*,[25] studies of these commentaries with contemporary Tibetan scholars of the Dge lugs pa school, and conversations with a Rnying ma scholar and with H.H. the Dalai Lama on some of the topics discussed in the sūtra.[26]

---

25 The version of Dpal 'byor lhun grub's text I have consulted is from Se ra Monastery (Buxaduar, 1968).

26 The Rnying ma teacher is Khamtul Rinpoche, an unofficial tutor to H.H. the Dalai Lama, who instructed me on various aspects of the Rnying ma approach to Buddhist scholarship and meditative practice. The studies with him and the conversation with the Dalai Lama took place

The oral commentaries have been particularly helpful in grappling with the thought of the sūtra. As Hans-Georg Gadamer states, contact with a tradition can help in bridging the gap between an ancient text and a modern interpreter. The Tibetan oral traditions are an invaluable resource for contemporary scholars seeking to comprehend a Buddhist text, particularly those written in the distant past, because the Tibetans imported, cultivated, and developed a rich oral tradition from India and continued to keep it alive through constant debate and re-examination. Although many contemporary scholars of Buddhism devalue this tradition and view those who take it seriously as a source as somehow less rigorous than textual or philological scholars, I suspect that this attitude is mainly due to lack of contact with the tradition. Although this is not the place to fully develop this idea, my experience with Tibetan oral traditions has been that many oral commentaries I have received have been as rigorous and tightly argued as any text (and much more so than many texts). In addition, discussions with different scholars at different times have led to an impression that there is a high level of consistency among various Tibetan teachers and that each learns the basic explanations thoroughly, gains a deep understanding of their philosophical ramifications through open-ended discussion and debate, and then the best put a personal stamp on their explanations. Anyone who overlooks this resource ignores a valuable means of helping to bridge the gap between ancient texts and ideas and the modern interpreter, since one can engage in dialogue with a living representative of the tradition to a degree not possible with a text.[27]

In addition to the textual and oral sources mentioned above, my study is informed by contemporary philosophical discussions, and the presentation of the hermeneutical theories of the sūtra brings in

---

during the summer and fall of 1988, while I was in India under the auspices of a grant from the American Institute of Indian Studies.

27 A good discussion of the value of this tradition to scholars can be found in Anne C. Klein, *Knowing, Naming, and Negation* (Ithaca: Snow Lion, 1991), pp. 37-8.

current issues and interpretive models in an attempt to draw the *Saṃdhinirmocana* and its commentaries into conversation with modern philosophy and religious studies. Each of these various sources has added to my understanding of the *Saṃdhinirmocana*, and it is hoped that by looking at a range of opinions and approaches the reader will become acquainted with a number of perspectives, each of which reveals something of the meaning and significance of the sūtra.[28]

COMMENTARIES ON THE SŪTRA

The commentaries on the *Saṃdhinirmocana-sūtra* in the Tibetan canon come from a wide variety of cultural and temporal milieux, beginning with the *Compendium of Ascertainments* (*Viniścaya-saṃgrahaṇī*) and the *Commentary on the Superior Sūtra Explaining the Thought* (*Ārya-saṃdhinirmocana-bhāṣya*),[29] both of which are attributed to Asaṅga, who lived in India around the third or fourth centuries A.D. and who is credited in Tibet with being the main founder of the Yogācāra school. The other Indian commentary, at-

---

[28] In this study, the term "meaning" will refer to what the author of a text intended to say, what sort of thought he/she was trying to convey through the words of a text, and "significance" will refer to how this is apprehended at different times, how it becomes related to other contexts, for instance, alien cultures and later times, where a text that was written for a particular audience comes to be interpreted in ways that were never intended by the original author(s). An example of this distinction could be, for instance, the difference between a commentary by a traditional Buddhist author like Wonch'uk or Asaṅga (who begin their works with the assumption that the author of the *Saṃdhinirmocana* is a fully enlightened Buddha and whose commentaries are attempts to explicate his intention, i.e., the thought of the Buddha) and a critique of the same sūtra according a Marxist or feminist analysis, which might find examples of class struggle or class oppression (in the case of a Marxist analysis) or misogyny and denigration of women (in the case of a feminist analysis), but these implications were probably never intended or perceived by the author(s). The latter two types of analyses look at the significance of a text, but my main goal in this study will be the more mundane task of searching for clues about what the authors of the *Saṃdhinirmocana* and its commentaries intended to convey with the words they wrote, to reappropriate their vision of the nature of reality in a way that hopefully both accords with their intentions and that is accessible to modern readers. For a discussion of the distinction between meaning and significance, see E.D. Hirsch, *The Aims of Interpretation* (Chicago: University of Chicago Press, 1976), pp. 1-16.

[29] Peking #5481, vol. 104, pp. 1-7; Tohoku #3981. Excerpts have been edited and translated by Lamotte in *Saṃdhinirmocana-sūtra: L'explication des Mystères*. The complete text is translated in John Powers, *Two Commentaries on the Saṃdhinirmocana-sūtra by Asaṅga and Jñānagarbha*, which also contains a complete translation of Jñānagarbha's commentary.

tributed to Jñānagarbha, comes from a period just after the apogee of development of Mahāyāna thought, around the eighth century A.D., and is concerned only with the eighth chapter of the sūtra. Asaṅga's commentary is the shortest extant commentary on the sūtra (consisting of eleven folios in the Sde dge version) and is not a major source of the present study because of its brevity and structure. It mainly summarizes large sections of text, focusing on particular issues and terms. It does not attempt to comment on the entire text, and many important ideas and terms are only briefly discussed (e.g., the sūtra's analysis of the nature of the ultimate). Some key terms and analyses are not even mentioned (e.g., the discussion of cognition-only—*rnam par rig pa tsam, vijñapti-mātra*—in the eighth chapter). Since it presents no clear statements on hermeneutics, its importance for this study is limited to its ideas about subsidiary topics.

By contrast, the text attributed to Jñānagarbha (entitled *Commentary on Just the Maitreya Chapter from the Superior Sutra Explaining the Thought, Ārya-saṃdhinirmocana-sūtre-ārya-maitreya-kevala-parivarta-bhāṣya*),[30] is a thorough and meticulous commentary on the eighth chapter of the sūtra. Like Asaṅga's text, however, its relevance to a discussion of hermeneutics is limited, since the eighth chapter is primarily concerned with meditation, and Jñānagarbha has little to say about the sūtra's hermeneutical theories.

The commentary by Wonch'uk (Tibetan: Wen tshegs; Chinese: Yüan-ts'e, 圓測) was composed in T'ang China by a Korean student of Hsüan-tsang who wrote in Chinese, but the only complete version of this text is in the Tibetan *Translations of Treatises*

[30] Peking #5535, vol. 109, pp. 196-211; Tohoku #4033. This has been studied and translated into Japanese by NOZAWA Jōshō in his *Daijō-Bukkyō Yuga-gyō no kenkyū* (*Studies in the Yogācāra School of Mahāyāna Buddhism*; Kyoto: Hōzōkan, 1957). This work contains the text of the "Maitreya" chapter of the *Saṃdhinirmocana-sūtra* and the Tibetan and Chinese texts of Jñānagarbha's commentary, along with the discussion of the eighth chapter of the sūtra from the commentary attributed to Byang chub rdzu 'phrul.

(*Bstan 'gyur*).[31] Another commentary, attributed to Byang chub rdzu 'phrul in the Sde dge edition of the Tibetan canon,[32] may have been written in Tibet, as Ernst Steinkellner suggests,[33] but it is difficult to place it because most of the evidence concerning the origin and authorship of this text is circumstantial.

The Extensive Commentary on the Profound Superior Sūtra Explaining the Thought (*'Phags pa dgongs pa zab mo nges par 'grel pa'i mdo'i rgya cher 'grel pa, Ārya-gambhīra-saṃdhinirmocana-sūtra-ṭīkā*) by Wonch'uk (613-696),[34] is the largest extant commentary on the *Sūtra Explaining the Thought.*[35] Wonch'uk was a monk

---

31 Four other Chinese commentaries are listed in the *Tung yü ch'uan teng mu lu* (T 2183, p. 55.1153a): (1) *Chieh shen mi ching shu*, by Hsüan-fan (ten *chüan*); (2) *Chieh shen mi ching shu* (T 1828), by Ling-yin (eleven *chüan*); (3) *Chieh shen mi ching shu*, by Ching-hsing; and (4) *Chieh shen mi shu*, by Yüan-hsiao (three *chüan*). None of these are extant. Another Chinese commentary that should be mentioned is Tao-lun's (ca. 650-730) *Yü ch'ieh shih ti lun chi*, a commentary on the *Yogācārabhūmi* (published as *Chieh shen mi ching chu*; Taipei, 1985), which comments on the portions of the sūtra contained in that work.

32 See *A Complete Catalogue of the Tibetan Buddhist Canons*, ed. UI Hakuju et al. (Tokyo, 1934), p. 670, #4358.

33 Steinkellner, "Who Is Byaṅ chub rdzu 'phrul?", pp. 236-241.

34 Regarding Wonch'uk's dates, see NAKAMURA Hajime, *Shin Bukkyō Jiten* (Tokyo: Seishin Shobo, 1961), p. 60. See also the "Enjiki" entry in the Hobogirin catalogue, ed. Paul Demiéville et al., Paris and Tokyo, 1978. For a more detailed discussion of the transmission of this text, see John Powers, "Accidental Immortality: How Wonch'uk Became the Author of the *Great Chinese Commentary*", *JIABS* #15.1, 1992, pp. 95-103. An outline of his life can be found in Ahn Kye-hyon, "Buddhism in the Unified Silla Period" (*Assimilation of Buddhism in Korea*, ed. Lewis Lancaster and C.S. Yu; Berkeley: Asian Humanities Press, 1991), pp. 10-11 and Oh Hyung-Keun, "The Yogācāra-Vijñaptimātratā Studies of Silla Monks" (also in *Assimilation of Buddhism in Korea*), pp. 105-130.

35 This commentary is number 5517 in the Peking edition and number 4016 in the Sde dge. All citations in the present study are from the version published by the Karmapa Centre in Delhi, entitled *Ārya-gambhīra-saṃdhinirmocana-sūtra-ṭīkā* (*'Phags pa dgongs pa zab mo nges par 'grel pa'i mdo'i rgya cher 'grel pa*; Delhi: Delhi Karmapae Choedhey, Gyalwae Sungrab Partun Khang, 1985, *mdo 'grel*, vol. *ti* [118], vol. *thi* [119], and vol. *di* [120].

The original Chinese text was in ten *chüan*, but the only extant version, in the *Dai-nihon Zokuzōkyō, hsü tsang ching* (大日本 續 藏 經; Hong Kong Reprint, 1922, pp. 134.d - 535.a) is missing the first portion of the eighth *chüan* and all of the tenth *chüan* of the original text. These have been reconstructed from the Tibetan translation of Fa-ch'eng (法 成 Tibetan: Chos grub) by INABA Shoju: *Enjiki Gejinmikkyōsho Sanitsububan no kanbunyaku* (Kyoto: Hōzōkan, 1949. See also Inaba's *Restoration of Yüan-tse's Chieh-shên-mi-ching-shu Through Its Tibetan Counterpart* (Kyoto: Heirakuji, 1972); reviewed by NAGAO Gadjin, in *Suzuki Gakujutsu Zaidan Kenkyū Nempō* #9, 1972, p. 95. Inaba discusses his methodology in his article, "On Chos-grub's Translation of the *Chieh-shên-mi-ching-shu*" (*Buddhist Thought and Asian Civilization*, ed. Leslie Kawamura and Keith Scott; Emeryville, CA: Dharma Press, 1977, pp. 105-113).

from Hsin-lo (新羅) in Korea who moved to Ch'ang-an (長安), then the capital of T'ang China. According to his memorial inscription at Hsi-ming (西明) Monastery,[36] he was born a prince of the Silla kingdom but renounced his royal heritage to become a monk. He traveled to Ch'ang-an, where he became one of the two main disciples of Hsüan-tsang (600-664),[37] the other being K'uei-chi (窺基, 632-682) of Tz'u-en (慈恩) Monastery.[38] Wonch'uk later became the abbot of Hsi-ming Monastery.

Wonch'uk's work is very different from the other commentaries on the sūtra in terms of style. While the commentaries of Jñānagarbha, Asaṅga, and Byang chub rdzu 'phrul all seem mainly to expound the author's thoughts concerning passages and terms, Wonch'uk provides a wide range of opinions, and some passages report ten or more conflicting explanations. For instance, he frequently cites Asaṅga Vasubandhu, and Sthiramati, Mādhyamika authors such as Nāgārjuna and Bhavya, as well as a number of sūtras and philosophical treatises (*śāstra*). He also cites many opinions of scholars whom he does not identify (referred to as "a certain person"—*kha cig*—in the Tibetan versions).

His commentary is also an unusual work for a traditional scholar in that his citations of opinions and quotations generally refer not only to an author, but also often cite the work from which it comes, and in many places he indicates the Chinese translation that

---

36 Written by Sung-fu, entitled *Ta-chou Hsi-ming ssu ku ta-te Yüan-ts'e fa-shih fo she-li t'a-ming ping hsu*.

37 For information about his life, see: Stanley Weinstein, *Buddhism Under the T'ang* (Cambridge: Cambridge University Press, 1987), pp. 24-31; Kenneth Ch'en, *Buddhism in China* (Princeton: Princeton University Press, 1964), pp. 235-38; and JAN Yün-hua, *A Chronicle of Buddhism in China, 581-960 A.D.* (Santiniketan: Visva-Bharati, 1966), pp. 20-21 and 33-4.

38 With respect to K'uei-chi, see: Stanley Weinstein, "A Biographical Study of Tz'u-en", in *Monumenta Nipponica* #15.1-2, 1959, pp. 119-49; Alan Sponberg, *The Vijñaptimātratā Buddhism of the Chinese Monk K'uei-chi* (Ph.D. dissertation, University of British Columbia; University Microfilms, 1979); Kenneth Ch'en, op. cit., pp. 320-21; and IIDA Shotaro, "The Three Stūpas of Ch'ang-an", in *Papers of the First International Conference on Korean Studies* (Soeul: The Academy of Korean Studies, 1980), pp. 486-7.

he was using.[39] This commentary is a massive compendium of Buddhist scholarship, and it contains a wide range of opinions that reflects Wonch'uk's own encyclopedic knowledge of Buddhist literature.

Wonch'uk's general approach is to cite a passage and then to preface his comments by dividing his explanation into sections.[40] He first places the passage he is discussing in the overall framework of the *Saṃdhinirmocana* and then explains its meaning. The explanatory portion of his commentary is often drawn from other texts, mainly by Yogācāra authors, and among these he primarily relies on Asaṅga and Vasubandhu. His explanations are often compendia of opinions. He may cite several interpretations, drawn from a variety of philosophical schools, and then he often indicates that he considers a particular one to be superior to the others.

His citations of Yogācāra authors are particularly interesting, because they indicate that Wonch'uk considered the *Saṃdhinirmocana-sūtra* to be the seminal work of the Yogācāra school, and his commentary tries to show the harmony between the teachings of the sūtra and the thought of Asaṅga and Vasubandhu. He attempts to place the sūtra within the continuum of Yogācāra thought and to show the connections between the *Saṃdhinirmocana* and the writings of later Yogācāras. It should be added, however, that his sources are not limited to Yogācāra texts, for he cites Mādhyamika writers such as Nāgārjuna, Bhavya, Candrakīrti, and Śāntarakṣita,

---

39 In the Chinese text Wonch'uk even cites the volume number according to the Chinese canon of many of his sources, but these are omitted in the Tibetan translation since they would be unnecessary to Tibetan readers.

40 This aspect of the structure of Wonch'uk's text is discussed by Ernst Steinkellner ("Who Is Byaṅ chub rdzu 'phrul?", p. 235), where he speculates that Wonch'uk's work may provide a key to determining the origin of the practice found among Tibetan authors of beginning texts with tables of contents (*sa bcad*) which divide their works into sections. Steinkellner writes:

To my knowledge...nobody so far has a clear idea of where this most successful and influential technique of literary analysis originated. In texts from the early period of the second spread of the religion it is already present and the question is still unanswered as to whether it is a Tibetan invention or a heritage. I myself have always looked for possible Indian models, but in vain....But in Yüan-ts'ê's text from the 7th century, translated in the early 9th century it is in use, fully developed, just as we know it from the much later Tibetan texts, and throughout the whole text.

as well as non-Mahāyāna texts such as the *Great Exposition* (*Mahā-vibhāṣā*).

The other extensive commentary on the sūtra is entitled *Explanation of the Superior Sūtra Explaining the Thought* (*'Phags pa dgongs pa nges par 'grel pa'i mdo'i rnam par bshad pa, Ārya-saṃdhinirmocana-sūtrasya-vyākhyāna*). It is the second-largest extant commentary on the *Saṃdhinirmocana-sūtra*, and it provides extensive explanations of the entire sūtra, especially the tenth chapter.[41] It is found in the "Miscellaneous" (*sna tshogs*) section of the Sde dge edition of the *Translations of Treatises* (*Bstan 'gyur* vols. *cho* and *jo*),[42] which is mainly comprised of texts composed by Tibetan authors of the eighth and ninth centuries. The name of the author is given as "Byang chub rdzu 'phrul" in the Sde dge edition of the canon, but no author is mentioned in the Peking edition. As Steinkellner has pointed out, Byang chub rdzu 'phrul is an epithet of the King Khri Srong lde brtsan, and a number of works are attributed to him in the Tibetan canon.[43]

---

41 *Ārya-saṃdhinirmocana-sūtrasya-vyākhyāna* (*'Phags pa dgongs pa nges par 'grel pa'i mdo'i rnam par bshad pa;* Delhi: Delhi Karmapae Choedhey, 1985). The particular focus of this work on the tenth chapter has been noted by Steinkellner ("Who Is Byaṅ chub rdzu 'phrul", pp. 247-8), who speculates that the stress laid on this particular chapter of the sūtra may have been due to the author's interest in the sections devoted to reasoning, which Steinkellner thinks may have proved useful to the scholar-monks who were propagating Buddhism in Tibet. See also: (1) Ariane MacDonald, "Une lecture des Pelliot Tibétain 1286, 1287, 1038, 1047, et 1290. Essai sur la formation et l'emploi des mythes politiques dans la religion royale de Sroṅ-bcan-sgam-po", in *Études Tibétaines dédiées à la mémoire de Marcelle Lalou* (Paris, 1971), pp. 190-391; (2) R.A. Stein, "Un ensemble sémantique Tibétain: créer et procréer, être et devenir, vivre, nourrir et guérir", in *BSOAS* #36, 1973, pp. 412-423; (3) Stein, "Saint et devin: un titre Tibétain et Chinois des rois Tibétaines", *JA* #269, 1981, pp. 231-275; and (4) Stein, "Tibetica Antiqua I", *BEFEO* #72, 1983, pp. 149-236; (5) H.E. Richardson, *A Corpus of Early Tibetan Inscriptions* (London, 1985), p. 40, 11.33ff.

42 In the Peking edition this section is called "Wondrous Treatises" (*ngo tshar bstan bcos*), and this commentary is found in vols. *co* and *cho*.

43 Steinkellner ("Who Is Byaṅ chub rdzu 'phrul"), pp. 238-9. For instance, Bu ston lists the author of the *Bka' yang dag pa'i tshad ma las mdo'i btus pa* (a discussion of reasonings found in the tenth chapter of the *Saṃdhinirmocana*) as Khri srong lde brtsan, and he later refers to the author as "Lha btsan po Byang chub rdzu 'phrul" (Steinkellner cites Lokesh Chandra, ed., *Bstan bsgyur gyi dkar chag, yid bzhin nor bu dbang gi rgyal po'i phreng ba*, in *The Collected Works of Bu-ston* (New Delhi, 1971, vol. 26, pp. 401-643), number 633.3 and 7).

Bu ston speculates that the author of this treatise was actually the translator (*lo tsa ba*) Cog ro Klu'i rgyal mtshan,[44] and in his *Catalogue of Translations of Treatises* (*Bstan 'gyur dkar chag*) he indicates that he thinks that the Byang chub rdzu 'phrul commentary corresponds to another commentary attributed to Khri srong lde brtsan in the *Lhan dkar* catalogue.[45] Steinkellner contends that it is unlikely that the commentary could have actually been written by Khri srong lde brtsan, since it is a text that indicates a high level of scholarly erudition on the part of its author. Because of this, it is improbable that a king could have acquired the breadth of technical knowledge evidenced in this work. For instance, the author of this commentary often goes into great detail in providing extensive divisions of terms, some of which extend to several levels of sub-divisions that in some cases span large sections of text. Steinkellner concurs with Bu ston's assessment that the author was actually the translator Cog ro Klu'i rgyal mtshan, and he adds that there would be no problem with an accomplished translator's composing a scholarly commentary that demonstrates a wide range of knowledge of Buddhist thought and literature.[46]

The author's general approach is to preface his remarks on a particular chapter by dividing it into sections and indicating the main thrust of each section. He then provides commentaries on in-

---

[44] Steinkellner (p. 238) translates the passage from Bu ston, which is found in NISHIOKA Soshu's edition of Bu ston's *Chos bsgyur dkar chag* ("*Putun bukkyōshi*"; in *Tōkyō Daigaku Bungakubu Bunka Koryū Kenkyū shisetsu Kenkyū Kiyō* #4 (1980), pp. 61-92; #5 (1981), pp. 43-94; #6 (1983), pp. 47-201); see especially #5, p. 55.7-15.

[45] See Steinkellner pp. 238-9. The passage in the *Catalogue of the Bstan 'gyur* is from Lokesh Chandra's edition, p. 633.6. Steinkellner speculates that the reason for Bu ston's equation of the two texts is that both are said to consist of forty sections (*bam po*).

[46] Bu ston's contention that the author is actually Klu'i rgyal mtshan is also cited by Ser shul dge bshes Blo bzang phun tshogs in his commentary on Tsong kha pa's *Legs bshad snying po* (entitled *Drang nges rnam 'byed kyi zin bris zab don gsal ba'i sgron me*; Mysore: Sere Byes Monastery, n.d., p. 29b.4), and he concurs with Bu ston's thought that the author is the translator (*lo tsa ba*) Cog ro Klu'i rgyal mtshan (although Ser shul dge bshes incorrectly cites the work in which Bu ston makes this assertion as the *Chos 'byung* rather than the *Chos bsgyur dkar chag*). If Bu ston's speculation is correct, this would mean that the probable time of composition of this text was during the reign of King Ral pa can (who ruled from 815-838), since according to Tsepon Shakabpa (*Tibet: A Political History*; New Haven: Yale University Press, 1967, p. 49) this was the time of Klu'i rgyal mtshan's greatest productivity.

dividual verses, but (unlike Wonch'uk) he does not cite every verse, nor does he comment on the entire text; rather, he seems to have chosen the passages that interested him and commented on those. In addition, he often goes into great detail concerning particular topics (such as the four analyses discussed in chapter ten of the *Saṃdhinirmocana*) while other topics mentioned in the sūtra are either not mentioned or only discussed briefly. Also, unlike Wonch'uk, he seldom cites other works or authors, and instead seems to be giving his own interpretations without reference to the opinions of others.

Both of these commentaries have proven to be useful in studying the thought of the *Saṃdhinirmocana-sūtra*. Their approaches and styles are very different, but taken together they complement each other, and each offers insights into the thought of this difficult text. Wonch'uk's commentary is a comprehensive discussion of practically every phrase and term of the *Saṃdhinirmocana* and is significant both for its detailed analyses and for the way that it places the sūtra in philosophical perspective by relating its thought to a wide range of Buddhist sources, particularly works by Yogācāra writers. Byang chub rdzu 'phrul's commentary is a masterpiece of traditional scholarship and provides incisive and cogent explanations for almost every passage of the sūtra. Unlike Wonch'uk's work, quotations from other sources are rare, and most of the opinions appear to reflect the author's own ideas. Both of these commentaries provide insights into the meaning of difficult and obscure passages, and they are invaluable resources for those who wish to explore the thought of the sūtra.

OUTLINE OF THE SŪTRA

The *Saṃdhinirmocana-sūtra* consists of ten chapters of unequal length, each of which deals with a specific subject or set of subjects, and each of which has a specific person who serves as the main interlocutor. With the exception of Subhūti, for whom the fourth chapter is named, the interlocutors are high-level Bodhisattvas. The introduction states that the Bodhisattvas present on the occasion of the teaching of the sūtra have all "progressed to the irreversible levels" (*phyir mi ldog pa'i sa bgrod pa*). According to Wonch'uk, the "irreversible levels" are the eighth through tenth Bodhisattva levels (*sa, bhūmi*), but Byang chub rdzu 'phrul[47] states that the term only refers to the eighth level. He adds that all of these Bodhisattvas have received prophesies that they will attain omniscience.

Although the introduction states that there are "innumerable" Bodhisattvas in the audience, there are only ten who speak in the sūtra. These are named at the conclusion of the introduction and are referred to by the sūtra as "great beings" (*sems dpa' chen po, mahāsattva*). The Second Dalai Lama thinks that they have all attained the tenth Bodhisattva level,[48] an idea that is echoed by Gung thang.[49] Wonch'uk, however, after reporting a similar opinion, declares that this is an incorrect idea that is found in the *Superior Sūtra Untying Knots* (*'Phags pa'i tshigs nges par 'grel pa'i mdo*, Paramārtha's Chinese translation of the sūtra) and the texts of the Sarvāstivādins.[50] He states that according to the author of the *Yogācāra-bhūmi* these "great beings" are fully enlightened in this very lifetime.

---

47 See Wonch'uk, vol. *ti* [118]), p. 195.3; and *Ārya-saṃdhi-nirmocana-sūtrasya-vyākhyāna* (*'Phags pa dgongs pa nges par 'grel pa'i mdo'i rnam par bshad pa;* Delhi: Delhi Karmapae Choedhey, 1985; attributed to Byang chub rdzu 'phrul in the Sde dge edition; no author is listed in Peking), vol. *cho* [205], p. 60.7.

48 This idea is found in Rgyal ba dge 'dun rgya mtsho's commentary on the difficult points of Tsong kha pa's *Essence of the Good Explanations* (entitled *Commentary on the Difficult Points of the Differentiation of the Interpretable and the Definitive from the Collected Works of the Foremost Holy Omniscient [Tsong kha pa], Lamp Thoroughly Clarifying the Meaning of the Thought*; *Rje btsun thams cad mkhyen pa'i gsung 'bum las drang nges rnam 'byed kyi dka' 'grel dgongs pa'i don rab tu gsal bar byed pa'i sgron me*; blockprint from the library of H.H. the Dalai Lama, n.d.), p. 6a.3.

49 Gung thang dkon mchog bstan pa'i sgron me (1762-1823), *Beginnings of a Commentary on the Difficult Points of [Tsong kha pa's] Differentiation of the Interpretable and the Definitive, the Quintessence of The Essence of the Good Explanations* (*Drang nges rnam 'byed kyi dka' 'grel rtsom 'phro legs bshad snying po'i yang snying*; Sarnath: Mongolian Lama Guru Deva, 1965), pp. 73.13-74.6.

50 Wonch'uk, vol. *ti* (118), pp. 202.1.

Although there is a disagreement concerning whether or not the Bodhisattvas who are the interlocutors of the sūtra have already attained enlightenment or are in the penultimate lifetime before attaining full enlightenment, Wonch'uk, Byang chub rdzu 'phrul, Asaṅga,[51] the Second Dalai Lama, and Gung thang all agree that they are at a very high level of attainment. They are at or near the completion of their training and have reached an advanced level of realization, which indicates that their questions will presumably deal with matters of concern to high-level Bodhisattvas. This idea, as we shall see, is important to the implicit appeals to authority made in the sūtra and is part of a pattern found in the text, which implies in a number of ways that it is a sūtra of definitive meaning, taught for advanced practitioners.

Some of the interlocutors of the first seven chapters—Gambhīrārthasaṃdhinirmocana, Vidhivatparipṛcchaka, Dharmodgata, Suviśuddhamati, Viśālamati, Guṇākara, and Paramārthasamudgata—are found in other Mahāyāna sūtras.[52] The interlocutors of the last three chapters—Maitreya, Avalokiteśvara, and Mañjuśrī—are well-known figures in the Mahāyāna Buddhist pantheon. Maitreya is the being who will become the next Buddha of the present era and is presently residing in the Tuṣita heaven in preparation for his final rebirth as a Buddha. Avalokiteśvara is the embodiment of compassion in Mahāyāna mythology, and Mañjuśrī is the embodiment of wisdom.

Among the interlocutors of the sūtra the only non-Bodhisattva is Subhūti, for whom the fourth chapter is named. Since Subhūti is said in several texts to be the most advanced of Buddha's Hearer (*nyan thos, śrāvaka*) disciples in realization of emptiness, this is

---

[51] See *Ārya-saṃdhinirmocana-bhāṣya*, pp. 6.7-8.2, which discusses their exalted spiritual attainments.

[52] Gambhīrārthasaṃdhinirmocana, Dharmodgata, and Suviśuddhamati appear in the *Avataṃsaka-sūtra*. The others play minor roles in other sūtras.

probably the reason for his inclusion among this distinguished assembly.[53]

The exalted status of the interlocutors serves to establish that this is an advanced teaching, and this idea is also confirmed by the fact that the setting of the sūtra is a celestial palace that fills countless worldly realms and that reflects the perfections of the Buddha who inhabits it.[54] This idea is expanded upon by Asaṅga's commentary on the sūtra, which states that it is

> (1) perfect in terms of color; (2) perfect in terms of shape; (3) perfect in terms of measurement; (4) perfect in terms of area; (5) perfect in terms of causes; (6) perfect in terms of nature; (7) perfect in terms of its master; (8) perfect in terms of servants; (9) perfect in terms of direction; (10) perfect in terms of resources; (11) perfect in terms of accomplishing activities; (12) perfect in terms of non-harmfulness; (13) perfect in terms of being free of opponents; (14) a perfect abode; (15) perfect in terms of the particulars of the master's abode; (16) perfect in terms of vehicle; (17) perfect in terms of entrance; and (18) perfect in terms of basis.[55]

In addition to the praises of the excellent qualities of the palace and the exalted attainments of its inhabitants, the idea that this is a teaching for advanced practitioners is also indicated by statements at the end of the last four chapters in which Buddha concludes the discourse by stating that it is a teaching of definitive meaning and should be apprehended as such, and he indicates the benefits that members of the assembly attain through hearing it.

Thus, in a number of ways the text is presented as a sūtra of definitive meaning both in terms of its structure and by means of statements that it is definitive. The setting of the sūtra is particu-

---

53 See the excellent note provided by Étienne Lamotte in *The Teaching of Vimalakīrti* (London: Pāli Text Society, 1976) pp. 54-5, which gives a brief biography of Subhūti that is drawn from a number of sources and indicates several places where he is said to be the greatest of Buddha's disciples in realization of emptiness. Wonch'uk (vol. *ti* [118], p. 359.5-6) also mentions this idea.

54 This is found at the begining of the sūtra, ranging from Stog pp. 4-8 (D pp. 2-5). See particularly the opening section, which describes in detail the wondrous qualities of the palace. All references to the sūtra in this study first cite the Stog Palace version (*The Tog Palace Edition of the Tibetan Kanjur*; Leh: Smanrtsis Shesrig Dpemzod, 1975-1978, vol. 63). References to the Sde dge version (D) are given after the page in Stog.

55 *Bhāṣya*, p. 5.5.

larly significant, since it establishes from the beginning that Buddha's instruction takes place in an exalted spot, a celestial palace, and the text praises the high attainments of the residents of the palace, who include the Buddha, an assembly of Hearers, and advanced Bodhisattvas.[56] The implication is that those present on the occasion of the teaching of the sūtra are Buddhist adepts, and so the discourse to follow will be for those of exalted spiritual status. The fact that the interlocutors include very advanced Bodhisattvas and the most accomplished of Buddha's Hearer disciples in the realization of emptiness also indicates that this is a teaching for advanced practitioners, and not for beginners.

This theme continues throughout the text, and there are numerous statements which indicate that the teachings of this sūtra are for the advanced and not for "children" (*byis pa, bāla*).[57] In addition, in the first four chapters the main interlocutors discuss the differences between the understandings of Superiors (*'phags pa, ārya*) and "children", and they indicate that the teachings of this text are in accordance with the understanding of Superiors. For example, in the concluding stanzas of the first chapter Buddha tells his audience,

> Even though the Conqueror taught the profound as not being the domain of children, as ineffable and non-dual,
> These children, obscured by ignorance, delight in elaborations of speech and abide in duality.
> Those who do not understand, or understand wrongly, are reborn as sheep or oxen.
> Having abandoned the speech of the wise, they are reborn here in cyclic existence for a very long time.[58]

The ways in which the sūtra seeks to establish its defintiveness will be an important concern of the discussion of hermeneutics in the

---

56 It should be noted that the setting is different in Paramārtha's version: his text indicates that the sūtra was spoken at the Vulture Peak (Gṛdhrakūṭa) in Rājagṛha (T 16.711b-c).

57 See, for example, chapter one, (beginning on Stog p. 10.2; D p. 6.2), which contrasts the awareness of Superiors to that of children.

58 Stog p. 13.5; D p. 9.4. A similar thought can be found in the concluding verses to chapter five.

fourth section of this study, which will look into some of the rules and assumptions underlying the sūtra's theories. The following sections of this study examine the hermeneutical thought of the sūtra from a number of perspectives in order to draw out both the thought of the text and how this relates to Buddhist notions of tradition and authority. In my presentation, I have tried to make the text of the sūtra itself a part of the discussion. In the following sections, the sūtra is quoted extensively in order to give the reader a sense of what it says, how it uses language, and how it seeks to persuade its readers of the correctness of its ideas. The quotations of the *Saṃdhinirmocana* are drawn from my translation of the sūtra, which is based on the Stog Palace edition of the Tibetan canon. I chose this text both for the exceptional clarity of its printing and for its style. It has very few errors and in many cases contains readings that I considered preferable to those found in the other complete Tibetan translation.[59] Since, however, the Stog Palace text is less readily available than the Sde dge version, for each quote I have indicated the corresponding page in that edition so that specialists can compare the two.

---

[59] In my article, "The Tibetan Translations of the *Saṃdhinirmocana-sūtra* and *Bka' 'gyur* Research", I argue that the New Translation texts can be divided into two groups: (1) Stog, the Them spangs ma edition brought to Japan by Ekai Kawaguchi, and a manuscript in the India Office Library in London; and (2) Sde dge, Peking, Lhasa, Co ne, Snar thang, and the edition used by Lamotte in preparing his critical edition. The version of the sūtra in the *Viniścaya-saṃgrahaṇī* also belongs to the second group. Anyone wishing to examine other textual variations may find a complete listing in my forthcoming critical edition of the sūtra, which arranges these two versions in parallel columns to facilitate comparison. All textual differences in the respective groups are listed in this critical edition.

CHAPTER TWO

THE TITLE OF THE SŪTRA

One of the initial difficulties confronting anyone wishing to translate the *Saṃdhinirmocana-sūtra* is the array of differing interpretations of its title found in Tibetan and Chinese translations and in commentaries. The purpose of this section is to discuss the range of interpretations of the title, the various ways in which it can be construed, and to indicate some of the problems they raise for translators. This has important ramifications for our present study, which is concerned with the sūtra's discussions of hermeneutics, since I intend to argue that the title of the sūtra reflects a concern with interpretation.

The full title of the sūtra in Sanskrit is "*Ārya-saṃdhi-nirmocana-sūtra*", which has been translated into Tibetan as "*'Phags pa dgongs pa nges par 'grel pa'i mdo*". The term "*ārya*" (Tibetan: *'phags pa*) means "honorable, respectable, noble...excellent",[1] and is often prefixed to the titles of texts in the Tibetan recensions of the Buddhist canon.[2]

The term *saṃdhi* derives from the Sanskrit root $\sqrt{}$*dhā*, "to connect", "to join", "to fasten", "to aim", "to direct towards" with the prefix (*upasarga*) *sam*. It was equated by Tibetan and Indian translators with the term *dgongs pa*, which means "to think, reflect, meditate, consider", "the act of thinking, reflection, cogitation", or "to purpose, intend".[3] *The Great Storehouse of Tibetan Terms* (*Bod*

---

1 M. Monier-Williams, *A Sanskrit-English Dictionary* (Delhi: Motilal Banarsidass, 1979), p. 152.

2 For examples, see UI Hakuju et. al., *A Complete Catalogue of the Tibetan Buddhist Canons* (Sendai, Japan, 1934), p. 58.

3 Sarat Chandra Das, *A Tibetan-English Dictionary* (Delhi: Motilal Banarsidass, 1970), p. 275. See also See D. Seyfort Ruegg, "Allusiveness and obliqueness in Buddhist texts", in *Dialectes dans les Littératures Indo-Aryennes*, ed. Colette Caillat (Paris: Institut de Civilisation Indienne, 1989), p. 323.

rgya tshig mdzod chen mo, a Tibetan-Tibetan-Chinese dictionary) states that *dgongs pa* is a term that is "an honorific for thinking or intention" (*bsam blo gtong ba'am sems pa'i zhe sa*).[4] M. Monier-Williams translates *saṃdhi* as "junction, connection, combination, union with…association, intercourse with…", and he states that *saṃ* $\sqrt{}$*dhā* means both (1) "to place or hold or put or draw or join or fasten or fix or sew together, unite…to combine, connect with…to bring together, reconcile" and (2) "intimate union, compact, agreement…a promise, vow…intention, design".[5] Franklin Edgerton states that it means "union, concord, conciliation", "intention", "esoteric meaning", and that *saṃ* $\sqrt{}$*dhā* means "the 'real' meaning of a Buddhist text or doctrine".[6]

The term *nirmocana* is a combination of the Sanskrit verbal root $\sqrt{}$*muc* or $\sqrt{}$*muñc* and the prefix *nir*, and was translated into Tibetan as *nges par 'grel pa*, a combination of the intensifying adverb *nges par*, "certainly, surely, really"[7] and the verb *'grel pa*, which means "to explain, comment upon", "to put in, arrange".[8] According to Monier-Williams, *nir* $\sqrt{}$*muc* means "to loosen, free from…liberate…to be freed or free one's self from, get rid of",[9] and Edgerton states that the compound *saṃdhi-nirmocana* means "setting forth, unfolding the real truth, fundamental explanation".[10]

As the above citations indicate, the terms *saṃdhi* and *nirmocana* have a wide range of possible meanings, and one finds corresponding differences among scholars who have translated and commented on the *Saṃdhinirmocana-sūtra*. The term *saṃdhi* is interpreted in a number of ways: (1) the Tibetan translators rendered it as *dgongs pa* in the New Translations,[11] which means "thought",

---

[4] *Bod rgya tshig mdzod chen mo* (Beijing: Nationalities Publishing House, 1986), p. 459.

[5] M. Monier-Williams, *A Sanskrit-English Dictionary*, p. 1144.

[6] Franklin Edgerton, *Buddhist Hybrid Sanskrit Dictionary* (Delhi: Motilal Banarsidass, 1979), p. 556.

[7] *Tibetan-English Dictionary*, p. 354.

[8] Ibid., p. 300.

[9] *Sanskrit-English Dictionary*, p. 556.

[10] *Buddhist Hybrid Sanskrit Dictionary*, vol. 2, p. 557.

[11] I refer to the New Translations in the plural in accordance with the argument in my article, "The Tibetan Translations of the *Saṃdhinirmocana-sūtra* and *Bka' 'gyur* Research", which

"intention", "purport", or "intended meaning";[12] (2) the Chinese translators rendered it as both "hidden", "profound", "secret" and "knot", "bond", "connection". Hsüan-tsang translates the title of the sūtra as "*The Sūtra Explaining the Profound Secret*" (*chieh shen mi ching*, 解深密經), while Bodhiruci translates it as "*Sūtra Unraveling the Profound Secret*" (*shen mi chieh t'o ching*, 深密解脫經), and Paramārtha translates it as "*Sūtra of the Knots of the Profound*" (*chieh chieh ching*, 解節經). Étienne Lamotte follows Hsüan-tsang's rendering, and translates the title as "*Explanation of Mysteries*" (*L'explication des Mystères*), and he cites a variety of terms in which *saṃdhi* indicates something hidden, mysterious, or abstruse.[13] He also states that the literal meaning of the title is "sūtra untying knots" (*sūtra détachant les nœuds*).[14] This is also reflected in Wonch'uk's contention that

> '*Nirmocana*' is *rnam par 'grel pa*; this means 'explain'. Therefore, in the master Paramārtha's *Tshigs nges par 'grel pa'i mdo'i brjed byang byas ba* [his translation of the *Saṃdhinirmocana-sūtra*], *nges par 'grel pa* [means] explain. *Tshigs* [means] hard and knot. With respect to that, hard [means] firm. Knot [means] bond. So just as there are hard and firm things and knots and bonds within the joints of wood and of humans, the profound thoughts of the teachings within this sūtra are also very difficult to realize and very difficult to untie; therefore, it cannot be realized and understood by ordinary beings and beginning Bodhisattvas, and thus it is 'hard and knotty'. Because this sūtra unties, it is called '*Tshigs nges par 'grel pa*'. Furthermore—because having included all the very subtle and difficult to understand meanings from among all the treatises of the Great Vehicle that are contained in this sūtra they are explained clearly—this sūtra is called '*Untying the Knots*' (*tshigs nges par 'grel pa*).[15]

In a later discussion of Paramārtha's translation of the title, Wonch'uk adds,

> In another way, with regard to this sūtra, [the term *saṃdhi*] is nominally designated from an example; therefore it is [translated as] 'word' or 'con-

---

demonstrates that there are two distinguishable translations of the sūtra in the New Translation (*skad gsar bcad*) format.

[12] See D. Seyfort Ruegg, "Purport, Implicature, and Presupposition: Sanskrit *Abhiprāya* and Tibetan *Dgoṅs pa/Dgons gźi* as Hermeneutical Concepts", *JIP* #13, 1985, p. 310.

[13] Lamotte, *Saṃdhinirmocana-sūtra*, pp. 12-13.

[14] Ibid., p. 12.

[15] Wonch'uk, vol. *ti* (118), p. 72.6. For the Chinese text of this passage, see *Chieh shen mi ching shu* (Taipei: Yuan kuang Buddhist Institute, 1985), pp. 2.2b-3a.

> nection'. So the connection between the meaningful words and things is like the interconnection of joints of bones.[16]

Wonch'uk also states that according to Vasubandhu Indian scholars recognized three meanings of the term *saṃdhi*: (1) a connection between two things (*dngos po gnyis mtshams sbyar ba*); (2) the connections of the joints of bones (*rus pa'i tshigs 'grel pa*); or (3) profound paths (*lam zab mo*).[17] He then states that translators rendered it according to the individual meanings of the words of the title, and so they understood the term *saṃdhi* to mean "the correct profound thought" (*yang dag par na dgongs pa zab mo*).

In an earlier section he indicated that in the case of the title of the *Saṃdhinirmocana-sūtra* "*saṃdhi*" refers to "statements in a secret manner" (*gsang ba'i tshul du gsungs*),[18] which accords with the Chinese translations of Hsüan-tsang and Bodhiruci, who used translation equivalents that mean "profound" or "secret".

Among the commentaries on the sutra, the most extensive explanation of the Sanskrit title is found in the introductory portion of the commentary attributed to Byang chub rdzu 'phrul, which indicates that *saṃdhi* has connotations of profundity and hiddenness and that the text helps one to cut the knots of the afflictive obstructions (*nyon mongs pa'i sgrib pa, kleśāvaraṇa*) and the obstructions to omniscience (*shes bya'i sgrib pa, jñeyāvaraṇa*).

> This [title] *Ārya-saṃdhinirmocana-sūtra* (*'Phags pa dgongs pa nges par 'grel pa'i mdo*) is designated according to the level of meaning. This [sūtra] definitely delineates the meaning of the profound thought and indirect thought of the Tathāgata and cuts all the knots of the afflictive obstructions and the obstructions to omniscience. Here, '*Ārya-saṃdhinirmocana*' is designated as the name of the sūtra.... With respect to that, '*ārya*' (*'phags pa*) means 'one who is very distanced from all sinful non-virtuous qualities.' '*Saṃdhi*' (*dgongs pa*) [refers to] the profound thought and indirect thought of the Tathāgata. Also, in one aspect the meaning of the words [refers] to the knots of the afflictive obstructions and the obstructions to omniscience. '*Nirmocana*' (*nges par 'grel pa*) [refers to] definite delineation. It refers to 'definite delineation of the profound thought and indirect thought of the Tathāgata'. Also, in one aspect the meaning of the

16 Wonch'uk, vol. *ti* (118), p. 72.6.

17 Wonch'uk, vol. *ti* (118), p. 72.6.

18 Wonch'uk, vol. *ti* (118), p. 4.6.

> words means to cut completely: this refers to 'completely cutting all of the knots of the afflictive obstructions and the obstructions to omniscience'. With respect to that, if the meaning of the words is brought together in a general way: it definitely unravels the profound thought of the Tathāgata and it cuts all of the knots of the afflictive obstructions and the obstructions to omniscience; hence, it both explains [Buddha's] thought and completely cuts knots.[19]

This passage reflects two ways in which *saṃdhi* can be understood: as referring to Buddha's hidden or intended thought or as a knot. In the former case, the title indicates that the sūtra explains Buddha's hidden thought, and the second rendering indicates that it is a text that aids one in eliminating the knots of the obstructions.

In my translation of the sūtra, I have chosen to render the term *saṃdhi* as "thought" in accordance with the Tibetan translations of the sūtra, primarily because this accords with the structure of the text itself, which consists of a series of questions by disciples of Buddha who ask him to explain the "thought" or "intention" (*dgongs pa, abhiprāya*) behind his earlier teachings. Throughout this sūtra he explains his thought, the hidden intention that lay behind the literal reading of the words he uttered in previous teachings. For example, in chapter seven the Bodhisattva Paramārthasamudgata says to Buddha,

> I am wondering of what the Bhagavan [Buddha] was thinking (*ci las dgongs te*) when he said, 'All phenomena are without entityness; all phenomena are unproduced, do not cease, are quiescent from the start, and are by nature in a state of nirvāṇa.' I ask the Bhagavan about the meaning of his saying, 'All phenomena are without entityness; all phenomena are unproduced, do not cease, are quiescent from the start, and are by nature in a state of nirvāṇa.'

Buddha replies,

> Paramārthasamudgata...your intention (*sems pa*) in asking the Tathāgata about the meaning of this is good. Therefore, Paramārthasamudgata, listen to my explanation (*bshad pa*) of my thought with respect to that in consideration of which I said, 'All phenomena are without entityness, all phenomena are unproduced, do not cease, are quiescent from the start, and are by nature in a state of nirvāṇa.'[20]

---

[19] Byang chub rdzu 'phrul, vol. *cho* (205), p. 8.2.

[20] Stog p. 46.2. Sde dge (D) p. 32.3.

In this passage, the question and answer indicate that when Buddha taught that 'all phenomena are without entityness' and so forth he was thinking (*dgongs te*) of something else and that he will now explain (*bshad pa*) his thought. Similar statements can be found in other parts of the sūtra. For instance:

> (1) In chapter eight (Stog p. 94.4; D p. 65.7) Buddha is asked to explain (*gsungs*) what he was thinking of (*dgongs te*) when he said, "A dirty pot, for example, an unclean mirror, for example, and an agitated pond, for example, are not suitable for viewing the signs of one's own face, and the opposites of those are suitable".
>
> (2) In chapter nine (Stog p. 138.4; D p. 95.7) Buddha is asked about the thought (*dgongs pa*) behind his statement, "Both the Hearer Vehicle and the Great Vehicle are one vehicle".
>
> (3) In chapter ten (Stog p. 157.4; D p. 109.1) Buddha is asked what he was thinking of (*ci las dgongs*) when he said, "Due to the power of the blessings of Tathāgatas the marvelous bodies of humans in the Desire Realm...[appear]".

As these passages indicate, in the *Saṃdhinirmocana-sūtra* Buddha is presented with questions concerning certain teachings that he has given in the past which are either conceptually difficult or contradictory with teachings that were presented at other times, and he is asked to explain what he was thinking of when he gave them. For this reason, I have chosen to translate *saṃdhi* as "thought" in preference to its other possible meanings.

This meaning is reflected in the use of *dgongs pa* in the Tibetan translations, whose authors apparently chose this rendering in order to reflect a meaning that resonates with the structure of the text. The Chinese translations, however, equated *saṃdhi* with terms like "profound" or "secret", "hidden", etc., which reflect another possible way of rendering this term. In addition, as Hakamaya has noted,[21] the possible meaning of *saṃdhi* as "connection", "knot",

---

[21] HAKAMAYA Noriaki, "The Old and New Translations of the *Saṃdhinirmocana-sūtra*: Some Notes on the History of the Early Tibetan Translations", *KDBK*, #42, 1984, p. 188. See also: (1) his discussions in *KDBR*, #17, 1986, pp. 1-17 and *KDBK*, #45, 1987, pp. 1-35 and (2) HARADA Satoru, "Analysis of the Tun-huang Manuscripts of the sGom rim dang po", *Report of the Japanese Association for Tibetan Studies*, #28, 1982, pp. 4-8, which points out that the name of Bodhisattva Zab mo'i dond bar mtshams ma las par 'grel pa in Stein Tib. #194, p. 46a.3-4 corresponds with Don zab dgongs pa nges par 'grel pa in the new translation (Sde dge, vol. *ngu*, p. 3a.3, Lamotte, p. 34, 1.12).

etc. is seen in the Old Translation fragment of the sūtra found in the caves of Tun-huang and now stored in the India Office Library, in which the name of the Bodhisattva Gambhīrārthasaṃdhinirmocana (who appears in the first chapter of the sūtra) is rendered as "Zab mo'i dond bar mtsams ma las par 'greld pa".[22] Ruegg also mentions that in a Tun-huang manuscript of Kamalaśīla's *Bhāvanākrama* the title of the sūtra is given as "*Bar mtshams ma las par 'grel pa*", which indicates that the translator of this text understood the title as referring to untying knots, rather than explaining [Buddha's] thought.[23] Also, as we have seen, Paramārtha's Chinese translation renders *saṃdhi* as "knot" (*chieh*: 節).

As Ruegg notes, however, even in cases where *saṃdhi* is rendered by terms that *can* connote "connection" or "knot" (such as the Tibetan terms *mtshams sbyor, bar mtshams, bar mtsams*, and *tshigs*), it is not absolutely certain that these *do* indicate these meanings, because

> this meaning may nevertheless have a semantic reference, just as English 'in connexion with' can mean 'with reference to, having in mind, intending'.[24]

The only conclusion that can reasonably be drawn from all these conflicting interpretations and translations is that the term *saṃdhi* has been viewed in a number of ways by Buddhist translators and commentators in India, China, and Tibet and that there are a number of plausible ways of understanding what it means in a given context. As I have indicated, my translation is guided by the context of

---

[22] Stein #194, p. 46a. See my forthcoming critical edition of the sūtra, which contains an edited version of both this text and Stein #683 (which has been correctly identified by Hakamaya as belonging to the *Saṃdhinirmocana*), excerpt one. The page numbers are out of sequence in these texts, but de la Vallée Poussin has provided a table containing the correct order (*Catalogue of the Tibetan Manuscripts from Tun-huang in the India Office Library*; Oxford, 1962, pp. 69-70). In my edited version the pages of Stein #194 and #683 are arranged in accordance with the order of the New Translation texts, and references to the corresponding pages in my critical edition of these texts are noted.

[23] See Ruegg, "Allusiveness and obliqueness", p. 308. The Tun-huang manuscript to which he refers is Stein #648, pp. 127a and 133a. The text of this can be found in my critical edition of the *Saṃdhinirmocana*, excerpt seven.

[24] Ruegg, "Allusiveness and obliqueness", p. 309.

the content of the sūtra, which is explicitly concerned with explaining the thought or intention of Buddha.

THE TERM "NIRMOCANA"

As with the term *saṃdhi*, there are differing opinions among the translators and commentators concerning how *nirmocana* should be interpreted. All of the Chinese translations mentioned above use the term *chieh* (解), which Soothill and Hodous indicate means "to unloose, let go, release, untie, disentangle, explain, expound".[25] Bodhiruci's translation of the title as "*Sūtra Unraveling the Profound Secret*" and Lamotte's contention that the title literally means "*Sūtra Untying Knots*" reflect the literal meaning of the term, which is derived from the root $\sqrt{}$*muc* or $\sqrt{}$*muñc*, meaning "to liberate", "to free", "to release", "to unravel", "to untie". These connotations are reflected in the passage from Byang chub rdzu 'phrul's commentary cited above, in which he states that this sūtra helps one to cut the bonds of the afflictive obstructions and the obstructions to omniscience. They are also reflected in Jñānagarbha's discussion of the title, which contains a similar statement:

> *Saṃdhinirmocana* means 'cutting the knots of the afflictive obstructions and the obstructions to omniscience' through definitely freeing (*nges par dkrol bas*) the profound thought [of Buddha]. It is a 'sūtra' because it is simply a complete statement of what is definite.[26]

Bodhiruci's translation and the commentaries of Byang chub rdzu 'phrul and Jñānagarbha reflect the literal meaning of *nirmocana*, which means "to liberate", "to free", "to unbind", "to untie", and they also reflect the fact that in the *Saṃdhinirmocana-sūtra* Buddha unties the conceptual knots created by his earlier contradictory or abstruse statements and, as Jñānagarbha and Byang chub rdzu 'phrul state, this helps the people in his audience to free themselves from the knots of afflictions.

---

[25] William Edward Soothill and Lewis Hodous, *A Dictionary of Chinese Buddhist Terms* (Delhi: Motilal Banarsidass, 1937), p. 412b.

[26] Jñānagarbha, *Ārya-maitreya-kevala-parivarta-bhāṣya* (*'Phags pa dgongs pa nges par 'grel pa'i mdo las 'phags pa byams pa'i le'u nyi tshe'i bshad pa*; Tohoku #4033, Ōtani University Press, *sems tsam* vol. 2 (*bi*)), p. 318b.5.

The Tibetan and Indian scholars who translated the sūtra into Tibetan, however, translated *nirmocana* as *nges par 'grel pa*, which means "to explain, comment upon".[27] Equating *nirmocana* with *nges par 'grel pa* is a case of a "meaning translation", and it apparently reflects the fact that throughout the sūtra Buddha is asked to explain the thought behind his earlier teachings, as is indicated by the fact that he uses verbs that mean "to explain", "to teach", or "to expound" to describe what he is doing. For example:

(1) When asked in chapter seven why he taught the idea of one vehicle (*theg pa gcig, ekayāna*) Buddha states that the path of purification is the same in all three vehicles (i.e., the Hearer vehicle, the Solitary Realizer vehicle, and the Bodhisattva vehicle), and he concludes (Stog p. 54.6; D p. 38.3), "Thinking of that, I explain that there is one vehicle" (*'di la dgongs nas ngas theg pa gcig tu bshad kyi*).

(2) Later in the same chapter (Stog p. 56.1; D p. 39.2) he says that his doctrine was,"explained with an intention [behind it]" (*bsam pa rnam par dag pas bshad pa*).

(3) At the conclusion of the chapter (Stog p. 72.1; D p. 50.4), Paramārthasamudgata asks, "Bhagavan, what is the name of this teaching in this form [of explanation] of doctrine that explains [your] thought?" (*bcom ldan 'das dgongs pa nges par 'grel pa'i chos kyi rnam grangs 'di la nges par bstan pa 'di'i ming ci lags*); this formula also occurs at the conclusions of chapters eight, nine, and ten.

(4) In chapter ten (Stog p. 152.3; D p. 105.3), Mañjuśrī asks Buddha to summarize his teachings: "Bhagavan, please teach the quintessential meanings (*gzung kyi don bstan du gsol*) by which Bodhisattvas enter into the indirect thought of the profound doctrines spoken by the Tathāgata" (*de bzhin gshegs pas gsungs pa'i chos zab mo rnams kyi ldem por dgongs pa la yang dag par 'jug par 'gyur zhing*),[28] to which Buddha replies: "Listen, Mañjuśrī, and I will explain to you all of the quintessential meanings (*gzungs kyi don ma lus par khyod la bshad do*), in order that Bodhisattvas may enter into that which I have said in indirect speech" (*byang chub sems dpa' rnams ngas ldem po ngag du gsungs pa la 'jug par bya ba'i phyir*).

---

[27] See, for example, Sarat Chandra Das, *A Tibetan-English Dictionary*, p. 300.

[28] For discussions of *ldem por dgongs pa* and related terms, see: (1) Étienne Lamotte, tr., *La Somme du Grand Véhicule d'Asaṅga* (Louvain, 1973), notes p. 23; (2) Walpola Rahula, tr., *La Compendium de la Super-Doctrine d'Asaṅga* (Paris, 1971), section II.2; (3) David S. Ruegg, "An Indian Source for the Tibetan Hermeneutical Term *Dgoṅs Gźi* 'Intentional Ground'", *JIP* #16, 1988, pp. 1-4; (4) Ruegg, "Purport, Implicature, and Presupposition", *JIP* #13, 1985, pp. 309-325; and (5) Ruegg, "Allusiveness and obliqueness", especially pp. 299-317.

As these examples indicate, throughout the sūtra Buddha and his interlocutors describe what he is doing as "explaining" or "teaching", and his interlocutors ask him to explain "of what he was thinking".[29] Both Buddha and his interlocutors also imply that there is a deeper or hidden meaning behind many of his utterances, which they assume he can and will explicate. As with my choice of the word "thought" to translate *saṃdhi*, my decision to translate *nirmocana* as "explaining" in accordance with the Tibetan translation of *nges par 'grel pa* is based on the structure of the text itself, in which Buddha "explains" his thought to his audience.

This meaning is also reflected in other Indian texts associated with Yogācāra, for instance: (1) the *Mahāyānasūtrālaṃkāra* (verse

---

[29] It should be noted also that the sūtra contains many more statements in which Buddha states that he is "explaining" (*bshad pa*) his thought or "teaching" (*bstan pa*), for instance:

(1) Buddha's statement in chapter two (Stog p. 15.7; D p. 10.4), "I am completely enlightened with respect to the ultimate, which has a character completely transcending all argumentation, and having completely realized it I also have explained and clarified it [for others], and I have opened it up, revealed it, and taught it" (*ngas ni don dam pa rtog ge thams cad las yang dag par 'das pa'i mtshan nyid mngon par rdzogs par sangs rgyas te / mngon par rdzogs par sangs rgyas nas kyang bshad cing gsal bar byas / rnam par phye / gdags pa byas / rab tu bstan to*).

(2) In chapter five, after being asked about the meaning of the secrets of mind, sentience, and consciousness, Buddha answers (Stog p. 34.7; D p. 23.6), "Viśālamati, I will explain (*bshad*) to you the secrets of mind, sentience, and consciousness".

(3) At the beginning of chapter six (Stog p. 40.2; D p. 27.4), Buddha says, "Guṇākara, I will explain (*bshad*) to you the character of phenomena".

(4) In chapter eight (Stog p. 92.7; D p. 65.2), Buddha is asked, "What are exalted wisdoms that know doctrines and that know meanings of Bodhisattvas who cultivate calming and insight?", to which he replies "Maitreya, I teach (*bstan mod kyi*) enumerations of exalted wisdom and insight extensively, but I will explain it briefly" (*mdor bstan to*).

(5) Later in the chapter (Stog p. 97.6; D p. 68.3), Buddha is asked to teach about emptiness, and he agrees to the request by answering, "Maitreya...I will fully explain to you the character of emptiness" (*byams pa...khyod la stong pa'i mtshan nyid rdzogs par bshad kyis*).

(6) In chapter nine (Stog p. 128.4; D p. 88.7), Buddha states, "[I] will explain to you (*khyod la bshad*) — collectively and specifically — the purities of the perfections".

(7) On Stog p. 137.2 (D p. 95.1), Buddha states, "I thoroughly explain (*rab bshad*) that the state of having abandoned all assumptions of bad states that are like something existing in the marrow...is the Buddha ground".

Of course, it is not surprising that Buddha states that he is "explaining" or "teaching", and one could undoubtedly find any number of examples in other sūtras that contain similar statements. The passages cited above do, however, serve to corroborate the idea that this is a text in which Buddha explains his thought, and that it is also a text in which he unravels the conceptual knots that his earlier teachings had created for some of his followers.

20.1), which indicates that the ability to figure out "how to explain the meaning of [Buddha's] profound thought" (*gaṃbhīrārthasaṃdhinirmokṣa, dgongs pa zab mo nges par 'grel pa*) is a mark of Bodhisattvas;[30] and (2) the *Bodhisattvabhūmi*, which discusses five "topics of explanation of the meaning of [Buddha's] profound thought by a Bodhisattva" (*bodhisattvasya gaṃbhīrārtha-saṃdhinirmocanatāyā adhiṣṭhāni*). These are: (1) [explaining] the profound, brilliantly profound sūtras spoken by the Tathāgata, associated with [teachings about] emptiness and dependent arising due to particular conditions; (2) understanding the faults [taught] in the *vinaya* and understanding how to remove the faults; (3) non-mistaken presentation of the characteristics of phenomena; (4) the names and divisions of hidden intentional doctrines; and (5) the qualities, meanings, etymologies, and divisions of all phenomena.[31]

This division accords with my contention that the term *saṃdhinirmocana* refers to explaining the hidden thought or intention behind Buddha's teachings, because in all of these cases Bodhisattvas explain the underlying thought of Buddha's teachings and terminology, and they explicate the purport, hidden assumptions, and underlying structures of these teachings. A similar idea is found in Ruegg's discussions of this and related terms, as when he writes,

> the term *saṃdhi* in the sense of 'indirect allusion' is found also in the title of the *Saṃdhinirmocanasūtra*, meaning literally 'Resolution of the intention [of the Buddha]'....In this Sūtra, Buddha is shown referring to persons who may not understand his deep intentional/allusive utterances (*dgoṅs te bśad pa = samdhā(ya) vacana* or °*bhāṣya*?), and who are attached only to the wording.[32]

As indicated above, my translation of the title as "*Sūtra Explaining the Thought*" in accordance with the interpretive Tibetan translation of "*Dgongs pa nges par 'grel pa'i mdo*" is based on a consideration of the internal structure of the text, because throughout the *Saṃdhinirmocana* Buddha is asked to explain of what he was thinking. My

---

[30] See Sylvain Lévi, *Mahāyāna-sūtrālaṃkāra* (Paris: Bibliothèque de l'École des Hautes Études, 1911, Tome II), p. 287.
[31] WOGIHARA Unrai, ed., *Bodhisattvabhūmi* (Tokyo: Seigo Kenkyūkai, 1936), p. 303.
[32] Ruegg, "Allusiveness and obliqueness", p. 308.

translation is also guided by several pertinent discussions in commentaries on the sūtra, for instance Wonch'uk's gloss of *nges par 'grel pa* with *rnam par bshad pa*,[33] "to explain, to declare, prove, enunciate"[34] and Byang chub rdzu 'phrul's statement that the title implies both that it cuts the knots of the obstructions and explains Buddha's thought.

> Because it definitely frees the profound thought of the Tathāgata and because it cuts all of the knots of the afflictive obstructions and the obstructions to omniscience, it both explains [Buddha's] thought and cuts all knots.[35]

This meaning is also reflected in Wonch'uk's statement that

> because in this sūtra the meaning of the very profound and hidden thought of all of the three vehicles which is difficult to unravel is revealed and clearly indicated, it is called '[*Sūtra*] *Explaining the Profound Thought*'.[36]

That the term *nirmocana* in the title can mean "explain" or "teach" is also seen in:

> (1) Byang chub rdzu 'phrul's comment that the phrase, "...this form [of explanation] of doctrine that explains [Buddha's] thought" (*dgongs pa nges par 'grel pa'i chos kyi rnam grangs 'di*; cited in example 5 above) "refers to the general presentation of the body of this sūtra that teaches the definitive meaning" (*nges pa'i don bstan pa'i mdo sde 'di'i lus rnam par gzhag pa*);[37]
>
> (2) Edgerton's statement that the compound *saṃdhinirmocana* means "setting forth, unfolding the real truth, fundamental explanation";[38]
>
> (3) Lamotte's translation of *nirmocana* as "explanation" (*explication*).

In choosing "explaining" over other possible equivalents I have followed the Tibetan translation, which appears to have been based on a consideration of the format of the sūtra. The choice of *rnam par 'grel pa*, "to explain, to comment upon" instead of *rnam par bkrol pa*, "to liberate, unravel, free" indicates that the Tibetan translators decided to use a term that reflected the *modus operandi* of the

---

33 Wonch'uk, vol. *ti* (118), p. 73.2; see also p. 212.1.

34 Sarat Chandra Das, *A Tibetan-English Dictionary*, p. 1252.

35 Byang chub rdzu 'phrul, vol. *cho* (205), p. 8.2.

36 Wonch'uk, vol. *ti* (118), p. 4.7.

37 Byang chub rdzu 'phrul, vol. *cho* (205), p. 268.6. A similar passage is found on p. 462.4.

38 *Buddhist Hybrid Sanskrit Dictionary*, vol. 2, p. 557.

text itself, which consists of questions about Buddha's thought and his explanations. While it is true that many of these explanations could also be seen as attempts to "unravel" conceptual knots or "free" his listeners from the bonds of the afflictive obstructions and the obstructions to omniscience, the fact that when Buddha is questioned about the thought behind his earlier teachings he responds by offering to "explain" himself indicates that the Tibetan translation reflects an important aspect of the architecture of the text. In the *Saṃdhinirmocana-sūtra* we find a number of explanations that attempt to show ways to reconcile apparent contradictions in Buddha's earlier teachings and to define his thought, and the translation "*Sūtra Explaining the Thought*" was chosen in order to indicate something of the format of the text and what it attempts to do, given that no single translation into English (or Tibetan) can reflect the dual meaning perceived by the commentators.

CHAPTER THREE

THE CONCEPT OF THE ULTIMATE

Throughout Buddhist literature, particularly in Mahāyāna texts, there are frequent references to the "ultimate" (Tibetan: *don dam pa*; Sanskrit: *paramārtha*), a term that expresses the final nature of all phenomena. Mahāyāna texts equate it with emptiness (*stong pa nyid, śūnyatā*), reality-limit (*yang dag pa'i mtha', bhūta-koṭi*), the selflessness of phenomena (*chos kyi bdag med, dharma-nairātmya*), the thoroughly established character (*yongs su grub pa'i mtshan nyid, pariniṣpanna-lakṣaṇa*), and other terms expressive of ultimate reality, but seldom attempt to provide descriptions of it. An important exception is the *Saṃdhinirmocana-sūtra*, which has an extended discussion of the ultimate in the first four chapters of the text which attempts to characterize it in both positive and negative terms and which also provides a series of analogies that indicate ways in which the ultimate may be understood conceptually. The purpose of the present section is to outline the ways in which the ultimate is characterized in the sūtra, the analogies it provides, and the conceptual difficulties these create when considered together. The discussion of the ultimate is important to our examination of the sūtra's theories of hermeneutics because, as I argue in Chapter 4, the sūtra's presentation of the differences between interpretable and definitive teachings in the seventh chapter is founded on the understanding of the ultimate outlined in the first four chapters. One of the interpretive models the sūtra provides for distinguishing interpretable and definitive teachings is the theory of the "three characters" (*mtshan nyid gsum, trilakṣaṇa*): the imputational character (*kun brtags pa'i mtshan nyid, parikalpita-lakṣaṇa*), the other-dependent character (*gzhan gyi dbang gi mtshan nyid, paratantra-lakṣaṇa*), and the thoroughly established character (*yongs su grub pa'i mtshan nyid, pariniṣpanna-lakṣaṇa*). As we saw above, the third character is equated with the ultimate, and the presentation of the three characters in the sixth and seventh chapters appears to be based on the discussion of the ultimate in the first four chapters, and so an excursus on the sūtra's explication of the ultimate is a necessary step on the way to understanding its hermeneutical theories.

The first four chapters of the sūtra concentrate on the nature of the ultimate, and each focuses on a particular aspect of it. The first chapter begins with a statement that the ultimate is "ineffable and of a non-dual character" (*brjod du med pa / gnyis su med pa'i mtshan nyid, anabhilāpya-advaya-lakṣaṇa*).[1] This idea is developed through a comparison of the character of the compounded (*'dus byas, saṃskṛta*) and the uncompounded (*'dus ma byas, asaṃskṛta*).[2] According to the Bodhisattva Gambhīrārthasaṃdhinirmocana, these two terms include all phenomena, but he states that the terms "compounded" and "uncompounded" are merely conventional designations used by Buddhas and Superiors (*'phags pa, ārya*) in order to express their understanding of reality. He adds that these are only conventional expressions and that in reality the compounded is not compounded and the uncompounded is not uncompounded.

> O son of good lineage, the so-called 'all phenomena' are of just two kinds, compounded and uncompounded. Concerning these, the compounded is not compounded, nor is the uncompounded uncompounded. The uncompounded is not uncompounded, nor is it compounded....The so-called 'compounded' is a term designated by the Teacher [i.e., Buddha]. This term, imputed by the Teacher, is a conventional expression arisen from mental construction. That which is a conventional expression

---

1 Stog p. 8.3 (D p. 5.3).

2 These two terms, compounded (*'du byas, saṃskṛta*) and uncompounded (*'du ma byas, asaṃskṛta*), constitute a common division that includes all phenomena. "Compounded" refers to phenomena that arise in dependence upon causes and conditions. The term literally means "put together" or "made", and its opposite term, uncompounded, refers to whatever is not produced in dependence upon causes and conditions. According to Asaṅga's *Abhidharma-samuccaya* (I.11), everything that is subject to arising (*utpāda*), extinction (*vyaya*), and abiding and change (*sthityanyathātva*) is the compounded.

Wonch'uk (vol. *ti* [118], p. 217.5) states that the "compounded" is so called because it is produced from the accumulation of many conditions. Quoting the *Mahāvibhāṣā* (*Bye brag tu bshad pa chen po*), he states: "Whatever phenomena subsist in terms of the activity of aggregation by causes and conditions and are related with such are compounded." Those that do not are uncompounded.

> arisen from mental construction is a non-established conventional expression of various mental constructions. Therefore, it is not uncompounded.... Because of their Superior's exalted wisdom and Superior's vision, Superiors perfectly realize the inexpressible, and because they are completely and perfectly enlightened with respect to the inexpressible reality, they nominally designate the 'compounded'.[3]

This passage indicates that the common division of phenomena into the two categories of "compounded" and "uncompounded" is merely a conventional one and is a nominal designation based on mental conventions. Gambhīrārthasaṃdhinirmocana adds that although Superiors completely understand the inexpressible reality, they use such conventionalities in order to communicate with ordinary beings who "have childish natures, obscured natures, and natures of disordered wisdom",[4] because such beings require conceptual designations.

The perception of ordinary beings is compared to that of the audience of a magic show in which a magician chants a special *mantra* that causes a pile of sticks and pebbles to appear as a herd of elephants, an army, jewels, etc. The audience of such a show is said to be completely convinced of the reality of the illusion, while other beings with superior faculties are able to perceive it but know it to be false.[5]

> For example, a skilled magician or his skillful student, located at a crossing of four great roads, having gathered grasses, leaves, twigs, pebbles, and stones, displays various aspects of magical activities, such as: a herd of elephants, cavalry, chariots, and infantry; collections of gems, pearls, *vaiḍūrya*,[6] conch-shells, crystal and coral; collections of wealth, grain, treasuries and granaries.
>
> When those sentient beings—who have childish natures, obscured natures, and natures of disordered wisdom, who do not realize that these are grasses, leaves, twigs, pebbles, and stones--see and hear those, they

---

3 Stog p. 8.6; D p. 5.5.

4 Stog p. 11.1; D p. 8.6.

5 This analogy is found in chapter one, beginning on Stog p. 10.6 (D p. 7.1). For a discussion of this analogy, see NAGAO Gadjin, "The Buddhist World-View as Elucidated in the Three-Nature Theory and its Similes", *EB* #16, 1983, pp. 1-18.

6 *Vaiḍūrya*, according to Chandra Das (*A Tibetan-English Dictionary*; Delhi: Motilal Banarsidass, 1970, p. 877), can refer to three different types of lapis-lazuli: (1) a yellow lapis-lazuli called a *mañjuri*; (2) a green lapis-lazuli called a *sugata*; and (3) a white lapis-lazuli called a *śūnya*.

> think this: 'This herd of elephants which is an appearance exists; the herd of horses which is an appearance, and cavalry, chariots, infantry, wealth, pearls, gems, conch-shells, crystal, coral, grain, treasuries, and granaries [all] exist.'
>
> Having thought this, they emphatically apprehend and manifestly conceive in accordance with how they see and hear. They also subsequently impute conventional designations: 'This is true; the other is false.' Later, these must be closely examined by them.
>
> When other sentient beings—who do not have childish or obscured natures and who have natures endowed with wisdom, who realize that these are grasses, twigs, pebbles, and stones—see and hear these, they think this: 'These which appear in this way are not herds of elephants, and these which appear in this way are not herds of horses, cavalry, chariots, infantry, wealth, pearls, gems, conch-shells, crystals, coral, grain, treasuries, granaries, and storehouses, and that with respect to which there arises a discrimination of a herd of elephants and a discrimination of the attributes of a herd of elephants and those with respect to which there arises discrimination of the attributes of collections of wealth, grain, treasuries, and storehouses are creations of magic.'
>
> Having thought: 'These deceive the eye,' they do not emphatically apprehend or manifestly conceive in accordance with how they see and hear, and thereupon they do not subsequently impute conventional designations: 'This is true, the other is false.' It is like this: They subsequently impute conventional designations in accordance with objects. Later it is not necessary that these [beings] closely examine those [conventional designations].

The people in the latter group are likened to Superiors, who see the mistaken appearances that other beings perceive when they look at phenomena, but Superiors know them to be false and so do not assent to the illusion. Because they are able to perceive the true nature of phenomena along with their false appearances, they create designations of "compounded" and "uncompounded" in order to indicate the differences between their perceptions and those of ordinary beings, to signal that what these ordinary beings perceive as reality is actually false. Even while making such distinctions, however, the Superiors know that ultimately these designations of "compounded" and "uncompounded" only operate on the level of conventionalities and do not express the true nature of reality.

> When those sentient beings—who do not have childish natures, who see the truth, who have attained the supramundane wisdom of Superiors, who directly cognize the inexpressible reality of all phenomena—see and hear these compounded and uncompounded things, they think: 'These com-

pounded and uncompounded things which appear are non-existent. Those with regard to which the discrimination of compounded and uncompounded and the discrimination of attributes of compounded and uncompounded operate are compositional signs that arise from mental construction, like a magician's illusions. These obscure the mind'....In that way, Superiors completely realize things as inexpressible by way of a Superior's exalted wisdom and a Superior's vision, and because they completely realize the ineffable reality they nominally designate [the terms] 'compounded' and 'uncompounded'.[7]

Wonch'uk[8] compares the magician to the basis-consciousness (*kun gzhi rnam par shes pa, ālaya-vijñāna*), which has created things that are unreal since beginningless time. The sticks and stones that serve as the basis for the illusions are compared to the seeds (*sa bon, bīja*) that reside in the basis-consciousness, and the jewels and so forth that the audience perceives are the results of those seeds. The perceptions of ordinary beings are controlled by their predispositions, and so they are unable to perceive reality as it is, just like the audience at the magic show which is affected by the power of the magician's *mantra* and is unable to see beyond the illusion. Until the point of Buddhahood, one's perceptions are influenced by the seeds deposited in the basis-consciousness and one's objects of experience are determined by them. A Buddha, by contrast, stands outside of the illusion but is able to perceive how ordinary beings apprehend reality. A Buddha's own perception, however, is free from the influence of predispositions, which enables him/her simultaneously to perceive the true nature of things and how they appear to others.

The Ultimate Transcends All Argumentation

The second chapter continues the discussion of the ultimate, stating that it is "a character that completely transcends all argumentation",[9] which seems to mean that those who argue about the ultimate and devise philosophical systems that attempt to categorize it are necessarily mistaken. In this chapter, "argumentation" (*rtog ge, tarka*) refers to intellectual gamesmanship and hair-splitting scho-

---

7 Stog p. 13.2; D p. 7.6.

8 Wonch'uk vol. *ti* (118), p. 238.3.

9 This begins on Stog p. 15.1 (D p. 10.3).

lastic quibbling, which enmesh people in disputation and prevent them from perceiving the ultimate.

Dharmodgata, the main interlocutor of this chapter, begins by describing a debate that he witnessed between proponents of various non-Buddhist systems, each of whom thought that his/her system accurately described the ultimate. These people are described as being involved in petty wrangling and as being overly attached to their mistaken systems. Byang chub rdzu 'phrul states that they are unable to understand the ultimate due to five faults: "(1) the fault of thorough searching (*kun tu tshol ba'i nyes pa*); (2) the fault of exaggerated pride (*mngon pa'i nga rgyal gyi nyes pa*); (3) the fault of exaggerated adherence (*mngon par zhen pa'i nyes pa*); (4) the fault of imputation (*'dogs pa'i nyes pa*); and (5) the fault of disputation (*rtsod pa'i nyes pa*)".[10] Wonch'uk states that their faulty views arise from mistakenly adhering to the view of true personhood (*'jig tshogs la lta ba, satkāya-dṛṣṭi*),[11] which leads them to other wrong views and causes them mistakenly to argue with their opponents on the basis of these wrong views.[12]

Their understandings are contrasted with the perceptions of Buddhas, who truly understand the ultimate. Buddhas know the ultimate to be beyond the realm of what can be described by words, something that cannot be argued about without missing its true nature, and because of this they are able to lead others to an understanding of it.[13]

---

10 Byang chub rdzu 'phrul, vol. *cho* (205), p. 89.5

11 The term "true personhood" (translated into Tibetan as "the transitory collection", *'jig tshogs*; Sanskrit: *satkāya*) refers to the constantly changing, impermanent collection of aggregates (*phung po, skandha*) that constitute the psychophysical personality and on the basis of which we designate "I" and "mine".

12 Wonch'uk (vol. *ti* [118], p. 276.3) comments: "Because those different [groups] were differently minded in terms of various kinds of views that arise from the root of the view of true personhood, each was discordant with the other." He adds that because of their discordance they did not have the teachings of the four noble truths in any way.

13 See for instance Stog pp. 15-16 (D p. 10), where Buddha states that he is completely enlightened with respect to the ultimate, and so he is able to reveal and teach it to others.

Dharmodgata states that the debate he witnessed took place in a distant world in which teachers of non-Buddhist systems had gathered to discuss the ultimate.

> They were considering, weighing, closely thinking about, and seeking the ultimate character of phenomena, but not having realized it, those whose minds had become different, who had two-pointed minds,[14] who had minds that were not in accord, who were debating and quarreling, disputed with each other, agitated each other, harmed each other, were malevolent toward each other, and rejected each other.
>
> When I had seen them thus in a diverse state, Bhagavan, I thought: 'Alas! Tathāgatas arise in the world and, due to their arising, the individual realization and actualization of an ultimate like this—which has a character completely transcending all argumentation—is indeed marvelous and astonishing'.[15]

Buddha agrees with this assessment of his understanding and then proceeds to give a number of descriptions, each of which indicates a different facet of the understanding of the ultimate, and each of which is designed to lead his audience to understand something of its nature. Each description appears to be a different way of looking at the ultimate through contrasting it with what is not ultimate. He states that:

> (1) "The ultimate is known by Superiors individually by themselves,[16] whereas the objects known mutually by ordinary beings [belong to] the realm of argumentation".
>
> (2) "The ultimate [belongs to] the signless realm, whereas argumentation [belongs to] the realm of signs".
>
> (3) "The ultimate is ineffable, whereas argumentation [belongs to] the realm of expression".
>
> (4) "The ultimate is completely devoid of all conventions, whereas argumentation [belongs to] the realm of conventions".[17]

---

[14] The phrase "two-pointed mind" (*blo gros...gnyis can, vimati*) refers to a mind that moves in two directions because of doubt (*the tshom, vicikitsā*). See *Ārya-saṃdhinirmocana-bhāṣya*, p. 10.7.

[15] Stog p. 15.2; D p. 9.7.

[16] Wonch'uk (vol. *ti* [118], p. 278.4) states that this means that: "Due to observing the object of suchness by way of a Superior's non-conceptual exalted wisdom, they manifestly realize their own internal nature".

[17] Wonch'uk (vol. *ti* [118], p. 290.6), in commenting on this passage, quotes Paramārtha's translation of the sūtra, the *Tshig nges par 'grel pa'i mdo*:

> Moreover, Dharmodgata, I explain that suchness is a complete elimination of four types of things, all: (1) seeing (*mthong ba*); (2) hearing (*thos pa*); (3) differentiation of distinctions

> (5) "The ultimate is completely devoid of all dispute, whereas argumentation [belongs to] the realm of dispute."[18]

After each of these descriptions of the ultimate, Buddha concludes that "whatever has a character completely transcending all argumentation is the ultimate." This theme repeats throughout the chapter, and it raises interesting questions concerning the sūtra's opinion of the value of Buddhist philosophy. Although the sūtra itself contains arguments for or against philosophical positions and refutes what it characterizes as wrong views, it exhibits a strong mistrust of discursive reasoning and argumentation. We are told repeatedly that the ultimate completely transcends all argumentation and that it is only realized by those whose understandings have also transcended the sphere of argumentation. If this is the case, it would seem that many prominent figures of Indian Buddhism who are revered for their great wisdom would fall short of the sūtra's standards. Asaṅga, for instance, wrote systematic philosophical texts that contained philosophical reasonings and arguments, and he wrote on the principles and rules of debate.[19] Vasubandhu was renowned as a debater, and his biographies contain stories of his prowess in argumentation.[20] He wrote a treatise on logic (the

---

> (*bye brag phyed pa*); and (4) consciousnesses (*rnam par shes pa*). But conceptuality and analysis arise within observing these four things.

Byang chub rdzu 'phrul (vol. *cho* [205], p. 91.6) states:

> [This passage] indicates that due to the faults of positing—in dependence upon conventions such as seeing and so forth—that living beings and so forth exist, one does not understand the ultimate. [The phrase,] 'in dependence upon conventions such as seeing and so forth' indicates that in dependence upon conventions of seeing, hearing, differentiating distinctions, and consciousness one posits selves, sentient beings, souls, and persons and so forth as existent due to apprehending [them] as enjoyers and agents. Also, due to positing [them] as selves, one does not understand the ultimate; therefore, this is the fault of positing [such a theory].

18 These five phrases are found on Stog pp. 16.2-17.4 (D p. 10.4-11.4).

19 See, for instance, Alex Wayman, "The Rules of Debate According to Asaṅga", in *JAOS* #78, Jan.-March, 1958, pp. 29-40 (which discusses a section of the *Yogācāra-bhūmi* that is concerned with the norms and conduct of scholastic debate), and Giuseppe Tucci, *Pre-Dignāga Buddhist Texts on Logic From Chinese Sources* (Baroda: Gaekwad Oriental Series, XLIX, 1929), which discusses logical treatises attributed to Asaṅga, Vasubandhu, and other writers.

20 This aspect of Vasubandhu's work is discussed by Stefan Anacker in *Vasubandhu: Three Aspects* (Ph.D. dissertation, University of Wisconsin, 1969), pp. 41-47, where he examines Vasubandhu's *Vādavidhi*, a text on logic (which Anacker translates on pp. 87-98). Bu ston

Vādavidhi), and although there are a number of passages in his works where he denigrates arguers, he utilizes the tools and methods of debate and philosophical reasoning.[21] Since the sūtra seems to be saying that people who engage in argumentation cannot realize the ultimate, does this mean that even these luminaries of Buddhist philosophy were unable to know it?

At first glance it may seem to be saying this, but upon closer examination of the text the situation is less clear. The sūtra does not say that *all* people who engage in argumentation are unable to realize the ultimate, and the fact that it singles out *certain* groups could indicate that some people who engage in argumentation could un-

---

(*History of Buddhism*, tr. E. Obermiller; Heidelberg, 1931, pp. 136-147) and Tāranātha (*History of Buddhism in India*, tr. Lama Chimpa and Alaka Chattopadhyaya; Simla, 1970, pp. 149-150 and 162-175) report stories of his debating prowess. A good biography is provided by Anacker (pp. 9-33), which includes some stories of his debating skills.

[21] Some examples of his attitudes toward arguers (*tarkika, rtog ge pa*) can be found in: (1) the *Karmasiddhiprakaraṇa* (Étienne Lamotte, "*Le Traité de l'Acte* de Vasubandhu (*Karmasiddhiprakaraṇa*)", *MCB* #4, 1935-36, p. 197), where he states: "You arguers do not understand in accordance with the meaning of scripture" (*rtog ge pa khyod rnams kyis lung gi don ji lta ba bzhin ma rtogs pas*); and (2) the concluding remarks of the *Madhyānta-vibhāga* (V.31; in Stefan Anacker, *Seven Works of Vasubandhu* [Delhi: Motilal Banarsidass, 1984], p. 462), where he states that the treatise is called "*Differentiation of the Middle and Extremes*" (*madhyānta-vibhāga*) "because it is not of the sphere of activity of argumentation and because it cannot be distinguished by disputants" (*tarkasyāgocaratvāt paravādibhirabhedyatvācca*).

In the conclusion of the *Viṃśatikā* (V.22; in *Seven Works of Vasubandhu*, p. 421), however, he seems to be saying that he himself is an arguer: "But it is not possible for people like me to consider [cognition-only; Skt. *vijñapti-mātratā*] in all of its aspects because it is not of the sphere of activity of argumentation" (*sarvaprakārā tu sā mādṛśaiścintayituṃ na śakyate / tarkāviṣayatvāt*).

In his commentary on this last passage, Vinītadeva (*Prakaraṇa-viṃśatikā-ṭīkā, Rab tu byed pa nyi shu pa'i 'grel bshad*; Peking #5566, vol. 113, p. 324.5.5, Ōtani Sde dge, *sems tsam* vol. 14, p. 195a.5) states that this means that the ultimate is an object of activity of Buddhas, which may be a way of explaining why Vasubandhu, a renowned Buddhist master, admits that he is unable to know cognition-only. If it can only be perceived by Buddhas, this could be a reason why Vasubandhu (despite being an advanced practitioner) is not able to realize it. Vinītadeva states:

> It is only an object of activity of the Buddhas, the Bhagavans...People like me, who do not perceive suchness, who are not free from the nets of conceptuality, are unable to imagine all the aspects of that cognition-only. If you think, 'Why is this,' [the root text] says, 'Because it is not an object of argumentation.' Thus, the ultimate is not an object of conceptual thought. 'Imagination' [refers to] argumentation. Therefore, it [i.e., the ultimate] cannot be imagined. Since cognition-only is the ultimate, how could it become an object of argumentation? If one were to think, 'Since those who do not perceive thusness are not able to imagine all the aspects, for whom are these objects of activity in all aspects,' [the root text] says, 'They are objects of activity of Buddhas'.

derstand the ultimate. In addition, the text states that Buddhas and Superiors present their understandings to ordinary beings in terms of conventional expressions in order to be able to communicate with them in ways that they can understand. For instance, in chapter one it is said that "Superiors nominally impute 'compounded phenomena' and 'uncompounded phenomena' because they have completely and thoroughly realized the fact that things are inexpressible, and they are completely and thoroughly enlightened with respect to the inexpressible reality",[22] which seems to indicate that because they have realized the ultimate they are able to use conventional expressions that teach their listeners something about it. Moreover, it appears that the sūtra is saying that it is precisely because of the fact that they understand the ultimate that they can designate terms that accurately express something of the nature of reality.

The discussion of the ultimate in chapter two also leaves open the possibility that some people who engage in argumentation may still be able to understand the ultimate. For instance, in the sūtra Buddha uses arguments to establish positions and to convince his audience, and he also states that Superiors are able to use conventional expressions to teach others about their understandings. Moreover, when he contrasts the understandings of Superiors and ordinary beings, the main distinction seems to be that the former are able to use conventional expressions to describe something of their non-conceptual understanding of the ultimate, whereas the latter are so caught up in conventionalities that they are unable to understand the ultimate, which completely transcends conventional expressions. Thus, when Buddha states that the ultimate is "known by Superiors individually by themselves, whereas the objects known mutually by ordinary beings [belong to] the realm of argumentation"[23] and that the ultimate is ineffable, while argumentation

---

[22] Stog p. 9.4; D p. 6.2.

[23] Stog p. 16.2; D p. 10.5. A similar idea can be found in Asaṅga's *Abhidharmasamuccaya* (Peking vol. 112, p. 241.1.8; Ōtani Sde dge, *sems tsam* vol 12, p. 53b.7):

"belongs to the realm of expression", these statements could be interpreted to mean that anyone who uses conventional expressions does not understand the ultimate, but Buddha himself is obviously using conventional expressions in this text to teach his understanding of the ultimate and to lead his audience toward full realization of it, and so it is difficult to imagine that the sūtra is trying to indicate that *anyone* who uses conventional expressions does not understand the ultimate. Rather, a more plausible conclusion is that it is saying that those whose understanding is limited only to conventions are unable to understand the ultimate, while those who understand the ultimate and become Superiors are able to use conventional expressions to speak of their understandings. Superiors can use arguments to establish their positions, but they are still aware of the limitations of conventional language and know that words are inadequate to convey the full existential reality of understanding of the ultimate.

This appears to be the import of a series of analogies that are provided near the end of the chapter. Buddha states that people who have only known hot and bitter tastes throughout their lives would be unable to imagine how something sweet would taste[24] and that people who have only known discursiveness would be unable to

---

> Why is the ultimate so called? Because it is the sphere of activity of the supreme exalted wisdom of Superiors (*ci'i phyir don dam pa zhes bya zhe na / 'phags pa'i ye shes dam pa'i spyod yul yin pa'i phyir ro*).

See also Asvabhāva's *Mahāyānasaṃgrahopanibandhana* (p. 282a.8; reported in Étienne Lamotte, *La Somme du Grand Véhicule d'Asaṅga* [Louvain, 1973], pp. 120-1): "The ultimate [is so called] because it is an object of attainment by supreme exalted wisdom" (*don dam pa ni ye shes mchog gis thob par bya ba'i phyir ro*).

24 This passage is found on Stog p. 17.4 (D p. 11.4). Wonch'uk (vol. *ti* [118], p. 307.2) explains this analogy as follows:

> Just as those persons who always only partake of bitter tastes are unable to understand, infer, or imagine the taste of honey, so also householders abide in cyclic existence for a long time and always partake of the taste of worldly agitation and coarse sufferings. Therefore, they are unable to understand, infer, or imagine the very auspicious taste of pure behavior, the bliss of thorough emergence [from the household life]. Therefore, the *Yogācāra-bhūmi* explains, 'When, out of correct faith, one thoroughly emerges from the home to the homeless [life], because of being released from the various forms of obstructors that are the afflictions of friends and relatives, the misfortunes that reside in a household, and great sufferings, this is the bliss of definite emergence.'

imagine the non-discursive understanding of Superiors. The clue here lies in the fact that while ordinary beings who are involved only in argumentation and discursive thought are said to be unable to imagine or relate to those who have transcended these, the opposite does not seem to be the case. Superiors seem to be able to understand the discursive thoughts of ordinary beings and are able to use conventional expressions to teach them something of the ultimate in terms that they can understand. The difference between the Superiors who use conventional expressions and arguments and ordinary beings is that the former group has directly experienced a reality that transcends conventionalities, while the latter is unable even to imagine such a reality. Superiors' teachings are based on their exalted understanding, whereas ordinary beings argue and create philosophical systems on the basis of a limited and partial understanding. According to Asaṅga, their inability to imagine the nature of the ultimate is a result of the power of previous argumentation, engaging in inference, and their fixed beliefs. He states that these beings "are unable to investigate, infer, or imagine" the non-discursive understanding of Superiors "due to the power of argumentation, the power of inference, and the power of belief".[25] Because they accustom themselves to fruitless disputation about the ultimate, they become involved in debate, acrimony, and anger, and thus they are unable to enter into actual understanding of the ultimate, which can only be understood through renouncing argumentation and cultivating the non-conceptual understanding gained by Superiors through meditation. The sūtra states that

> because of involvement with discursiveness and manifestly delighting in discursiveness for a long time, [beings are] unable to investigate, infer, or imagine the internal, non-discursive happiness of Superiors.[26]

Byang chub rdzu 'phrul thinks that this

> indicates that due to the faults of dispute—in which there is attachment and anger with respect to one's own and others' positions which are posited in a mutually discordant way—one does not understand the

[25] *Bhāṣya* p. 11.3.
[26] Stog p. 17.7; D p. 11.6.

> ultimate. [The phrase,] 'mutually discordant positings' [indicates that] one disputes due to positing discordant tenet systems and textual systems through the power of exaggerated adherence to doctrines, attachment to one's own position, and anger toward the positions of others on this basis. One who is attached to positions and who disputes due to exaggerated adherence to doctrines does not understand the ultimate; therefore, just these are the faults of argumentation....Argumentation arises with respect to discordances [caused by] non-realization or wrong realization, but because this [i.e., realization of the ultimate] is the opposite of that [i.e., argumentation,] all disputation is completely eliminated.[27]

This commentary does not state that argumentation *per se* is bad, but rather that argumentation based on anger and exaggerated adherence to a particular philosophical position is to be avoided because it interferes with realization of the ultimate. This leaves open the possibility that someone who has realized the ultimate could engage in debate with others provided that his/her actions were not based on anger or acrimony, although it also seems to be a warning against the possible pitfalls of such activity.

Buddha sums up the discussion of the second chapter with the following verse:

> The signless realm that is individually [known by Superiors]
> Is ineffable and is completely devoid of conventions.
> The ultimate reality is free from dispute.
> It is a character completely transcending argumentation.[28]

THE ULTIMATE TRANSCENDS SAMENESS AND DIFFERENCE

Chapter three develops the idea that the ultimate transcends argumentation, and it indicates that even some Bodhisattvas are guilty of not being able to see the ultimate forest for the trees of conventionalities. It opens with a statement by the Bodhisattva Suviśuddhamati that the ultimate is "profound and subtle, having a character completely transcending sameness and difference".[29] He relates a story of a group of beginning Bodhisattvas whom he saw arguing about whether the character of the compounded and the character of the ultimate are different or non-different. He states that some Bodhi-

---

27 Byang chub rdzu 'phrul, vol. *cho* (205), p. 92.2.
28 Stog p. 18.4; D p. 12.3.
29 Stog p. 18.6; D p. 12.4.

sattvas held that they are different, and some held that they are non-different, and others were simply confused, having no idea which group was correct and which was mistaken. Buddha indicates that both groups are mistaken, since the character of the ultimate and the character of the compounded are neither different nor non-different.

> Because even all these children of good lineage in this way do not realize the subtle ultimate having a character completely transcending compounded things, as well as difference and non-difference, they are childish, foolish, unclear, unskilled, and are not properly oriented.[30]

Asaṅga elaborates on this by saying that they understand what is unimportant but do not realize what is important because they reason by way of faulty reasonings that lack correct consequences.

> In the third [chapter], Bodhisattvas who abide in the level of engagement through belief[31] mentally consider the ultimate improperly, having become obscured by the two obscurations: (1) obscuration with respect to imputations; and (2) obscuration with respect to reasonings. Obscuration with respect to imputations is a result of being estranged from sūtras of definitive meaning. Obscuration with respect to reasonings is a result of not directly understanding the branches of reasons (*gtan tshigs, hetu*) and so forth.[32]

Buddha then outlines a series of correct reasonings which show that either position (that the nature of the ultimate and the nature of the compounded are different or that they are non-different) results in contradiction.[33] In the first reasoning, Buddha indicates that if the ultimate and the compounded were non-different, then even ordi-

---

[30] Stog p. 19.1; D p. 13.4.

[31] The "level of engagement through belief" (*mos pas spyod pa'i sa, adhimukticaryā-bhūmi*) refers the first two Buddhist paths, the path of accumulation (*tshogs lam, sambhāra-mārga*) and the path of preparation (*sbyor lam, prayoga-mārga*), in which one's practice is motivated by desire to emulate the exalted states of beings in the higher levels.

[32] *Bhāṣya* p. 11.3. Byang chub rdzu 'phrul (vol. *cho* [205], p. 98.5) has a similar comment: he states that even though they are at the level of engagement through belief they are unable to understand the ultimate due to two types of obscurations: "(1) obscuration with respect to imputations (*gdags pa la shin tu rmongs pa*); and (2) obscuration with respect to reasoning (*rigs pa la shin tu rmongs pa*)."

[33] These reasonings are also discussed by 'Jam dbyangs bzhad pa (1648-1721) and Ngag dbang dpal ldan (b. 1797) in their presentations of the two truths. See Guy Newland, *The Two Truths in the Mādhyamika Philosophy of the Ge-luk-ba Order of Tibetan Buddhism* (Ph.D. dissertation, University of Virginia, 1990), pp. 82-89 and Donald S. Lopez, *A Study of Svātantrika* (Ithaca: Snow Lion, 1987), pp. 213-217.

nary beings would perceive the ultimate, since they perceive the compounded. If this were the case, then they would not be ordinary beings (since they would understand the ultimate, which is only done by Superiors). Buddha adds that they would also attain nirvāṇa and the highest enlightenment, and so there would be no need to engage in meditation or religious practice, since all ordinary beings would have already attained the primary goals of such practice.

> Suviśuddhamati, if the character of the compounded and the character of the ultimate were not different, then even all ordinary beings would see the truth, and while [still] ordinary beings they would attain the highest achievement and would attain blissful nirvāṇa. Moreover, they would have manifestly and completely realized unsurpassed, perfect enlightenment.[34]

In the second reasoning Buddha shows that the character of the compounded and the character of the ultimate are also not different. If they were different, then the realization of a Superior who has understood the ultimate would not eliminate false ideas concerning the compounded, because realization of the ultimate would have as its referent something different from the compounded. The ultimate would be different from compounded phenomena, and so the ultimate nature of an object could have nothing to do with the object itself. This would mean that if one were to understand the ultimate character of a particular object, one would still not understand the final nature of the object, since these would be different factualities. If this were possible, there would be no way to reach enlightenment, since realization of the ultimate would not eliminate mistaken apprehension of false conventionalities, because the two would be of different entities.

> If the character of the compounded and the character of the ultimate were different, then even seers of truth would not become separated from characterizations of the compounded. Since they would not have separated from the signs of the compounded, even seers of truth would not be completely released from the bondage of characterizations...seers of truth would not have attained the highest achievement, would not have attained

[34] Stog p. 20.5; D p. 13.7.

> blissful nirvāṇa, and also would not have manifestly and completely realized unsurpassed, perfect enlightenment.[35]

Buddha indicates that these conclusions are unacceptable. Ordinary beings are not seers of truth, and seers of truth are free from the bonds of mistaken conceptualizations. Thus, both those who think that the compounded and the ultimate are different and those who think they are the same are mistaken, since either position leads to unacceptable consequences. The upshot of this argument seems to be that any statement one makes concerning the ultimate will be unable to characterize it accurately. Although logically it would seem that the ultimate and the compounded must be either the same or different (since these two states of affairs are mutually exclusive), the sūtra warns us not to imagine that either of these extremes expresses the relation between the ultimate and the compounded. Instead, the sūtra seems to be advising readers to beware of choosing one position at the expense of the other. Also, it seems that the true relation of the two is not something that can be properly expressed in words, since the sūtra never attempts to resolve the apparent conflict between its statements that the ultimate and the compounded are not different and that they are not non-different. The conclusion of this section seems to be that any attempt verbally to express the relation of the two or to form a conception of it will err on the side of one extreme or the other because "the ultimate, which has a character completely transcending difference and non-difference, is subtle...profound...and difficult to understand".[36] It must be sought through meditation that moves beyond such limiting and distorting categories and perceives the ultimate as it is, free from conceptions about its nature.

The sūtra draws out other undesirable consequences that would result from holding either that the ultimate and the compounded are different or that they are non-different. Buddha states that if they were not different, then the ultimate would not be different from the afflicted character of the compounded.

---

[35] Stog p. 20.7; D p. 14.1.

> If the character of the compounded and the character of the ultimate were not different, then it is the case that just as the character of the compounded is included in the afflicted character, so also the character of the ultimate would be included in the afflicted character.[37]

On the other hand, if they were different, then the ultimate could not be the general character (*spyi'i mtshan nyid, sāmānya-lakṣaṇa*) of compounded phenomena. This implies that the ultimate is a quality or property that is found in compounded phenomena, which is borne out by Buddha's statement, "the ultimate character does not differ in all characters of compounded things".[38] He adds that the ultimate is the "mere absence of self" (*bdag med pa tsam, nairātmyamātra*) and the "mere absence of inherent nature" (*rang bzhin med pa tsam, niḥsvabhāvamātra*) of compounded phenomena,[39] and he concludes that

> if the character of the compounded and the character of the ultimate were different, then just the mere absence of self and just the mere absence of inherent nature of compounded phenomena would not be the ultimate character [of those phenomena], and the afflicted character and the purified character would also become simultaneously different characters.... It is also the case that the characters of compounded phenomena differ and do not not differ, and so yogis also search for an ultimate beyond all compounded things as they are seen, as they are heard, as they are differentiated, and as they are known, and the ultimate is distinguished by being the selflessness of compounded things. The afflicted character and the purified character also are not simultaneously different characters. Therefore, the character of the compounded and the character of the ultimate are not suitable as being either 'non-different' or 'different'.[40]

This passage indicates that the ultimate is a characteristic of compounded phenomena, a property or trait that pervades all of them. This property is said to be their selflessness and absence of inherent nature, which in Mahāyāna Buddhist thought is the final nature of phenomena. The idea that the ultimate is a quality or characteristic of compounded phenomena is developed through a series of analogies that Buddha uses to indicate the relation between the ultimate

---

36 Stog p. 26.3; D p. 17.6.
37 Stog p. 22.5; D p. 15.2.
38 Stog p. 23.7; D p. 16.1.
39 Stog p. 24.1; D p. 16.2.
40 Stog p. 24.1; D p. 16.2.

and the compounded. In each of these the ultimate is compared to a quality or characteristic of something, a property that is essential to it but which can be discussed separately from the thing it characterizes, although the two cannot be separated in fact.

In the first analogy, the relation between the ultimate and the compounded is compared to the relation between a conch and its white color. As Wonch'uk states,[41] in this analogy the conch is an example illustrating the character of compounded phenomena (*'du byed rnams kyi mtshan nyid kyi dper*), and whiteness is compared to the ultimate truth (*don dam pa'i dben pa*) "because it pervades all the nature of the form [of the conch]". He adds that "the ultimate and conventionalities exist in mutual dependence".[42] This implies that there is a necessary connection between the two and that neither could exist without the other, just as neither the conch nor its whiteness could exist independently of the other. The white color of the conch is not different from the conch, since it is a quality that pervades it. On the other hand, it is also not exactly the same as it, since they can be differentiated by thought and can be discussed separately. Since they are intimately related, however, one could not be eliminated without eliminating the other. (If one were to color the conch black, for instance, one would not eliminate the whiteness, but would only obscure it.) One cannot eliminate the whiteness, since it pervades the whole conch, but that does not mean that the whiteness *is* the conch, since there are other aspects of the conch that are not its color, such as its shape, texture, taste, etc., and these cannot be equated with the white color of the conch.

This analogy is extended to several other relationships, and the point of these examples is to show that the ultimate and the compounded are intimately related (but are not completely the same) and that realization of the actual relation of these two and understanding of the nature of the ultimate is the means to attain liberation and to eliminate the bonds of assumptions of bad states (*gnas*

---

41 Wonch'uk vol. *ti* (118), p. 347.3.

42 On p. 352.1.

ngan len gyi bcings pa, dauṣṭhulya-bandhana).[43] Buddha concludes this discussion with the statement,

> Similarly, Suviśuddhamati, it is not easy to designate the character of the compounded and the character of the ultimate as being either different characters or non-different characters.[44]

A TIBETAN INTERPRETATION OF THE RELATION BETWEEN THE TWO TRUTHS

According to Gung thang, the main idea of this chapter is that the two truths are different isolates (*ldog pa tha dad*), within being one entity (*ngo bo gcig*).[45] This means that they can be separated by thought, like a conch and its white color, but they are one entity. The example of the conch and its color is also cited by 'Jam dbyangs bzhad pa[46] in a discussion of the relation between the two truths, the conventional truth (*kun rdzob bden pa, saṃvṛti-satya*) and the ultimate truth (*don dam bden pa, paramārtha-satya*). According to the Dge lugs pa tradition, the relationship is one of sameness of entity and difference of isolates. 'Jam dbyangs bzhad pa cites passages from this section of the *Saṃdhinirmocana-sūtra*, and he states that the two truths must be seen as being related within being of one nature, like a conch and its white color.

An "isolate" (*ldog pa*) is something that can be isolated or differentiated by thought and discussed separately from the thing it characterizes, as in the case of the whiteness of a conch and the conch of which it is a quality.[47] They cannot be separated in fact, since they are mutually dependent. The whiteness of the conch, for example, could not exist apart from the conch, nor could the conch exist without its color.

---

43 The passage in the sūtra ranges from Stog pp. 21-22 (D p. 14).

44 Stog p. 26.2; D p. 17.4.

45 Gung thang dkon mchog bstan pa'i sgron me (1762-1823), *Bstan bcos legs bshad snying po las sems tsam skor gyi mchan 'grel rtsom 'phro rnam rig gzhung brgya'i snang ba* (Lhasa: *Gung thang gsung 'bum*, n.d., vol. *kha*), pp. 8-9.

46 'Jam dbyangs bzhad pa, *Dbu ma chen mo* (Buxaduar: Gomang, 1967), pp. 525ff. This reference is from a draft translation of the text by Guy Newland, which he kindly lent to me.

47 See, for example, Jeffrey Hopkins, *Meditation on Emptiness* (London: Wisdom, 1983), pp. 347-9 and 413-5.

Although the idea that the relation between compounded phenomena and the ultimate is one of sameness of entity and difference of isolates is an ingenious solution to the conceptual conflict of the sūtra's statements that they are neither different nor non-different, I suspect that this solution might be too neat and that it undermines something of the intent of the text. It does show a way to reconcile the apparent contradiction involved in stating that the two are neither different nor non-different, and it does not contradict the words of the sūtra, but if the author(s) had wanted to present such a neat solution there would be no reason not to. Instead, the text stresses that the ultimate is difficult to discuss, difficult to realize, and that it cannot be grasped by conceptual thought or accurately described by words.

The sūtra seems to avoid any attempt at resolution of the conceptual difficulties created by its conflicting statements except by offering analogies, and instead it urges us to look beyond words and conceptions in order to realize the ultimate. The Dge lugs pa formulation of the relation between the ultimate and compounded phenomena fixes it in a conceptually apprehendable and verbally expressible way, but the *Saṃdhinirmocana-sūtra* presents conceptual antinomies as problems that cannot be resolved conceptually. The intent of this procedure seems to be to forestall attempts to conceptualize the nature of the ultimate, to prevent people from thinking that they have understood the ultimate through formulating philosophical ideas about it. The text even warns that some Bodhisattvas imagine that they know the ultimate through conceptual systems and that they argue with others on the basis of limited understanding. Buddha says of such Bodhisattvas,

> Because even all these children of good lineage in this way do not realize the subtle ultimate having a character completely transcending compounded things, as well as difference and non-difference, they are childish, foolish, unclear, unskilled, and are not properly oriented.[48]

---

[48] Stog p. 20.2; D p. 13.5.

The ultimate, Buddha concludes, can only be known through non-conceptual insight, and I suspect that part of the intent of the sūtra is to warn its readers against facile explanations concerning the ultimate by presenting apparently contradictory statements that cannot be resolved conceptually and that might lead people beyond attempts to discuss it and toward direct realization of it.

THE ULTIMATE IS EVERYWHERE OF ONE TASTE

The fourth chapter continues the discussion of the ultimate by explaining how it is "a character that is everywhere of one taste" (*thams cad du ro gcig pa'i mtshan nyid*).[49] It is compared to space (*nam mkha', ākāśa*), which pervades everything and is undifferentiated in all compounded things. As with the statement in the previous chapter that "the ultimate character does not differ in all characters of compounded things", this indicates that the ultimate is a quality of compounded phenomena, a trait that characterizes all of them, although it is subtle and difficult to perceive.

Buddha then indicates that the ultimate has an important function in the context of religious practice, because it is "an object of observation for purification" (*rnam par dag pa'i dmigs pa, viśuddhālambana*).[50] He equates it with thusness (*de bzhin nyid, tathatā*) and the selflessness of phenomena (*chos kyi bdag med, dharmanairātmya*), and he adds that it is an object of observation that leads to advanced states of spiritual attainment.

> Subhūti, monks who practice yoga, having completely realized thusness, the ultimate, the selflessness of phenomena of one aggregate, do not [have to] seek individually for thusness, the ultimate, the selflessness of phenomena in those [phenomena] which are other than that....Those [monks who practice yoga] understand and realize the ultimate, whose character is everywhere of one taste, through just relying on the exalted wisdom that is non-dual with the scope of thusness, and not in another way. Therefore, Subhūti, you should know by this form [of explanation] also that that which has a character that is everywhere of one taste is the ultimate.[51]

---

[49] Stog p. 30.2; D p. 20.3.
[50] Stog p. 30.6; D p. 21.1.
[51] Stog p. 31.2; D p. 21.5.

Unfortunately, the sūtra does not elaborate on how the ultimate functions as an object of observation for purification, nor does it clearly delineate what an object of observation for purification is. The term appears again in chapter seven, where it is stated that only the ultimate is an object of observation for purification and that the ultimate is the thoroughly established character (*yongs su grub pa'i mtshan nyid, pariniṣpanna-lakṣaṇa*),[52] but this passage also gives no further clues concerning how an object of observation for purification functions.

The commentaries, however, do provide some indications concerning what it means to say that the ultimate is an object of observation for purification. Byang chub rdzu 'phrul, for example, states not only that the ultimate is to be equated with suchness and the selflessness of phenomena, but also that it is something which leads to enlightenment and serves to counteract exaggerated pride (*mngon pa'i nga rgyal, abhimāna*), which the sūtra indicates is an obstacle that interferes with correct understanding. Byang chub rdzu 'phrul comments that

> due to correctly knowing suchness, the ultimate, the selflessness of phenomena, which is a character that is everywhere of one taste, one perceives it....Because Superiors [know] the other-dependent character by way of a Superior's knowledge and perception, that which completely

---

[52] See Stog p. 48.4 (D p. 33.7). A statement that the ultimate should be equated with the thoroughly established nature is also found in Vasubandhu's *Madhyānta-vibhāga-bhāṣya* (chapter III.10; Stefan Anacker, *Seven Works of Vasubandhu*, p. 441; Ōtani Sde dge, *sems tsam* vol. 2, p. 12a.6): "You should know that the ultimate truth is just the thoroughly established nature" (*paramārthasatyamekasmātpariniṣpannādeva svabhāvādveditavyam; don dam pa'i bden pa ni yongs su grub pa'i ngo bo nyid gcig pur rig par bya'o*).

This section of the *Madhyānta-vibhāga-bhāṣya* is concerned with the functions of the ultimate, the thoroughly established nature, in meditative practice. This presentation concurs with how it is presented in the *Saṃdhinirmocana*, i.e., as an object of observation that, when taken to mind in meditation, can lead to exalted spiritual states and to enlightenment. In the same section Vasubandhu also states that

> the ultimate is known through three things: object, attainment, and achievement (*arthaprāptiprapattyā hi paramārthastridhā mataḥ*)....It is an ultimate object because suchness serves as an object of an ultimate wisdom. It is an ultimate attainment because its [attainment] is nirvāṇa, which serves as the ultimate aim. It is the ultimate achievement because its [achievement] is the path, which serves as the ultimate object (*arthaparamārthastathatā paramasya jñānasyārtha iti kṛtvā / prāptiparamārthaṃ nirvāṇaṃ paramo 'rtha iti kṛtvā / pratipattiparamārtho mārgaḥ paramo 'syārtaḥ iti kṛtvā*).

> enlightens, which is perceived as being inexpressible, is thoroughly established suchness, the ultimate, the selflessness of phenomena, and it has a character that is everywhere of one taste. Therefore, it is an antidote to exaggerated pride in terms of apprehended objects, this ultimate that has a character which is everywhere of one taste.[53]

In his commentary on Tsong kha pa's *Essence of the Good Explanations* (*Legs bshad snying po*), Dpal 'byor lhun grub explains that the term "object of observation for purification" refers to the ultimate, which does not have either production or disintegration.[54] Citing Vasubandhu's commentary on the *Differentiation of the Middle and the Extremes* (*Madhyānta-vibhāga*), he comments that

> that suchness which is the object of the exalted wisdom purifying the two obstructions [i.e., the afflictive obstructions and the obstructions to omniscience] is the thoroughly established character and is an object of observation for purification.[55]

In an oral commentary on this section of Dpal 'byor lhun grub's text, Geshe Palden Dragpa stated:

> The only thing that is a true ultimate is that which is taken as the object of a path that will purify obstructions. Since other-dependent natures (*gzhan gyi dbang gi ngo bo nyid, paratantra-svabhāva*) do not have that quality of being an object of observation for a path of purification, they lack the entity of the ultimate....The true object of observation must be something that—through observing it again and again—will purify the afflictions. That is not true with other-dependent natures. Because emptiness has this effect of purifying obstructions, it is the main object of meditation.

Wonch'uk's commentary contains a similar idea. He states that "through the power of observing this object one also attains mental purification", and he adds that according to the *Bstan bcos rnam par bshad pa'i tshig le'ur byas pa* an object of observation for purification has three aspects: (1) it is permanently changeless (*rtag tu rnam par 'gyur ba med*); (2) it is a nature of virtue and happiness (*dge dang bde ba'i ngo bo nyid*); and (3) it manifestly accomplishes

---

53 Byang chub rdzu 'phrul, vol. *cho* (205), p. 112.5.

54 *Legs bshad snying po'i dka' 'grel bstan pa'i sgron me* (Delhi: Rong tha mchog sprul rnam pa gnyis, 1968), p. 47.2-5.

55 Dpal 'byor lhun grub, p. 48.1. See also the discussions of this term in the *Madhyānta-vibhāga* (ed. YAMAGUCHI Susumu; Nagoya: Hajinkaku, 1934), pp. 11.22-12.6, 46.9-15, and 113.18-22.

everything (*thams cad mngon par 'grub par 'gyur*).[56] He adds that a commentary on this text contends that

> because the ultimate truth is free from sameness and difference, you should know that it is an object of observation for purification. Why is this? Because through the power of observing this object one obtains mental purification.[57]

According to these sources, the ultimate is an "object of observation for purification" in the sense that when one meditates on it it serves to purify the mind by removing obstructions. According to the sūtra, it is a quality that pervades all phenomena and is "everywhere of one taste", which seems to mean that it is something that is of an undifferentiable nature in all phenomena. It is compared to space, which is the same everywhere, lacks distinctions, and is all-pervasive. It is also something that is unchanging, that is neither created nor destroyed, a quality that permanently characterizes all compounded phenomena.

> In permanent, permanent time and in everlasting, everlasting time,[58] whether Tathāgatas appear or do not appear, the element of the reality of phenomena only thoroughly abides, and [it is] not otherwise.[59]

---

[56] Wonch'uk vol. *ti* (118), p. 406.2.

[57] Wonch'uk vol. *ti* (118), p. 406.2.

[58] Tsong kha pa (*Legs bshad snying po*; Sarnath: Pleasure of Elegant Sayings Printing Press, 1973, p. 17.10) reports that Wonch'uk states that these terms (*rtag pa rtag pa'i dus, nityakāla* and *ther zug ther zug gi dus, śāśvatakāla*) imply respectively a backwards looking orientation and a forward looking oriention. Tsong kha pa (p. 17.18) also states that Wonch'uk glosses "permanent, permanent time" as "former, former time" (*snga ma snga ma'i dus*) and that "everlasting, everlasting time" is glossed as "later, later time" (*phyi ma phyi ma'i dus*), but these glosses are not found in any of the four places (vol. *ti* [118], pp. 416, 512, 525, and 567) where Wonch'uk mentions the terms *rtag pa rtag pa'i dus* and *ther zug ther zug gi dus*, with the exception of p. 525.6, where Wonch'uk says that someone else's (*kha cig*) opinion equates *ther zug ther zug* with *phyi ma phyi ma*, but he does not claim this position as his own.

On p. 416.5 Wonch'uk states: "The suchness that is of one taste is (1) without oneness in the past from the beginning; therefore [the sūtra says,] 'permanent, permanent time'. It is (2) without oneness in the future; therefore [the sūtra says,] 'everlasting, everlasting time'". On p. 567.6, in a discussion of the uncompounded (*'dus ma byas, asaṃskṛta*) he states: "Because it abides as the reality of phenomena in permanent, permanent time and in everlasting, everlasting time, it is uncompounded".

[59] Stog p. 33.2; D p. 22.6.

Concluding Remarks

When we add these statements to those of the previous sections, we can see that although the sūtra began by warning us that the ultimate is ineffable and cannot be expressed in words it has made a number of statements about it, each of which is supposed to tell us something of its nature and functions. It is a quality of phenomena that is imperceptible to ordinary beings but which is known directly by Superiors through their exalted wisdom and vision. It is also all-pervasive and omnipresent, since it is said to characterize all compounded phenomena. It is permanent and changeless. It has no distinctions or differentiations, an idea that is also expressed in positive terms by the statement that it is "everywhere of one taste". It is non-dual and completely transcends any attempts to characterize, describe, or discuss it, and it is not something about which we can legitimately argue. It eludes any attempt to categorize it through verbal or conventional designations, and those who attempt to discuss or debate its nature tend to miss the reality of the ultimate.

Its main importance for religious practice, however, lies not in its elusiveness and resistance to categorization, but its function as an "object of observation for purification". If it were merely a quality that could only be perceived by Superiors but not by ordinary beings it would probably be of interest primarily as a sort of anomaly, something that is seen by one group but not by another. The ultimate, however, is an object of observation that when meditated on leads to the state of a Superior and the realizations associated with that state. Thus, through cultivating understanding of the ultimate one can transform oneself from an ordinary being into a Superior, can eliminate afflictions, and can progress toward complete enlightenment. This is what the sūtra seems to be urging its readers to do. If we discuss the ultimate, categorize it, argue about it, and construct philosophical systems around it, we will direct our attention away from meditating on it. If, on the other hand, we take it as an object of observation in meditation, this can lead to advanced states of realization and can initiate a process of meditative training that culminates in the attainment of Buddhahood.

The presentation of the ultimate in the sūtra contrasts sharply with some discussions of it by contemporary scholars, especially those who see its equivalent term, the thoroughly established character, as a state of awareness, a perfected level of understanding in which false imputational characters no longer operate. An examination of the literature discussing the ultimate in relation to Yogācāra (and the thoroughly established character in relation to the three natures [*trisvabhāva*] theory)[60] indicates that this is a prevalent notion in contemporary Buddhist scholarship. An example of this idea can be found in John Keenan's article, "Buddhist Yogācāra Philosophy as Ancilla Theologiæ", where he states that the thoroughly established character (which the *Saṃdhinirmocana-sūtra* equates with the ultimate) is

> awakening both to the true suchness of all things in the silence of ultimate meaning and also to the dependent co-arising of all human constructs and notions in terms of the other-dependent pattern.[61]

According to Keenan's presentation, the thoroughly established character is not a quality that pervades all phenomena and that is their true nature (as it is said to be in the *Saṃdhinirmocana-sūtra*), but instead is a state of awareness that is attained when one eliminates imputations (*kun brtags, parikalpa*). This is certainly not the way that it is presented in the sūtra, and I know of no Yogācāra treatise that presents the thoroughly established character as a state of awareness rather than as a quality that is found in all phenomena.

Keenan's presentation is similar to the model advocated by Gadjin Nagao, who contends that the thoroughly established character is something that is "consummated" or "perfected" by the contemplative practice of Buddhist meditators. He thinks that the Yogācāra idea of the three characters is based on a "principle of convertibility" in that when the imputational character (*kun brtags*

---

60 This division is also referred to as the "three characters" (*mtshan nyid gsum, trilakṣaṇa*).

61 *Japanese Religions* #15.5, 1988, p. 37.

pa'i mtshan nyid, parikalpita-lakṣaṇa) which is falsely attributed to the other-dependent character (*gzhan gyi dbang gi mtshan nyid, paratantra-lakṣaṇa*) is eliminated through meditative practice, this results in the conversion and perfection of the other-dependent character. Through this process it is transformed into the "consummated" or "perfected" nature (his translation of *yongs su grub pa'i mtshan nyid, pariniṣpanna-lakṣaṇa*) In his article, "The Buddhist World-View as Elucidated in the Three-Nature Theory and Its Similes", he writes that the term

> *pariniṣpanna* or "consummated" means perfect, real, and existent; and connotes 'reality', 'truth', 'real existence', or 'the absolute'. It does not mean that this reality exists in an ontological sense or that it is to be perceived epistemologically. It is a reality completely perfected or "consummated" by a practitioner through arduous practice.[62]

Like Keenan, Nagao thinks that the ultimate is not a quality of phenomena that is their ultimate nature (as the *Saṃdhinirmocana-sūtra* contends), but rather is something brought about by a religious practitioner. This corresponds to the understanding of the three characters that Alan Sponberg terms the "pivotal model", because in this conception the other-dependent is the basis for the false creation of imputations. According to this idea, it is the basis that is transformed or converted into the "consummated" nature.[63] In his article, "The Logic of Convertibility", Nagao argues that

> [t]he world is considered to be constituted of these three natures that are also called three "characteristics" (*lakṣaṇa*). The world, however, must remain at all times one and the same; therefore, the fact that the world is constituted of three natures does not mean that there are three worlds or

---

62 *The Eastern Buddhist* #16, 1983, p. 2.

63 Alan Sponberg, "The Trisvabhāva Doctrine in India and China: A Study of Three Exegetical Models", *Bukkyō Bunka Kenkyū-jo Kiyō*, #21, 1982, pp. 97-119. Unlike Nagao, Sponberg does not attribute this model to the *Saṃdhinirmocana*, but he does indicate that it is the model found in "classical Yogācāra" and cites the *Mahāyāna-saṃgraha* as an example of a text that upholds it (see pp. 99-101). His analysis of this model is similar to that of Keenan when he writes,

> Notice carefully the axial position of the Dependent in this analysis. This pivotal role of the Dependent is the most distinctive feature of the *trisvabhāva* doctrine in Classical Yogācāra. The Dependent can be mistaken to be something totally Imaginary; or, it can be understood in its true or Consummate nature (p. 100).

> three different realities side by side; it means that there is a world that is convertible from one nature to another.[64]

He goes on to state that the world always remains the same, but the world a particular person inhabits depends on whether or not that person has converted or perfected the other-dependent into the "consummated". As will be more fully developed in the next section, the *Saṃdhinirmocana* presents the three characters as aspects in terms of which phenomena may be viewed, not as alternative modes of constructing reality, which seems to be Nagao's notion, since he thinks that "there needs to be a conversion of the imagined nature of the world into the consummated nature".[65] A similar idea is seen in his statement, "the three natures are thus not lateral in their relationship but are convertible realities".[66] This is particularly clear when he writes,

> It is again this one and the same world that is characterized as "other-dependent"....It is in this world of dependent origination that we make our continual rounds of birth and death and it is therein that we become liberated from saṃsāra. Hell, and likewise the heaven, too, are to be found in this world, not elsewhere. It is the world itself that converts. Thus, the three-nature theory accounts for the structure of this world and sets forth the ground on which these conversions occur.[67]

The discussion of the three characters in the next section will consider the ontological and epistemological status of the imputational character and the other-dependent character in detail, but since the present section is mainly concerned with the ultimate, a term that in the *Saṃdhinirmocana-sūtra* is equivalent to *pariniṣpanna*, my comments will focus on that particular character.

As we have seen, the sūtra describes the ultimate as a quality of phenomena that characterizes all compounded things. It is said to be equivalent to the absence of self in phenomena, and in the sixth and seventh chapters we are told that the thoroughly established character is the non-existence of the imputations that are imputed to other-

---

64 "The Logic of Convertibility", in *Mādhyamika and Yogācāra* (Albany: SUNY Press, 1991), p. 131.
65 Ibid., p. 131.
66 Ibid., p. 135.
67 Ibid., p. 131.

dependent phenomena. In none of these descriptions is there any inkling that the thoroughly established character is something that is the result of a process of conversion of the other-dependent character. In addition, Nagao's contention that it does not exist in an ontological sense appears to contradict the sūtra's statements that it is a quality that pervades all phenomena at all times and that is their true nature. According to Nagao, it is not a quality of things that is present at all times, but rather a state of awareness that is reached by advanced practitioners. In his view, they "transform" the ordinary world and "consummate" it through their meditative practice, and so

> [t]he sages and enlightened ones also live in this one, unchanging world. But, because they are enlightened and are free of all false imagination and attachment, for them, the world is no longer imagined and contaminated; it is pure and "consummated". The world in which they live their lives differs in no way from our world. For them, too, summer is hot and winter is cold; willows are green and flowers are red. Due to their deep insight and detachment, however, only the pure and real world is manifested to them; the imagined world does not appear. It is in this sense that the one, unchanging world is referred to as possessing a "consummated" nature. It is "consummated" in the sense that it has assumed a nature of perfection owing to the long, assiduous training of the enlightened sages. In other words, the consummated world is established anew by them.[68]

I have quoted Nagao at length in order to demonstrate the extent to which his model differs from that presented in the *Saṃdhinirmocana*. It should also be noted that Nagao's ideas have influenced other recent studies, such as Stephen Kaplan's "A Holographic Alternative to a Traditional Yogācāra Simile", in which he cites Nagao's principle of convertibility with approval and agrees with his assessment that in the three natures schema *paratantra* is converted into

---

[68] Ibid., p. 4. It should be noted that although Nagao's interpretation appears to be at variance with that found in the *Saṃdhinirmocana* (and, as I will argue below, with other Yogācāra presentations of these ideas), it is fully in line with the Zen idea of how one transforms one's understanding of the world through practice. This observation is significant because Nagao indicates that his presentation accords with Zen understandings of how the world remains the same but is perceived differently by those who are enlightened (see "The Buddhist World-View", p. 4 note 2). I suspect that his concept owes more to Zen than to Yogācāra.

parinispanna.[69] Another example of a presentation that assumes this model can be found in Ian Harris' work, *The Continuity of Madhyamaka and Yogācāra in Indian Mahāyāna Buddhism*, in which he states that

> *paratantra* has a pivotal role in the theory. It can be externalised through imaginative activity as the imagined nature (*parikalpitasvabhāva*), while in its pristine condition it is necessarily uncontaminated. In this circumstance it is referred to as the accomplished nature (*parinispannasvabhāva*). The accomplished nature of course represents a level of knowledge in which independent existence of self and other are precluded and there is perfect union of knower and known, epistemology and ontology.[70]

Oddly enough, he backs up this statement with a quotation from the *Triṃśikā* which is at variance with his thesis but that accords with the presentation of the *Saṃdhinirmocana*,

> The thoroughly established character is the perpetual absence of the former [i.e., the imputational] in the latter [i.e., the other-dependent].[71]

I have attempted to establish that the convertibility model is prevalent in contemporary discussions of the three natures doctrine, but a question remains as to where the scholars cited above got this idea. As the discussion of the ultimate in the earlier sections of this chapter reveals, there is no sense in the *Saṃdhinirmocana* that the ultimate (or its equivalent term the thoroughly established character) is either a state of awareness or the result of meditative training. This is very clear in the sūtra's statement that

> in permanent, permanent time and in everlasting, everlasting time, whether Tathāgatas appear or do not appear, the element of the reality of phenomena only thoroughly abides, and [it is] not otherwise.[72]

---

[69] Stephen Kaplan, "A Holographic Alternative to a Traditional Yogācāra Simile", in *JIABS*, pp. 56-78. See also his earlier article, "*Paratantra* and *Parikalpita* as Epistemological Concepts in Yogācāra Buddhism and Holographic Psychology", in Nathan Katz, ed., *Buddhist and Western Psychology* (Boulder: Prajñā Press, 1983), especially pp. 218-20.

[70] Ian Charles Harris, *The Continuity of Madhyamaka and Yogācāra in Indian Mahāyāna Buddhism* (Leiden: E.J. Brill, 1991), p. 147.

[71] The Sanskrit passage (*Triṃśikā* 21b) reads: *niṣpannas tasya pūrvena sadā rahitatā tu yā*; quoted by Harris, p. 147. My translation differs slightly from Harris'. See also Harris, p. 107, where he expresses a similar thought.

[72] Stog p. 33.2; D p. 22.6.

This summarizes an important aspect of how the ultimate and the thoroughly established character are presented in the sūtra: these terms refer to a quality or aspect of phenomena that is independent of human activity. It is permanently and always the final nature of phenomena and it is not "consummated" or "perfected" by the actions of Tathāgatas or of any other beings. It is simply the true nature of reality.

Although he cites the *Saṃdhinirmocana-sūtra* near the beginning of his article, "The Buddhist World-View as Elucidated in the Three-Nature Theory" as one of the "main sources" used in his study,[73] Nagao's view of the relation of the thoroughly established character and compounded phenomena appears to be fundamentally at variance with that presented in the sūtra. While the sūtra states that it is the eternal, unchanging reality that pervades all phenomena and that it has nothing to do with the actions or realizations of individual beings, Nagao thinks that it is something that is brought about through the efforts of meditators. In his view, it appears that if there were no enlightened sages there would be no thoroughly established character, since for him it is something that must be "consummated" through the effort of religious practitioners.

The *Saṃdhinirmocana-sūtra*, as we have seen, rejects this view: according to the sūtra, it is an "object of observation for purification", something that exists permanently at all times, the ultimate reality that pervades all phenomena, and so it is something that meditators can take as their meditative object in order to eliminate obstructions. If it were something that is brought about through individual effort, as Nagao contends, it could not serve this function, since it would be the end result of meditative practice, rather than an object that facilitates it.

I can see no way of reconciling the two positions. For Nagao and others who accept his model (or variations on the model), the ultimate (the thoroughly established character) is something brought about through meditative training, a state of mind that allows en-

---

73 "The Buddhist World-View", p. 1 note 1.

lightened sages to perceive the world in a "consummated" aspect, while for the sūtra it is an ineffable, permanent quality of phenomena that is in no way dependent on individual effort for its actualization. It is simply the true nature of phenomena, and because of this it can serve as an object of observation for purification that one can use to bring about advanced levels of realization. Moreover, since the thoroughly established character, the ultimate, is also equated with the selflessness of phenomena, it is difficult to imagine how the sūtra's presentation of the ultimate could be reconciled with Nagao's interpretation, since in Mahāyāna Buddhist philosophy the selflessness of phenomena is a quality that characterizes all phenomena at all times and is not something that is brought about through meditative training. Rather, meditative training enables sages to perceive the true nature of phenomena directly, to understand that they lack self and that this is their final nature.

It would also be difficult to reconcile the sūtra's discussion of the ultimate and that of Nagao in light of the analogies presented in the third chapter of the *Saṃdhinirmocana* illustrating the relation between the ultimate and compounded phenomena. In these analogies, the ultimate is compared to the whiteness of a conch, the yellowness of gold, the melodiousness of a musical instrument, etc. In all of these analogies, the ultimate is compared to a quality that is present in a thing and is not something that is brought about through individual effort. No effort is required to make a conch white, or gold yellow: these qualities are present in conchs and gold, just as, according to the sūtra, the ultimate is always present in all compounded phenomena. There is no need for sages to "consummate" or "perfect" it through their meditative practice, since, according to the sūtra, it is just what it is in "permanent, permanent time" and in "everlasting, everlasting time". In other words, the ultimate character of phenomena is a quality that is present in them at all times, something that is not brought about or transformed through personal effort.

Although it is clear that Nagao's model is at variance with that of the *Saṃdhinirmocana*, it seems unlikely that a scholar of his stature would simply make up such a model without some basis. After researching statements about the three natures in Yogācāra treatises, my conclusion is that most Indian texts that I have seen are in accord with the presentation found in the sūtra (and that many are ambiguous enough to be read in more than one way), but it is worth mentioning a passage in the *Mahāyānasaṃgraha* that may support Nagao's hypothesis, one that he discusses in "The Buddhist World-View". The statement occurs in a passage which discusses analogies that explain the three natures in which Asaṅga states,

> What example is there for this subject [the three natures]? The example of auriferous clay (*kāñcanagarbha mṛttikā*). Thus, in the auriferous clay, one ascertains three things: the earth element (*pṛthivīdhātu*), the earth (*pṛthivī*), and the gold (*kāñcana*). In the earth element, the earth which is not found there is perceived, while the gold which is found there is not perceived. When one burns the earth element with fire, the earth does not appear, while the gold does appear. The earth element, when it appears as earth, has a false appearance; when it appears as gold, it has a true appearance. Consequently, the earth element enters into two parts at once [participates at once in the earth and the gold]. In the same way, when one has not burned perception (*vijñapti*) with the fire of intuitive wisdom (*nirvikalpakajñāna*), the false imaginary nature (*abhūtaparikalpitasvabhāva*) contained in this perception appears, while the true absolute nature (*bhūtapariniṣpannasvabhāva*) does not appear. When one burns perception with the fire of intuitive wisdom, the true absolute nature contained in this perception appears, while the false imaginary nature does not appear. Consequently, the dependent nature which is composed of the false imaginations of perception enters into the two parts at once [participates at once in defilement and purity] and is similar to the earth element in auriferous clay.[74]

In this example, we see a real basis (auriferous clay) that is transformed through the action of purifying it of dross elements, after which the pure gold ore shines forth with its innate lustre. This is comparable to Nagao's model, except for the fact that in the analogy the dross elements that are eliminated are real and not imagined.

---

[74] Étienne Lamotte, *La Somme du Grand Véhicule d'Asaṅga*, pp. 125-126. The translation is my rendering of Lamotte's French translation. I have eliminated many of Lamotte's reconstructions of Sanskrit terms in order to make the passage more readable.

As with Nagao's model, one thing is converted into another thing, and the latter is the result of purifying it of adventitious elements that keep its luminous potential from being realized. This analogy is mentioned by Nagao in "The Buddhist World-View", where he concludes that its purport is that just as gold is purified through wisdom, so enlightened sages purify *paratantra* through meditation, and thus

> when burned away by the fire of non-discriminative wisdom, the one world is transformed into the consummated world of the enlightened ones, and the consummated nature is fully manifested.[75]

While it is clearly plausible to draw such a conclusion from this analogy, it should be noted that there are other analogies in the *Mahāyānasaṃgraha* that oppose Nagao's ideas, such as the analogy in Chapter III.8 in which Asaṅga uses the classical image of the rope perceived as a snake.[76] In this analogy, a person in a dimly lit room looks at a coiled rope and mistakenly thinks that it is a snake. Upon re-examining this perception, the rope is revealed for what it is, and the snake-cognition disappears.

In the analogy, the rope is compared to the other-dependent character, the basis on which the mistaken idea of a snake is imputed. The non-existence of the snake that is imputed is the thoroughly established character. Asaṅga's conclusion is significant for our present discussion: he indicates that the rope itself is not a real thing, but is merely a composite of various qualities, such as color, odor, and tangibility.

> One enters that [i.e., cognition-only] in the same way [that one identifies] a rope which in the darkness seems to be a snake. Since it does not exist, the snake seen in the rope is an illusion (*bhrānti*). Those who recognize that it does not exist reject the notion of a snake (*sarpabuddhi*) and adhere to the notion of a rope (*rajjubuddhi*). But the rope itself, if one reduces it to its subtle elements, is an illusion, because its specific characteristics are color, odor, flavor, and tangibility.

---

[75] Nagao, "The Buddhist World-View", p. 10.

[76] Lamotte, *La Somme du Grand Véhicule d'Asaṅga*, pp.163-164. As with my translation of the previous passage from this text, I have eliminated many of Lamotte's reconstructions of Sanskrit terms in order to make the passage more readable.

> Thus, when one denies all reality to the six kinds of mental utterances which appear as words or things—just as one rejects the notion of snake [through the notion of rope]—one should also abolish, through the notion of absolute nature (*parinispannasvabhāvabuddhi*), the notion of Nothing-but-cognition (*vijñaptimātratābuddhi*) [subjacent to the mental utterances], just as one rejects the notion of the rope through the notion of color, etc.

This is quite different from Nagao's contention that

> [o]nly when attachment and false imagination are removed is the one unchanging world thoroughly purified and consummated as the pure world; that is to say, the imagined nature has been changed or converted into the consummated nature.[77]

Although this analogy appears to contradict Nagao's model, he cites it in support of his theories and interprets it as implying that a real thing (the rope) is the basis upon which one perceives both the illusion of the snake and the reality of the rope, which is the hemp from which it is made.

> In this simile, the 'snake' is, of course, to be equated with the imagined nature, the 'rope' with the other-dependent nature, and the 'hemp' with the consummated nature. Both 'snake' and 'rope' are negated to reach the final, substantial reality, 'hemp'.[78]

Not only is this interpretation not mentioned in the *Mahāyānasaṃgraha*, but at no point does Asaga intimate that the hemp from which the rope is made should be equated with the thoroughly established character. Nor is there any indication in this passage or anywhere else in the text that the thoroughly established character is a "substantial reality". On the contrary, Asaṅga appears to be using this analogy to deny the very notion of substance. He uses the analogy to indicate that the rope is merely a nominally designated entity that is a creation of thought, not that the hemp from which it is made is a real substantial entity that is found when one eliminates the idea of rope. The hemp is just as much a creation of the mind as the rope and is no more real. The notion of "hemp" is just as much an abstraction as the idea of a "rope", and one's mental creation of

---

77 "The Buddhist World-View", p. 5.
78 "The Buddhist World-View", p. 9.

this idea is based on a composite of elements, such as the way it appears, smells, feels, etc.

To return to our discussion of Nagao's ideas in relation to the *Saṃdhinirmocana*: as we have seen, there is a pronounced difference between his understanding of the thoroughly established character and the presentation found in the sūtra. It is significant that although he mentions the sūtra as a source, he seldom cites it in support of his theories. Rather, his argument seems to be based on a particular reading of a few analogies in other Yogācāra texts, at least one of which, as we have seen, could be read as being concordant with his model.

Our discussion of Nagao's ideas has taken us into a number of issues not directly raised by the *Sūtra Explaining the Thought*, but it has been useful in outlining some of the issues that are at stake in its presentations of the ultimate and the three natures. Since the topic of the three natures as presented in the sixth and seventh chapters of the sūtra is based on the presentation of the ultimate in the first four chapters, our discussion hopefully provides a useful transition to the discussion of the three natures in the following section. In order definitively to evaluate Nagao's theories, it would be necessary to examine a wide range of literature to see how exactly the three natures are presented, but such a study clearly exceeds the limits of the present work. The main goal of the preceding discussion has been to demonstrate the discrepancies between Nagao's interpretations and the presentation of the *Sūtra Explaining the Thought* in order to make clear exactly where the sūtra stands. The concept of the ultimate is one that still requires a great deal of study before definite conclusions can be reached concerning what it means in Buddhist literature. It may be that there are other texts which contain presentations concordant with Nagao's, but since the present study is limited to the *Saṃdhinirmocana-sūtra* a wider examination of other sources exceeds my self-imposed limitations. It is hoped that others will go beyond what has been presented here to consider other works and that future studies will add to our understanding of this concept, a concept that is crucial to understanding the ontology, epistemology, and meditation theory of Mahāyāna Buddhism.

CHAPTER FOUR

HERMENEUTICS AND TRADITION

In recent years a number of studies discussing "Buddhist hermeneutics" have appeared in journals and books, but with a few notable exceptions (such as John Maraldo's "Hermeneutics and Historicity in the Study of Buddhism"),[1] most have not seriously discussed the propriety of using the term hermeneutics in relation to Buddhist philosophy. This seems to me to be a major oversight, since I know of no term in any Asian language that exactly corresponds to the Western term "hermeneutics". This does not mean, of course, that hermeneutical concerns are not found in Buddhist thought, but rather that we should be wary of uncritically appropriating Western terminology without first considering whether or not this is justifiable. Since in this section I propose to discuss the hermeneutical theories of the *Saṃdhinirmocana-sūtra*, it will be useful to begin with a short excursus on how I understand the term "hermeneutics" and why I think that it is legitimate to use it in conjunction with a discussion of the *Saṃdhinirmocana*.

The etymology of the term hermeneutics is connected with Hermes, the messenger of the Greek gods and the intermediary between the gods and humanity. His task was to translate the wishes and commands of the gods into the language of humans, a task that required him to be conversant both with the language and idioms of humans. His intermediary position required him to know how to translate, convey, and explicate the messages sent from the gods to human beings. He had to understand for himself the intentions behind the gods' pronouncements and commands and how these could best be conveyed to humans, who neither spoke the gods'

---

[1] John C. Maraldo, "Hermeneutics and Historicity in the Study of Buddhism", *EB* #19.1, 1986, especially pp. 21-6.

language nor shared their worldview. It is significant that in Greek mythology Hermes is considered to be the inventor of language and writing (the principal tools by means of which we apprehend meaning and communicate it to others), because the discipline of hermeneutics is concerned with uncovering and explicating the meaning of utterances. As Paul Ricoeur states,

> The hermeneutical problem was first raised within the limits of *exegesis*, that is, within the framework of a discipline which proposes to understand a text—to understand it beginning with its intention, on the basis of what it attempts to say.[2]

The modern usage of the term hermeneutics derives from the Greek verb *hermēneuō*, which means "to interpret or explain" and the Greek noun *hermēneia*, which means "interpretation" or "explanation".[3] In both the classical Greek usage and in its modern meanings, hermeneutics is concerned with interpretation of the meaning of utterances (whether verbal, non-verbal, or written), and from very early times a distinction has been made between actual commentary and exegesis and the rules, methods, and theories governing them, which fall within the domain of hermeneutics. In Western thought, the term hermeneutics has strong connections with biblical interpretation, the discipline of articulating rules and methodologies for determining the meanings of scriptural statements and transmitting those meanings to readers of scripture.

According to Richard Palmer, the earliest example of this usage of the term occurs in the title of a book by J.C. Dannhauer that presents principles for interpretation of Christian scriptures, entitled *Hermeneutica sacra sive methodus exponendarum sacrarum litterarum*, published in 1654.[4] Palmer notes that until fairly recently the term hermeneutics has been primarily connected with biblical exegesis, but since the time of Schleiermacher (1768-1834)

---

2 Paul Ricoeur, "Existence and Hermeneutics", in *The Conflict of Interpretations*, ed. Don Ihde (Evanston: Northwestern University Press, 1974), p. 3.

3 See Henry George Liddell and Robert Scott, *A Greek-English Lexicon*, 9th ed. (1940), I, p. 690.

4 Richard E. Palmer, *Hermeneutics* (Evanston: Northwestern University Press, 1969), p. 34.

its range has been extended to the point where it is now viewed by many philosophers as being

> fundamental to all the humanities—all those disciplines occupied with the interpretation of the *works* of man. It is more than merely interdisciplinary, for its principles comprise a theoretical foundation for the humanities.[5]

Palmer distinguishes six divisions within the field of hermeneutics: (1) principles of biblical exegesis; (2) general philological methodology; (3) the science of linguistic understanding; (4) the methodological foundations of the human sciences (*Geisteswissenschaften*); (5) phenomenology of existence and existential understanding; and (6) systems of interpretation whose purpose is to determine the meanings behind myths and symbols.[6] He admits that there may be more divisions than this and that there is considerable overlapping and mutual influence between the various groups, but he thinks that each category represents a distinguishable trend in hermeneutics.

The first group, in Palmer's view, is primarily concerned with the rules and methods proper to interpretation of scripture, with developing viable and consistent standards to enable students of scripture to get at the meaning of sacred texts. The second group consists of biblical scholars who are concerned with philological questions related to Bible study. They propose to treat the Bible as literature and to use the same tools of study and exegesis that are used on other texts. As Spinoza expressed this approach, "The norm of biblical exegesis can only be the light of reason common to all".[7] According to Spinoza and other proponents of Rationalism, the Bible contains universal rational and moral truths, and the task of exegesis is to find the truths intended by the writers of scriptures and translate them in ways acceptable to enlightened reason.

The third group, represented primarily by Schleiermacher and his disciples, "reconceived hermeneutics as a 'science' or 'art' of

---

5 Ibid., p. 10.

6 Ibid., p. 33.

7 *Tractatus theologico-politicus* (1670), chapter 7; cited in Palmer, p. 38.

understanding".[8] For them, hermeneutics is concerned with determining and articulating the conditions that make understanding itself possible. The fourth group is represented by Wilhelm Dilthey (1833-1911), who championed the idea that hermeneutics properly understood can serve as the methodological foundation for all the human sciences and who wanted to find the principles underlying human understanding. Through this program, he hoped to determine the basic structures of understanding common to all the human sciences. The fifth group, represented by Martin Heidegger (1889-1976) and Hans-Georg Gadamer (b. 1900), sees understanding and interpretation as fundamental modes of human existence and proposes a phenomenological investigation of the ontological dimensions of understanding. In Heidegger's terminology, his purpose was to uncover how *Dasein* (literally, "Being-there", or human being) comes to understand itself, to find the processes of understanding and interpretation through which man can come to know the structure of his own being. The sixth division of hermeneutics is represented by Paul Ricoeur, who defines hermeneutics as a discipline primarily concerned with textual exegesis. He states, "We mean by hermeneutics the theory of rules that govern an exegesis, that is to say, an interpretation of a particular text or collection of signs susceptible of being considered as a text".[9]

In each of these cases, hermeneutics is conceived as being the rules and methodologies used in interpretation, rather than the act of interpretation itself. This distinction has also been noted by Maraldo, who distinguishes between textual exegesis and discussions of methods and rules for interpretation.

> In all Western developments of the term, hermeneutics is a highly reflective and self-conscious discipline that focuses on methods and principles of interpretation as opposed to interpretation or exegesis itself. In the modern sense of the term, an interpretive scheme or strategy is not "hermeneutical"

---

8 Palmer, p. 40.

9 Paul Ricoeur, *De l'interprétation*, p. 18, translated by Palmer, p. 43.

> unless it reflects an awareness of the problems of authorship, historical distance, and the historical position of the interpreter.[10]

This is an important distinction, and it will be used in the present section, which will be mainly concerned with the principles of interpretation outlined in the *Sūtra Explaining the Thought* and their ramifications for Buddhist philosophy. Another important concern of this chapter will be to examine the similarities and differences between Western approaches to hermeneutics and the theories presented in the sūtra and its commentaries. The aim of this study will be to look into the principles of interpretation as outlined in the sūtra in an attempt to determine how these compare with some Western formulations as well as their ramifications for the study and exegesis of Buddhist literature and for human understanding.

The first goal of this section will be to justify appropriating the term "hermeneutics" to describe an important focus of the sūtra. I will then outline the hermeneutical issues the text faces, how it proposes to resolve them, and how its resolutions were further explicated by some of the scholars who commented on the sūtra. Throughout this section, I will also attempt to show the connections between the thought of the first seven chapters of the sūtra and to indicate how the discussion of theories of interpretation in the seventh chapter is built upon the analysis of the nature of the ultimate (*don dam pa, paramārtha*) in the first four chapters. Some other important concerns of this chapter will be to show the com-

---

[10] John C. Maraldo, "Hermeneutics and Historicity in the Study of Buddhism", pp. 23-4. See also: (1) Maraldo, p. 26; (2) Ernst Steinkellner, "Remarks on Tantristic Hermeneutics", in L. Ligetti, ed., *Proceedings of the 1976 Csoma de Körös Symposium* (Budapest, 1978, Bibliotheca Orientalia Hungarica no. 23), pp. 445-458; and (3) Michael M. Broido, "Killing, Lying, Stealing, and Adultery: A Problem of Interpretation in the Tantras", in Donald S. Lopez, ed., *Buddhist Hermeneutics* (Honolulu: University of Hawaii Press, 1988), p. 82. On p. 83, Broido makes a statement that provides a good cautionary note for scholars trying to explicate "Buddhist hermeneutics":

> This important distinction cannot perhaps be made completely hard-and-fast, but it is essential that we nevertheless try to keep it in mind; for otherwise there will be nothing to prevent the study of Buddhist hermeneutics from becoming the study of absolutely anything within Buddhism. It is not difficult to see that this confusion is rampant in much work on Buddhist hermeneutics.

plex interrelationship between reason and authority in the sūtra and its commentaries and to analyze how implicit norms of tradition and notions of authority influence the thought of the text.

THE CASE OF *THE SŪTRA EXPLAINING THE THOUGHT*

The purpose of the foregoing discussion of hermeneutics was to set the stage for discussing the hermeneutical theory of the *Sūtra Explaining the Thought*. One problem immediately presents itself: since the term hermeneutics has its roots in Greek mythology and was later appropriated by Western philosophy to include such non-Buddhist tasks as exegesis of the Bible and the methodological foundations of the *Geisteswissenschaften*, what possible connection could this have with Buddhist philosophy? Or, to express the question another way, what term or terms in Buddhist philosophy correspond closely enough with the term hermeneutics to justify appropriating it for Buddhist studies?

As mentioned above, in this study a distinction will be drawn between texts that present rules for interpretation and others that simply interpret without explicating the theories in terms of which interpretations are formulated. All texts probably contain either explicit or implicit interpretations, but for our present purposes the focus will be on Buddhist texts that attempt to establish rules and methodologies in terms of which scriptures may be explicated. As Robert Thurman has pointed out, questions concerning interpretation are of crucial importance in Buddhism, since the Buddhist canon contains a huge number of texts that are considered by the tradition to have been spoken by Buddha, although these often contain contradictory and apparently incompatible doctrines.[11] When Buddhism spread to other countries, the size and scope of the Buddhist canon made it necessary for Buddhist scholars to devise sys-

---

[11] See Robert Thurman, "Buddhist Hermeneutics", *JAAR*, XI.VI.1, 1978, pp. 19-21. See also Étienne Lamotte, "The Assessment of Textual Interpretation in Buddhism" (in *Buddhist Hermeneutics*), pp. 16-17 for a discussion of the problems that the perceived self-contradictions of Buddha presented for Buddhist exegesis and hermeneutics.

tems in terms of which the differences could be reconciled that would allow them to distinguish consistently which texts and teachings would be normative for their particular traditions and which would be held to be of "interpretable meaning" (*drang ba'i don, neyārtha*).

In Tibet, one of the most influential texts that explicate rules for interpretation is Tsong kha pa's *Essence of the Good Explanations* (*Legs bshad snying po*), which is one of the main sources for the present study. The first part of this text, entitled "Mind-Only" (*sems tsam, citta-mātra*) outlines the rules for interpretation in the Mind-Only (or Yogācāra) school and is based on the *Sūtra Explaining the Thought* and on some of the main treatises of Asaṅga, Vasubandhu, and their commentators. In the first part of this text, Tsong kha pa cites passages from the sūtra and from Yogācāra treatises and evaluates various interpretation theories in Buddhist literature in order to formulate ground rules for interpretation according to the Yogācāra tradition. This text spawned a number of commentaries in Tibet that attempted to draw out the implications of Tsong kha pa's thought, and the process continues today in Tibetan monastic universities. A part of the curriculum studied in these monastic universities is called "The Interpretable and the Definitive" (*drang nges*), which is partly concerned with explicating the rules that govern interpretation of scriptures, and students in these universities are still debating the ramifications of Tsong kha pa's text. Since Tsong kha pa's work and part of the study based on it are concerned with explicating rules that govern interpretation of Buddhist scriptures, a plausible comparison can be made between this subject and Western biblical hermeneutics, since both are concerned with rules for interpreting the scriptures of their respective traditions.

In Indian literature, however, it is more difficult to find terms that correspond to Western usages of the term hermeneutics. One of the few examples of an Indian term that has some of the connotations of this word is the term "explaining the thought" (*saṃdhi-*

nirmocana) as it is used in the *Saṃdhinirmocana-sūtra*, in which Buddha not only explains what he was thinking of when he made some of his earlier statements, but also expounds general rules for determining the meaning of other scriptural statements and how to understand the thought behind them.

As we saw in the discussion of the meaning of the title in chapter two, the *Saṃdhinirmocana-sūtra* is a text in which Buddha is asked to explain what he was thinking of when he made certain statements. In the sūtra Buddha is confronted with a number of problematic teachings he had given previously and asked to make clear his underlying intention. Throughout most of the text, he discusses various matters of doctrine and responds to questions on specific points, but the most important section for the discussion of hermeneutics in the sūtra occurs in the seventh chapter, in which he provides general rules for interpreting some of his earlier statements. Since, as we have seen, hermeneutics is mainly concerned with articulating rules for interpretation, it seems to me that this term accurately describes an important focus of this chapter, which, among other things, sets forth principles for interpreting the thought behind certain of Buddha's statements.

The occasion for Buddha's outlining of these rules is a series of questions presented to him by the Bodhisattva Paramārthasamudgata, who asks:

> The Bhagavan [Buddha] spoke, in many ways, of the own-character (*rang gi mtshan nyid, svalakṣaṇa*) of the [five] aggregates...the [six] sense spheres, dependent arising, and the [four] sustenances...the own-character of the [four] truths...the constituents...the [four] mindful establishments... the [four] thorough abandonings, the [four] bases of magical emanations, the [five] powers, the [five] forces, and the [seven] branches of enlightenment....
>
> The Bhagavan also said that all phenomena are without entityness and that all phenomena are not produced, do not cease, are quiescent from the start, and are by nature in a state of nirvāṇa.
>
> Therefore, I am wondering of what the Bhagavan was thinking when he said, 'All phenomena are without entityness; all phenomena are unproduced, do not cease, are quiescent from the start, and are by nature in a state of nirvāṇa.' I ask the Bhagavan about the meaning of his saying, 'All phe-

> nomena are without entityness; all phenomena are unproduced, do not cease, are quiescent from the start, and are by nature in a state of nirvāṇa.'[12]

The format of this question indicates that there is a discrepancy between Buddha's teachings on the aggregates and so forth and his subsequent statements which indicated that "all phenomena are without entityness; all phenomena are unproduced, do not cease, are quiescent from the start, and are by nature in a state of nirvāṇa". The sūtra unfortunately does not spell out exactly what this discrepancy is, nor does it explicitly state that there is a contradiction between the two sets of teachings, but the format of Paramārthasamudgata's question, "I am wondering of what the Bhagavan was thinking when he said..." indicates that the two sets of teachings are in conflict and that there is a need for Buddha to explain the thought (*dgongs pa, abhiprāya*) behind them.[13] Thus, after quoting this passage in his commentary, Wonch'uk states that Paramārthasamudgata's question implies that

> because earlier Buddha spoke of the thirteen original types of phenomena—the aggregates, the sense spheres, the constituents, etc.—as existent by way of their own entityness and later spoke of all phenomena as unproduced by way of their own entityness, as unceasing, etc., the two teachings: (1) speaking of [the thirteen types of phenomena] as naturally existent; and (2) later speaking of [all phenomena] as without entityness are mutually contradictory. Therefore, the meaning of [Paramārthasamudgata's question] is, '[I] do not understand of what the Bhagavan was thinking in speaking of non-entityness and so forth.'[14]

---

[12] Stog p. 45.1; Sde dge edition (D) p. 31.3.

[13] For a detailed discussion of the term *dgongs pa*, which I render as "thought", see David S. Ruegg (who favors "intention, intended meaning, purport"), "Purport, Implicature, and Presupposition: Sanskrit Abhiprāya and Tibetan Dgoṅs pa/Dgoṅs gźi as Hermeneutical Concepts", *JIP* # 13, 1985, pp. 309-325. See also his meticulously researched and tightly argued article, "Allusiveness and Obliqueness in Buddhist Texts: *saṃdhā, saṃdhi, saṃdhyā* and *abhisaṃdhi*", in *Dialectes dans les Littératures Indo-Aryennes*, ed. Colette Caillat (Paris: Institut de Civilisation Indienne, 1989) and "An Indian Source for the Tibetan Hermeneutical Term Dgoṅs gźi 'Intentional Ground'", *JIP* #16, 1988, pp. 1-4. These terms are also discussed by Étienne Lamotte, "The Assessment of Textual Interpretation in Buddhism", p. 20. See also his note 40, p. 26, for a short bibliography of discussions of these terms.

[14] Wonch'uk, vol. *ti* (118) p. 552.4.

A similar idea is expressed in the *Essence of the Good Explanations* when Tsong kha pa quotes Paramārthasamudgata's question and states his intent in asking it in a paraphrase which makes clear that the sūtra implies that there is a contradiction between the two sets of teachings being discussed:

> This asks the following question: If the statements in some sūtras that all phenomena are without entityness etc., and the statements in some sūtras that the aggregates and so forth have an own-character, etc., were left as they are verbally, they would be contradictory. However, since [the Buddha] must be without contradiction, of what were you [Buddha] thinking when you spoke of non-entityness, etc.?[15]

---

[15] *The Essence of the Good Explanations* (*Legs bshad snying po*; Sarnath: Pleasure of Elegant Sayings Printing Press, 1979), p. 5.9. See also Donald Lopez ("On the Interpretation of the Mahāyāna Sūtras", in *Buddhist Hermeneutics*, p. 57), who states that the sūtra teaches that in the discourses mentioned by Paramārthasamudgata Buddha described the aggregates etc. as being "established by way of their own character". This statement is not, however, found in the sūtra; rather, Lopez conflates a later Dge lugs pa interpretation of the passages in question with the actual words of the sūtra. An examination of the seventh chapter reveals that the only places where this expression (i.e., "established by way of [a thing's] own character) is used in this part of the *Saṃdhinirmocana* are two sections in which Buddha asserts that imputations "do not exist by way of their own character" (see Stog pp. 47.6 and 49.4).

This is an example of a failure on Lopez' part to distinguish between what the sūtra itself says and what later Dge lugs pa exegetes interpreted it as implying. Another example can be found on p. 60, where he states that Buddha tells Paramārthasamudgata that he taught the third wheel because some trainees of the second wheel had misinterpreted his intention and fallen to an extreme of nihilism. In fact, in the sūtra it is Paramārthasamudgata who presents to Buddha the new vocabulary of the three wheels and indicates why each of the wheels was taught, and at no time does he state that some trainees of the second wheel fell to an extreme of nihilism. At no time in the seventh chapter does Buddha use the vocabulary of the three wheels. In addition, the idea that the sūtra contends that some second wheel trainees fell to an extreme of nihilism due to misunderstanding Buddha's final thought is also a Dge lugs pa interpretation of the purport of the sūtra's teachings, but Lopez fails to indicate that his source is not the sūtra but a particular sectarian interpretation of it. Lopez' article, although it contains some excellent insights into the importance of the *Saṃdhinirmocana* for Buddhist hermeneutics, must be read with great care because of such oversights. He seldom gives any indication that he understands the differences between the readings of Tibetan Dge lugs pa interpreters and what the sūtra actually says, and since the Dge lugs pas interpreted the sūtra for their own purposes as part of a hierarchical schema of Buddhist teachings which placed Prāsaṅgika-Madhyamaka at the top, great caution should be excercised by anyone who uses Dge lugs pa sources in interpreting this text.

A good study of the differences between the words of the sūtra and Dge lugs pa interpretations (along with detailed analyses of the motivations behind particular interpretations) can be found in Jeffrey Hopkins' forthcoming *Reflections on Reality*. When reading Dge lugs pa materials that comment on the *Saṃdhinirmocana-sūtra* and Yogācāra treatises, it is particularly important to be aware that an implicit assumption of Dge lugs literature is that the sūtra and

Both the phrasing of the question in the sūtra and Tsong kha pa's paraphrase of it indicate that there was a perceived conflict between the two sets of teachings and that Paramārthasamudgata is asking Buddha to outline a way to reconcile them. The perception of conflict between different sets of doctrines within a religious tradition is often the occasion for doctrinal and terminological innovation that attempts to explain away the apparent contradictions and reconcile one set of teachings with the other. As Robert Carroll writes, "dissonance gives rise to hermeneutics."[16] Moreover, cognitive psychology has shown that when such contradictions occur with regard to things to which an individual is deeply committed (such as religion), the experience of dissonance can be especially traumatic and will motivate people to find ways to reconcile or alleviate the contradiction. As Robert Wicklund and Jack Brehm express this, "When a person holds two cognitions that are in a dissonant relationship, the amount of dissonance he experiences is a direct function of how important those cognitions are to him."[17] In some cases where the perception of dissonance is strong enough, this may cause people to re-evaluate and even reject cognitions that are seen as conflicting with other strongly held convictions and in other cases may lead to a rejection of the authority upon which the original cognition was based.

In this passage, however, there is no apparent perceived need to reject the authority of Buddha's words just because some of his

---

the thinkers of the school that it inspired (e.g., Asaṅga and Vasubandhu) all spoke with one voice and shared a philosophical system that was in agreement in all important respects. They also assume that the system of Prāsaṅgika-Madhyamaka is the supreme Buddhist philosophical system and interpret other schools in light of this assumption. (Tsong kha pa and his followers even think that Asaṅga, being an advanced Buddhist practitioner, actually embraced Prāsaṅgika-Madhyamaka, but wrote from a Yogācāra point of view for the benefit of Buddhists who lacked the mental capacity to understand Prāsaṅgika.) Given these assumptions, which require Dge lugs pa exegetes to overlook differences in thought, style, etc. among different texts and authors, it is important to weigh their interpretations carefully and make clear the distinctions between their words and those of the texts they are considering.

16 Robert P. Carroll, *When Prophecy Failed* (New York: Seabury, 1979), p. 124.

17 Robert A. Wicklund and Jack W. Brehm, *Perspectives on Cognitive Dissonance* (New Jersey: Lawrence Erlbaum Associates, 1976), p. 2.

teachings are in conflict. Rather, Paramārthasamudgata is asking Buddha to provide explanations that will show a way to reconcile the doctrinal conflicts brought about by the teachings concerning non-entityness, etc., which appear to contradict his teachings on the aggregates, etc. This process of conflicts between old doctrines and paradigms and new paradigms and resolutions operates in all living religions, in which changing historical circumstances and new paradigms (such as the teachings on non-entityness) lead to cognitive conflicts. Unless these conflicts prove fatal to the religion, new paradigms and resolutions will be formulated to reduce the dissonance, but these often contain problems of their own, which in turn lead to further developments in religious paradigms and doctrines. Throughout this process of adaptation and innovation, the members of a religion will also strive to remain faithful to their tradition, and the dialectic of adaptation and continuity governs the process of development of religious organizations. As George Lindbeck describes this process, "Anomalies accumulate, old categories fail, and with luck or skill...new concepts are found that better serve to account for the data. If they are not found, the consequences can be intellectually and religiously traumatic."[18] All religious traditions undergo change, but at the same time struggle to retain their identity, and disagreements about which adjustments are appropriate are part of the hermeneutical process. According to Gadamer,

> [t]he hermeneutical problem only emerges clearly when there is no powerful tradition present to absorb one's own attitude into itself and when one is aware of confronting an alien tradition to which he has never belonged or one he no longer unquestioningly accepts.[19]

Although Gadamer's statement of the problem is perhaps too strong for this situation (since there is no evidence that the tradition itself is being called into question, but only that conflicting doctrines are being reconciled), it does hint at the problem that the

---

[18] George Lindbeck, *The Nature of Doctrine* (Philadelphia: Westminster Press, 1984), p. 8.
[19] Hans-Georg Gadamer, *Philosophical Hermeneutics*, tr. David E. Linge (Berkeley: University of California Press, 1976), p. 46.

sūtra is addressing, that of a perceived cognitive dissonance between two sets of teachings that was apparently strong enough to prompt the question raised by Paramārthasamudgata and to require new hermeneutical strategies and innovations in vocabulary to alleviate the problem. The tone of the questioning indicates, however, that the text was written at a time when traditional authority was still decisive, and there is no perceived need to reject the authority of Buddha because some of his teachings are in conflict.

Innovations in vocabulary are often attempts to reconcile apparent conflicts through proposing new terminology that either provides greater precision in making doctrinal distinctions or that enables sets of conflicting doctrines to be reconciled by means of the new terminology. The solution proposed by the *Sūtra Explaining the Thought* does both by introducing the vocabulary of the three "non-entitynesses" (*ngo bo nyid med pa, niḥsvabhāva*) of phenomena and the three "characters" (*mtshan nyid, lakṣaṇa*) of phenomena and stating that when Buddha gave his earlier teachings he was thinking of these.

> Paramārthasamudgata, thinking of three types of non-entityness of [phenomena]—the non-existence of an entityness in terms of character, the non-existence of an entityness in terms of production, and an ultimate non-entityness—I taught, 'All phenomena are without entityness.'[20]

He expands on this statement by equating each of these non-entitynesses with one of the three characters of phenomena.

> Paramārthasamudgata, if you ask, 'What is the non-entityness in terms of character of phenomena', [I reply,] 'It is the imputational character.' Why? It is thus: that [imputational character] is a character posited by nominal terminology and does not subsist by way of its own character. Therefore, it is said to be 'without entityness in terms of character.'
>
> Paramārthasamudgata, if you ask, 'What is the non-entityness in terms of production of phenomena,' [I reply,] 'It is that which is the other-dependent nature of phenomena.' Why? It is thus: Those [other-dependent phenomena] arise through the force of other conditions and not by themselves; therefore, they are said to be 'without entityness in terms of production.'

---

[20] Stog p. 47.3; D p. 32.7.

> "Paramārthasamudgata, if you ask, 'What is the ultimate non-entityness of phenomena,' [I reply,] 'Those dependently arisen phenomena that are without entityness due to being without entityness in terms of production are [also without entityness due to being] without the entityness of the ultimate.' Why? Paramārthasamudgata, I teach that that which is the object of observation for purification in phenomena is the 'ultimate', and since the other-dependent character is not the object of observation for purification, it is said to be 'without the entityness of the ultimate.'
>
> [Moreover,] Paramārthasamudgata, that which is the thoroughly established character of phenomena is also called the 'ultimate non-entityness.' Why? Paramārthasamudgata, that which in phenomena is the selflessness of phenomena is called their 'non-entityness'. It is the ultimate, and since the ultimate is distinguished by [being] the non-entityness of all phenomena, it is called the 'ultimate non-entityness'.[21]

The use of the term "character" to describe each of these non-entitynesses is reminiscent of the use of the same term to describe the ultimate (*don dam pa, paramārtha*) in relation to compounded phenomena (*'dus byas, saṃskṛta*) in the discussion of the ultimate in the first four chapters of the sūtra. In these chapters, the ultimate is described as being a characteristic or quality of phenomena, and so it is not surprising that in the seventh chapter the ultimate (which is equated with the thoroughly established character and the selflessness of phenomena) is again described in this way. In the above quoted passage, Buddha also describes two other characters of phenomena, the imputational character (*kun brtags pa'i mtshan nyid, parikalpita-lakṣaṇa*) and the other-dependent character (*gzhan gyi dbang gi mtshan nyid, paratantra-lakṣaṇa*), and he indicates that, like the ultimate, these are aspects in terms of which phenomena can be viewed and which are characteristics of compounded things. As Stephen Kaplan has noted, these are not ontological realities, but rather aspects of phenomena in terms of which things can be experienced.

> The Yogācāra doctrine of the three *svabhāvas* is not intended to divide the world into three distinct and separate ontological domains. Rather, the three

---

21 Stog p. 47.4; D p. 33.1.

> nature doctrine is intended to indicate that there is only one world and it can be known—experienced—in three ways.[22]

The ultimate is described in the sūtra as being a quality of phenomena that can be conceptually distinguished from the things that it characterizes and that can be discussed separately (like a conch and its white color) although they cannot be separated ontologically. This does not seem to be true of the case of the relation between imputational characters described in the sūtra and compounded phenomena, however, since the sūtra's discussion of imputational characters describes them as being completely unreal, like a sky-flower, and as being merely posited by terms and thought.[23] The

---

[22] Stephen Kaplan, "A Holographic Alternative to a Traditional Yogācāra Simile: Analysis of Vasubandhu's Trisvabhāva Doctrine", *EB* #23, 1990, p. 59.

[23] I qualify my discussion of imputational natures with the phrase "as described in the sūtra" on the basis of an important point made by Tsong kha pa, which is that the sūtra hints that not all imputations are non-existent. Tsong kha pa divides imputations into two types, existent and non-existent, and Jeffrey Hopkins points out that if there were no existent imputations this would contradict the sūtra's statement on Stog p. 59.2 that some beings develop a view of nihilism that causes them mistakenly to think that all phenomena do not exist, and this leads them to deprecate each of the three characters of phenomena, including the imputational character. If some imputations did not exist it would be impossible to deprecate imputations, since a person who viewed them as non-existent would be correct. According to Tsong kha pa (*Legs bshad snying po*, Sarnath ed., p. 13.11), when the sūtra compares imputations to sky-flowers (which are completely non-existent), this "is an example of their merely being imputed by thought and is not an example of their not occuring among objects of knowledge". It should not be taken to mean that they are completely non-existent like sky-flowers. Hopkins points out that space, for example (which is defined in the sūtra as "a mere absence of the entityness of forms" that "pervades everywhere"), is an imputation that exists, and the sūtra's references to it treat it as such. Moreover, it must belong to the class of imputations, since it is described as being uncompounded (and so it cannot be an other-powered nature, since these are compounded in the sense of being produced by other causes and conditions), but it is not a thoroughly established nature (since the sūtra states that a thoroughly established nature must be an object of observation for purification, and space is not). Since it is described as pervading everywhere, it must exist, since it is incomprehensible that something that is all-pervasive is also non-existent. For a discussion of Buddhist understandings of the term "space", see Thomas E. Wood, *Mind Only: A Philosophical and Doctrinal Analysis of the Vijñānavāda* (Honolulu: University of Hawaii Press, 1991), p. 246 n. 17.

To return to our previous point, however, the descriptions of imputations in the sūtra characterize them as non-existent, but the sūtra's statement that a view which treats all imputations as completely non-existent is mistaken indicates that it agrees with Tsong kha pa's point that there are some that do exist, although it does not elaborate on this. Nor does it indicate any examples of existent imputations. For this reason, I have chosen to limit the extension of the discussion of imputations to those specifically mentioned in the sūtra in order to leave open the possibility that some imputations are not completely non-existent.

overall impression that the sūtra gives is that the imputational characters it describes are conceptual overlays falsely attributed to things, like the hairs and so forth seen by people with faulty vision or the yellow hue that colors the perceptions of people with jaundice. In the verses at the end of chapter six, imputational characters are described as being "phenomena that have a non-existent character", and Byang chub rdzu 'phrul asserts that they are "utterly non-existent in terms of both truths".[24]

Although they are perceived, the state of affairs that they indicate is merely a deception caused by misconceptions, and so, while the ultimate is described as being an essential and inseparable quality of a thing (like the color of a conch), there would seem to be no reason that the imputational characters described in the sūtra could not be eliminated without changing the ontological status of the things to which they are attributed (as, for instance, if the condition that causes a person with jaundice to see things as yellow is removed, that person will no longer perceive them as having a yellow hue, but the elimination of the false conception of yellowness will not eliminate the objects that one had previously perceived as being yellow). Buddha describes the relation between the three characters as follows:

> The imputational character is to be viewed as being like the faults of clouded vision that exist in the eye of a person who has clouded vision. It is like this: For example, the other-dependent character is to be viewed as being like the signs of clouded vision of that very [being], which appear as: the signs of a hair-net, or flies, or sesame seeds; or an appearance of either a sign of blue, a sign of yellow, a sign of red, or a sign of white.... When the eyes of just that very being become purified and faults of clouded vision that have formed in the eyes do not exist, the thoroughly established character is to be viewed as being like the object of operation which is the natural object of operation of that person's eyes.[25]

This passage indicates that the imputational character as described in the sūtra is something falsely or mistakenly attributed to other-

---

[24] Stog p. 44.5; D p. 30.7; Byang chub rdzu 'phrul, vol. *cho* (205), p. 213.5.
[25] Stog p. 41.1; D p. 28.2.

dependent phenomena, but that when one views the thoroughly established character imputations no longer appear. The sūtra explains that this is because the thoroughly established character is an "object of observation for purification", which according to the sūtra means that it is an object that when meditated on serves to eliminate obstructions. In the context of the discussion of the three characters, this means that when one takes the thoroughly established character as one's object of observation, this can serve to eliminate the false views of imputations. Buddha continues,[26]

> That which is the non-establishment—of the objects of activity of conceptuality, that is to say, the foundations of imputational characters and those which have the signs of compounded phenomena—as that imputational character, that which is just the absence of entityness of only that [imputational] nature, that which is the absence of a self of phenomena, which is suchness, the object of observation for purification, is the thoroughly established character.

In other words, the thoroughly established character, the ultimate truth, is an absence of a quality that is attributed to other-dependent characters. This quality, the imputational character, is a conceptual overlay that people mistakenly attribute to other-dependent phenomena, although in reality they do not possess this quality. Moreover, the attribution of the imputational character is not merely erroneous; it is also psychically and spiritually harmful and is an obstruction that prevents progress on the Buddhist path.

Buddha then elaborates on his earlier discussion of imputational characters as being "non-entitynesses in terms of character" by stating that when he spoke of all phenomena as being unproduced, unceasing, and quiescent from the start it was in consideration of the fact that imputational characters do not exist by way of their own character, and so they cannot be said to be produced. Since they are not produced, they cannot cease, and so they are also "quiescent from the start". He adds that the ultimate is also unproduced and so forth because it does not arise in dependence upon

[26] Stog p. 64.3; D p. 45.7.

causes and conditions, is not compounded, and is just the absence of a self of phenomena. The selflessness of phenomena is always the true nature of phenomena, never changes into something else, is devoid of all obstructions, and so it also is quiescent from the start and by nature in a state of nirvāṇa. Thus, Buddha tells Paramārthasamudgata,[27]

> Thinking of the ultimate non-entityness that is distinguished by [being] the selflessness of phenomena, I taught, 'All phenomena are unproduced, unceasing, quiescent from the start, and by nature in a state of nirvāṇa.' Why? It is thus: the reality, the uncompoundedness, the freedom from all obstructions in phenomena, which is the ultimate non-entityness and which is distinguished by [being] the selflessness of phenomena, abides in permanent, permanent time and everlasting, everlasting time. That which abides in permanent, permanent time and everlasting, everlasting time, due to [being] just that reality, is uncompounded. Because it is uncompounded, it is not produced. It is unceasing. Because it is devoid of all obstructions, it is quiescent from the start. That is by nature in a state of nirvāṇa. Therefore, also thinking of the ultimate non-entityness that is distinguished by [being] the selflessness of phenomena, I taught, 'All phenomena are unproduced, unceasing, are quiescent from the start, and are by nature in a state of nirvāṇa.'

These passages indicate the outlines of how Buddha explains the thought behind his statements that all phenomena are unproduced and so forth. He states that when he made these pronouncements he was thinking of specific aspects of phenomena, and his remarks were made with reference to these, although he did not explicitly make this point. Thus, although he made sweeping statements that "all phenomena are unproduced, do not cease, are quiescent from the start, and are by nature in a state of nirvṇa", he was thinking of specific ways in which phenomena are unproduced and so forth. The vocabulary innovations of the three characters and three non-entitynesses indicate the thought behind his earlier statements and provide models in terms of which the contradictions implicit in them can be reconciled.

---

[27] Stog p. 49.6; D p. 34.7.

Thus, Buddha indicates that when he declared that all phenomena are unproduced he was thinking that the imputational characters described in the sūtra are unproduced in the sense that they are without entityness in terms of character and are like a sky-flower (which is completely non-existent), and so they cannot be said to be produced. Other-dependent phenomena are unproduced in the sense that they are not produced by their own power, but require other causes and conditions for their production. The thoroughly established character is unproduced in the sense that it is uncompounded and is just the selflessness of phenomena, which does not come into being due to causes and conditions and is always the final nature of phenomena. Looked at in these ways, these three characters are said to be "unproduced", and if they are unproduced they must also be unceasing (since they are not produced in the first place), and so they can also be said to be "quiescent from the start" and "by nature in a state of nirvāṇa". Byang chub rdzu 'phrul comments that

> the imputational character is a character that is posited in the manner of names and terminology but is not posited by way of its own character; therefore, since it is utterly non-existent in terms of both truths, it is a non-entityness due to being a non-entityness in terms of character. The other-dependent character is produced by the power of other conditions but is not [produced] by way of its nature; therefore—since it exists merely [like] a magician's illusions in terms of conventional truths—it is a non-entityness due to being a non-entityness in terms of production, and—since it does not have ultimate non-entityness because it is not an object of observation for purification—it is not an ultimate non-entityness because it is not an ultimate truth; thus, it is a non-entityness. Also, the thoroughly established character is the ultimate, and the ultimate is distinguished by being the non-entityness of all phenomena, and—because it is both the ultimate truth and a non-entityness—it is a non-entityness due to being the ultimate non-entityness.[28]

Paramārthasamudgata expands on Buddha's answer by stating that Buddha had a thought behind his earlier teachings and that when he spoke of the non-entityness in terms of character of phenomena he

---

[28] Byang chub rdzu 'phrul, vol. *cho* (205), p. 213.5.

was referring to imputational characters, which are merely imputed by names and terminology and have no real mode of subsistence. When he said that phenomena lack entityness in terms of production he was speaking of other-dependent characters, which serve as the bases of imputations. These lack entityness in terms of production in the sense that they depend upon other causes and conditions for their production and are not produced autonomously.

The vocabulary innovations of the three non-entitynesses and the three characters allow the *Sūtra Explaining the Thought* to reconcile the apparent conflict of Buddha's earlier statements and to provide an exegetical model by means of which one can posit the thought behind them. As Paramārthasamudgata explains it,

> I offer the meaning of what the Bhagavan said as follows: Those which are posited by nominal terminology—to the objects of activity of conceptuality, that is to say, the foundations of imputational characters and those which have the signs of compounded phenomena—as the character of entities [such as] 'form aggregate' or attributes [such as 'the production of form'] and that which is posited through nominal terminology as the character of entities or the character of attributes [such as] 'the production of the form aggregate,' 'the cessation [of the form aggregate],' 'the abandonment and knowledge [of the form aggregate]' are imputational characters. In dependence upon those, the Bhagavan designated the non-entityness, in terms of character, of phenomena.
>
> Those which are the objects of activity of conceptuality, that is to say, the foundations of imputational characters and those which have the signs of compounded phenomena, are other-dependent characters. In dependence upon those, the Bhagavan designated the non-entityness, in terms of production, of phenomena, and, in addition, [designated] the non-entityness in terms of the ultimate....
>
> That which is the non-establishment—of the objects of activity of conceptuality, that is to say, the foundations of imputational characters and those which have the signs of compounded phenomena—as that imputational character, that which is just the absence of entityness of only that [imputational] nature, that which is the absence of a self of phenomena, which is suchness, the object of observation for purification, is the thoroughly established character. In dependence upon that, the Bhagavan, in addition, designated the ultimate non-entityness of phenomena.
>
> Just as this is applied to the form aggregate, so this should be applied similarly to the remaining aggregates. Just as this is applied to the aggregates, so this should be applied similarly to each of the sense spheres that are the twelve sense spheres. This should be applied similarly to each of the limbs of existence that are the twelve limbs of existence. This should be

> applied similarly to each of the sustenances that are the four sustenances. This should be applied similarly to each of the constituents that are the six constituents and the eighteen constituents.[29]

As a strategy for interpreting Buddha's teachings, this has a wide range of application, since the aggregates, sense-spheres, and so forth include all phenomena. As a framework for interpreting cognitive experience, it also has wide-ranging applications. In laying out the terminology of the three non-entitynesses and the three characters, the *Saṃdhinirmocana-sūtra* has provided a way to reconcile apparently contradictory statements, and it also provides what could be called an "epistemological hermeneutic" that could apply to a broad spectrum of cognitive phenomena. I use the term "epistemological hermeneutic" to describe this model because it outlines a framework for interpreting the presuppositions, veracity (truth value, reliability, validity), and nature of knowledge and a way of categorizing cognitive experience. For example, the sūtra's categorization of imputational characters as false conceptions superimposed on other-dependent phenomena is a description of a particular way of perceiving and relating to our surroundings, one that is determined by false conceptions of reality that influence how and what we experience. The sūtra itself implicitly makes this connection, which indicates that its teachings have ramifications beyond the limited goal of reconciling the two sets of teachings mentioned above.

Thus, the sūtra's statements that imputational characters are attributed to other-dependent phenomena in terms of names and conceptions is a description of how most people view reality, and when one's understanding is structured in terms of mistaken conceptual imputations one could be said to be apprehending reality on the level of the mistaken imputational characters described in the sūtra. Such apprehension is erroneous, misunderstands the true nature of the objects of one's experience, and involves attributing to

---

[29] Stog p. 63.6; D p. 44.3.

objects qualities that they lack. Wonch'uk makes this point when he writes,

> Why is it called 'imputational'? Because conceptual mental consciousness, having immeasurable aspects, just gives rise to error, it is termed 'imputational'. Because while [phenomena] do not truly have their own character it merely conceptually apprehends [them] in that way, it is [called] 'imputational'.[30]

As a description of a particular way of experiencing, this indicates that when one's perceptions operate on the level of imputational characters, one engages in superimposing qualities onto phenomena that they do not possess. When, however, one understands compounded phenomena as being produced in dependence upon causes and conditions, one apprehends them in terms of the other-dependent character, which refers to a phenomenon's being produced by causes and conditions. As Buddha describes this character in chapter six of the sūtra,

> The other-dependent character of phenomena...is just the dependent arising of phenomena. It is thus: Because this exists, that arises; because this is produced, that is produced.[31]

A person who understands compounded phenomena in terms of the other-dependent character perceives them as being produced by other causes and conditions and does not imagine that they are produced by way of their own nature. This represents a significant advance in understanding and indicates that one has eliminated some of the false conceptions in terms of which one previously perceived things.[32]

---

30 Wonch'uk, vol. *ti* (118), p. 496.4.

31 Stog p. 40.5; D p. 27.6.

32 This conception of the other-dependent character is at odds with the presentation of the three natures in Ian Charles Harris' work, *The Continuity of Madhyamaka and Yogācāra in Indian Mahāyāna Buddhism* (Leiden: E.J. Brill, 1991, p. 106), in which he contends that the other-dependent is so named in the *Saṃdhinirmocana* because "the first characteristic [i.e., the imputational] is dependent upon it and it acts as the support for the imagined characteristic". As we have seen, the sūtra clearly indicates that it is called "other-dependent" because it depends on other cause and conditions, not because something other depends on it.

The next decisive advance in understanding comes when one perceives the non-existence of imputational characters that were previously superimposed onto other-dependent phenomena. At this point, one perceives objects in a manner that is free from certain types of mistaken imputations. One overcomes the afflictions that resulted from previous misunderstanding of the true nature of phenomena through taking to mind the thoroughly established character, which is said to be the ultimate non-entityness and an object of observation for purification of obstructions.

In its presentation of the level of understanding attained by those who perceive phenomena in terms of the thoroughly established character, the sūtra describes the broad outlines of the sort of realization that can free sentient beings from the illusions which mire them in ignorance and delusion. When we perceive the non-existence of the imputational characters that were superimposed onto other-dependent phenomena, then we can perceive objects in terms of the ultimate truth, because the fact that phenomena are utterly devoid of imputational characters is the ultimate truth. One who perceives the absence of imputational characters that are imputed to other-dependent phenomena knows the ultimate.

The applicability of the three characters schema to cognitive experience indicates the range of the hermeneutical theory of the *Sūtra Explaining the Thought*. The intent of the discussions of strategies of interpretation presented in the text is not simply to provide guidelines for interpreting certain texts and teachings, but to suggest new ways of viewing the world which, if properly understood, can radically transform one's consciousness and overturn deeply rooted misconceptions about the nature of reality. This attitude accords with Ricoeur's idea that the world is the ultimate referent of a text,[33] since the aim of Buddhist teachings is to bring about the elimination of one's illusions and misconceptions about

[33] Paul Ricoeur, *Interpretation Theory* (Fort Worth: Texas Christian University Press, 1976), pp. 36-7.

the world and to replace them with understanding that accords with reality. This focus has been noted with respect to Buddhist hermeneutics by Étienne Lamotte, who states that sound hermeneutics in Buddhism is based not on theoretical understanding, but on direct knowledge of reality.[34] This is certainly true of the *Sūtra Explaining the Thought*, which stresses the importance of direct personal understanding and the soteriological benefits gained by those who contemplate its teachings.

The hermeneutical principles outlined in the *Sūtra Explaining the Thought* are not merely guidelines for textual exegesis; rather, the goal of Buddhist doctrine is to present guidelines for re-interpreting all of one's experience, to reorient one's perceptions and understandings in such a way that one is no longer confused and deluded by false appearances and mistaken conceptions. In this sense, the referents of Buddhist teachings are the world and one's perceptions of it.

Of course, the same claim could be made for many (or perhaps most) religious texts, but I think that the distinctive feature of the *Saṃdhinirmocana-sūtra* is its presentation of a comprehensive worldview in terms of which Buddhist practitioners are to interpret all aspects of their experience and reorient their attitudes and perceptions. Other Buddhist texts, such as the corpus of texts that outline the rules of monastic discipline, also provide guidelines for changing one's lifestyle and reorienting one's thinking, but the *Saṃdhinirmocana* proposes a model for fundamental and comprehensive restructuring of the worldviews and cognitions of the trainees of the sūtra that if fully actualized will profoundly influence every aspect of cognitive experience. This attitude is reflected in the sūtra in Buddha's explanations of the cognitive and existential ramifications of his teachings on the three non-entitynesses and the three characters:

---

[34] Étienne Lamotte, "The Assessment of Textual Interpretation in Buddhism", in *Buddhist Hermeneutics*, p. 23.

> The Tathāgata teaches them doctrines stemming from non-entitynesses in terms of character and ultimate non-entitynesses in order that [those beings] become averse toward all compounded phenomena, become separated from desire, become completely released, pass beyond the afflictions that are the afflictive emotions, pass beyond the afflictions that are actions, and so that they pass beyond the afflictions that are lifetimes. Because, hearing these doctrines, they do not conceive other-dependent characters to be the imputational character, they believe and understand non-entitynesses in terms of production [that is to say, other-dependent phenomena] to be without the entity of character and without the entity of the ultimate, whereupon they realize, just as it is, [the other-dependent nature]....On this basis, they develop aversion toward all compounded phenomena, become completely free from desire, become completely released, and become released from the afflictive afflictions, the afflictions that are actions, and the afflictions that are lifetimes. With respect to that, Paramārthasamudgata, through just this path and through just this procedure, even sentient beings who have the lineage of the Hearer vehicle attain the unsurpassed accomplishment and blissful nirvāṇa. Through just this path and through just this procedure, sentient beings who have the lineage of the Solitary Realizer vehicle and those who have the lineage of the Tathāgata vehicle attain the unsurpassed accomplishment and blissful nirvāṇa.[35]

As this passage indicates, Buddha's intention in presenting the terminological innovations of the three non-entitynesses and the three characters is not only to provide an exegetical schema through which contradictions in his earlier statements can be reconciled, but also to facilitate a reorientation of the perceptions of sentient beings whose understanding of reality is mistaken. The ultimate aim expressed in this passage is a soteriological one, involving first overcoming misconceptions, desires, and afflictions through eliminating the wrong views that give rise to them and then leading those who follow this training to a transformation of the way they view reality that culminates in the attainment of nirvāṇa.

[35] Stog p. 53.3; D p. 37.3.

CHAPTER FIVE

THE THREE WHEELS OF DOCTRINE

The discussion of the thought behind Buddha's conflicting teachings is further developed by Paramārthasamudgata in a section near the end of the seventh chapter where he characterizes the doctrinal differences in Buddha's teachings in terms of "wheels of doctrine" (*chos kyi 'khor lo, dharma-cakra*). In what appears to be a summary of the discussion of the doctrinal conflicts caused by Buddha's teachings asserting the non-entityness and so forth of phenomena and the resolutions proposed by the vocabulary innovations of the three characters and the three non-entitynesses, he indicates that Buddha has given specific teachings to certain groups of trainees, and he implies that each group was presented with teachings that conform to its level of understanding. The first wheel of doctrine that he describes consists of teachings spoken at the Deer Park in Sarnath, which were given to Hearers (*nyan thos, śrāvaka*) and which were primarily articulated in terms of the four noble truths.

> Initially, in the area of Vārānasī in the Deer Park [called] 'Sage's Alighting', the Bhagavan turned a wheel of doctrine for those who were engaged in the Hearer vehicle, fantastic and marvelous, which none—god or human—had turned in a similar fashion in the world, through teaching the aspects of the four noble truths.[1]

Paramārthasamudgata states that this wheel of doctrine "is surpassable, provides an opportunity [for refutation], is of interpretable meaning, and serves as a basis for dispute."[2] The description of these teachings indicates that they include Buddha's teachings concerning the aggregates and so forth and that they were presented for a particular group for a particular purpose. An underlying assumption behind this description is that Buddha taught them such doc-

---

1 Stog p. 69.4; D p. 48.5.

2 Stog p. 69.6; D p. 48.7.

trines for their own benefit, although they did not represent his final thought and thus were of interpretable meaning.

The second wheel of doctrine consists of teachings given to Mahāyānists in which Buddha taught that phenomena lack entityness, are unproduced, do not cease, are quiescent from the start, and are by nature in a state of nirvāṇa. These teachings are not correct on the literal level, however, and need to be explained in terms of the three types of non-entityness of phenomena.

> During the second period, based on the absence of entityness of phenomena and based on the absence of production, the absence of cessation, quiescence from the start, and [the fact that phenomena] are by nature in a state of nirvāṇa, the Bhagavan turned a second wheel of doctrine, for those engaged in the Great Vehicle, very fantastic and marvelous, in an elaborative way. Furthermore, that wheel of doctrine turned by the Bhagavan is surpassable, provides an opportunity [for refutation], is of interpretable meaning, and serves as a basis for dispute.[3]

This passage indicates that the second wheel consists of Buddha's statements that all phenomena lack entityness, production, etc., which were the source of the doctrinal conflicts discussed above. These teachings appeared to contradict his earlier teachings regarding the aggregates, etc., teachings that were spoken with reference to "aspects of the four noble truths". As Blo bzang dkon mchog explains the doctrinal conflict,

> The middle turning of the wheel indicated [in the *Saṃdhinirmocana-sūtra*]—the Mahāyāna sūtras on the profound, the perfection of wisdom—is not literal because, thinking of the non-entityness of the first of the three natures—imputations, other-dependent natures, and thoroughly established natures—and thinking of the non-entityness in terms of production of the second [i.e., other-dependent natures], and thinking of the ultimacy and non-entityness of the third [i.e., thoroughly established natures, Buddha] said that all phenomena lack entityness. Therefore [the middle wheel] is not suitable to be literal because in that case [Buddha] would have spoken deprecatingly of all three natures.[4]

Since the teachings presented in the second wheel were not acceptable on the literal level, Buddha turns a third "wheel of doctrine" in

---

3 Stog p. 69.7; D p. 48.7.

4 Blo bzang dkon mchog (in his *Grub mtha' rtsa ba'i tshig ṭik shel dkar me long*, a word commentary on 'Jam dbyangs bzhad pa's *Great Exposition of Tenets*; *Grub mtha' chen mo*; Delhi: Chophel Legden, 1978), p. 123.2; tr. Jeffrey Hopkins, unpublished manuscript, p. 207.

the *Sūtra Explaining the Thought* in which he introduces new vocabulary and doctrines (for example, the three characters and the three wheels) that provide the keys to understanding the thought behind his earlier teachings for those of his followers who had been confused by his second wheel teachings and who saw them as being in conflict with the teachings of the first wheel.

> During the third period, based on the absence of entityness of phenomena and based on the absence of production, the absence of cessation, quiescence from the start, and [the fact that phenomena] are by nature in a state of nirvāṇa, the Bhagavan turned a third wheel of doctrine for those who are engaged in all vehicles, extremely fantastic and marvelous, through the distinctiveness of thorough differentiation. This wheel of doctrine is unsurpassable, does not provide an opportunity [for refutation], is of definitive meaning, and does not serve as a basis for dispute.[5]

According to these passages, both the second and third wheels are "based on the absence of entityness of phenomena and based on their absence of production" and so forth, which indicates that the focus of both is the same set of teachings, but the second wheel is described as being of interpretable meaning, while the third wheel is of definitive meaning. The third wheel is described by Paramārthasamudgata as the wheel in which Buddha teaches "through the distinctiveness of thorough differentiation" because in this wheel Buddha explains what he was thinking of when he gave the teachings of the middle wheel. He differentiates the three non-entitynesses and indicates that the first two wheels are of interpretable meaning while the third is of definitive meaning.[6] Dpal 'byor lhun grub comments that third wheel teachings are "unsurpassable" (*bla na ma mchis pa, anuttara*) because there are no sūtras of definitive meaning that are superior to them. They "do not provide an opportunity [for refutation]" (*skabs ma mchis pa, anavakaśa*) because there is no opportunity for opponents validly to dispute them in

---

[5] Stog p. 70.3; D p. 49.2.

[6] It should be noted that this distinction between interpretable and definitive teachings is not unique to the *Saṃdhinirmocana-sūtra* and is found at least as early as *Aṅguttara* I.60. For a discussion of these terms, see Étienne Lamotte, "The Assessment of Textual Interpretation in Buddhism", p. 17 and David S. Ruegg, "Allusiveness and Obliqueness in Buddhist Texts", especially pp. 297-9.

terms of the literal readings of the teachings. They are of "definitive meaning" (*nges pa'i don, nītārtha*) because they "need not be interpreted as something else and are definitive as that meaning" (*'di'i don gzhan du drang mi dgos shing don der nges pa'o*).[7] Tsong kha pa comments that the statement that the third wheel does not involve controversy

> should be taken as [meaning] that since the [sūtra] indicates the existence or non-existence of entityness, there is no place for controversy when scholars analyze whether the meaning of the sūtra is or is not delineated in that way.[8]

Wonch'uk[9] states that the first wheel includes doctrines in which Buddha "thoroughly teaches the causes and effects of cyclic existence and nirvāṇa in the Deer Park for those inclined toward the Hearer vehicle; this is 'the wheel of doctrine of the four truths'." The second wheel includes "teachings of the superior Perfection of Wisdom [Sūtras] to sixteen congregations at the Vulture Peak and so forth to those who are inclined toward the Bodhisattva vehicle; this is the wheel of doctrine of absence of character" (*mtshan nyid med pa'i chos kyi 'khor lo*). The teachings of the third wheel, however, are those teachings that are for "those inclined toward all vehicles".

> Because in this sūtra the meaning of the very profound and hidden thought of all of the three vehicles which is difficult to unravel is revealed and clearly indicated, it is called '[*Sūtra*] *Explaining the Profound Thought*'.[10]

These third wheel teachings, according to Wonch'uk, are taught both in pure lands such as Padmagarbha (*padma'i snying po*) and in impure places. The main example of such teachings is the *Sūtra Explaining the Thought*, and Wonch'uk states that such teachings are called "the Mahāyāna wheel of doctrine of definitive meaning" (*nges pa'i don theg pa chen po'i chos kyi 'khor lo*). He adds that the

---

7 *Legs bshad snying po'i dka' 'grel bstan pa'i sgron me* (Buxaduar: Sera Monastery, 1968), p. 31.5.

8 *Legs bshad snying po*, Sarnath ed., p. 27.4.

9 Wonch'uk, vol. *ti* (118), p. 4.2.

10 Wonch'uk, vol. *ti* (118), p. 4.7.

teachings of this vehicle "are the thought of the teachings of Tathāgatas."[11] In his discussion of the sūtra's statements concerning the three wheels in the seventh chapter, he states:

> Those teachings of the four truths are teachings spoken in the first [period]. Those teachings of absence of character are teachings of the second period. Those complete and perfect teachings of reasonings of existence or non-existence—stemming from the three types of entityness, the three types of non-entityness, and so forth—are teachings of the third period....The first wheel teaches that [phenomena] are existent while holding back [the doctrine of] emptiness; the second wheel teaches that [phenomena] are empty while holding back [the doctrine of] existence, but the third wheel completely teaches reasonings of emptiness and existence; therefore, it is said to be of 'definitive meaning'.[12]

The third wheel is said in the sūtra to be beneficial for sentient beings who listen to these teachings and copy, memorize, and recite them and is said to produce spiritual benefits for all lineages of Buddhists, i.e., those of the Hearer, Solitary Realizer, and Bodhisattva vehicles. According to Dpal 'byor lhun grub, this wheel is taught "for the sake of taking care of trainees of the three lineages",[13] an idea that is also expressed in the concluding statement of the seventh chapter of the sūtra, which contains an outline of the benefits received by those who were present when this chapter of the *Sūtra Explaining the Thought* was taught.

> When this teaching of the ultimate, the definitive meaning, was set forth, 600,000 beings generated the unsurpassed, completely perfect mind of enlightenment; 300,000 Hearers [attained] the eye of doctrine that, with respect to phenomena, is undefiled and free from stains; 150,000 Hearers released their minds from contaminations in terms of non-attachment; 75,000 Bodhisattvas attained the forbearance of the doctrine of non-production.[14]

This passage indicates that part of the sūtra's claim to authoritativeness is based on the sensibleness and efficacy of its teachings. Through outlining the spiritual advances made by those in the audience who heard the teachings of the *Saṃdhinirmocana*, it indicates

---

[11] Wonch'uk, vol. *ti* (118), p. 4.5.
[12] Wonch'uk, vol. *thi* (119), p. 142.6.
[13] Dpal 'byor lhun grub, *Legs bshad snying po'i dka' 'grel bstan pa'i sgron me*, p. 30.3.
[14] Stog p. 72.3; D p. 50.6.

that people reading this sūtra should listen to and contemplate the teachings it presents because of the spiritual benefits to be derived from them.

The implicit claims of authoritativeness in the sūtra also derive from a number of other sources. Throughout the text there are both implicit and explicit claims made by the sūtra about its definitiveness. Beginning with the introduction, this is presented as a text for advanced practitioners, and the place where it is taught is described as being a vast celestial palace that reflects the supreme state of realization of the Buddha. In addition, the residents of the palace and the audience of the sūtra are described as being very advanced practitioners, and the interlocutors (except for Subhūti) are Bodhisattvas who have attained a high level of understanding. (Subhūti is presumably a member of this august assembly because of being recognized in Pāli literature as the most advanced of Buddha's Hearer disciples in understanding of emptiness).

The authority of the Buddha and his teaching abilities are also important elements of the sūtra's implicit arguments for its authoritativeness. When the first two wheels are described, the audience is told that these wheels were taught for particular congregations, and behind this statement is the Mahāyāna Buddhist doctrine of "skill in means" (*thabs la mkhas pa, upāya-kauśalya*, an idea that is discussed in the ninth chapter of the sūtra), which holds that Buddha teaches each individual or group what will be most beneficial.[15] In addition, the Mahāyāna tradition in general views Buddha as omniscient (an idea that is discussed in the tenth chapter of the sūtra), and so he is able to know precisely the nature of the predispositions of each individual and group and adapt his teachings accordingly. Thus, given the statements indicating that Buddha's teachings of interpretable meaning in the first two wheels were concordant with the spiritual needs and predispositions of their respective audiences, the assembly present at the teaching of the *Saṃdhinirmocana* apparently should conclude that, since Buddha teaches everyone what

[15] For a discussion of this idea in relation to Buddhist hermeneutics, see Étienne Lamotte, "The Assessment of Textual Interpretation in Buddhism", p. 21.

is most beneficial, they should know that the doctrines they are hearing are ideally suited to them.

In general, Buddhism asks for a level of assent directly proportioned to the evidence, and the implicit arguments of the text give Buddhists in the audience (and those who belong to traditions that hold the *Saṃdhinirmocana* to be authoritative) a number of reasons to accept it as definitive. The text is taught by Buddha, and the appeal of the sūtra is mainly based on his personal authority, but there are also implicit appeals based on the sensibleness of the sūtra's teachings. Although throughout the text Buddha simply declares the definitiveness of his teachings without arguing against rival viewpoints (including rival viewpoints that he himself had presented on other occasions), there is also an undercurrent of thought in the text that indicates that those in the audience will be convinced not only by the authority of the Buddha who is presenting the teachings but by their apparent persuasiveness. When the teachings of the first two wheels are said to be "surpassable", of "interpretable meaning" and to serve as a "basis for dispute", whereas the third wheel is "unsurpassable", of "definitive meaning" and does not serve as a "basis for dispute", this indicates that the audience should find the third wheel teachings more compelling and convincing than those of the other two wheels. The sense of the reasonableness of the teachings of the sūtra is also fostered by the presentation of analogies throughout the text, which demonstrate the superiority of the sūtra's discussion of the ultimate in the first four chapters and its presentation of interpretable and definitive teachings in the seventh chapter.

The implicit claim of the sūtra's multi-faceted arguments for its own definitiveness—which is based on the personal authority of Buddha, the reasonableness of its doctrines, the persuasiveness of its analogies, as well as the sūtra's own claims of definitiveness—requires the assumptions that this is a teaching given by the supreme authority for Buddhists and that these teachings can effectively reconcile the conceptual difficulties that arose from his earlier teachings and will advance the spiritual progress of those who embrace the worldview outlined in the sūtra. Thus, the congregation that is listening to these new teachings (and later traditions that accept them as authoritative) have good reasons in a traditional context for confidence in the teachings of the third wheel.

The qualification "in a traditional context" is an important one, since in Buddhism community, tradition, and authority are important. Each interpretive community (such as the Yogācāra school, which takes the *Saṃdhinirmocana* as authoritative) chooses which texts, persons, interpretations, and strategies are authoritative, and belonging to a particular interpretive community involves at least in part accepting this framework as normative. Operating within a traditional context determines the sort of evidence on which one relies. If, for instance, one is a biblical fundamentalist, one will view the doctrine of virgin birth as being definitive, even though virginity and pregnancy are incompatible states of affairs. If the primary authority is Buddha, then whatever he says will appear to a devout traditional Buddhist as possessing a high degree of authority. Given such an attitude, Buddhists will seek for interpretational schemas that accord with this assumption, and whatever momentary doubts they may entertain will be seen as being merely due to their own imperfections in understanding.

This attitude is expressed in a passage in the seventh chapter in which the reactions of various types of beings to the sūtra's teachings are described. Some are criticized for thinking that the doctrines of the *Saṃdhinirmocana* are demonic in origin because they conflict with the teachings with which they are familiar, while others are praised for accepting the new pronouncements with simple faith because they know that the sūtra's teachings are given by Buddha, and his teachings must be beneficial and authoritative, even if people of limited understanding cannot fathom how this can be so.

> When those sentient beings...who are honest and have an honest nature, who are unable to remove conceptuality, who do not abide in holding their own view to be supreme hear this doctrine, although they do not understand, just as it is, this which I explained with a thought behind it, they develop belief and experience faith with respect to this doctrine. They believe: 'These sūtras are taught by the Tathāgata, and are profound, bril-

> liantly profound, possessing [the doctrine of] emptiness, difficult to perceive, difficult to understand, unanalyzable, not an object of activity of argumentation, known by the wise who finely analyze and by the discerning.'
>
> Apprehending that they do not understand the meaning of those sūtras and what they teach, they say: 'The enlightenment of the Bhagavan is profound; the reality of phenomena is also profound; therefore, the Tathāgata alone knows; we do not understand. The doctrine that is taught by the Tathāgatas works on sentient beings by way of their various beliefs. Our understanding and perception are merely [like] cowprints [compared to that of the Tathāgatas], whereas the Tathāgata's knowledge and perception are infinite.'[16]

In other words, they understand that since these teachings (which appear to conflict with what they have previously heard) are taught by Buddha, they are authoritative, even if they are unable to comprehend them. They know that if they are unable to see the harmony of thought in Buddha's contradictory statements, this is because their understanding is limited. Because of their attitude of reverence for the teachings and the Teacher, Buddha states that "on this basis, they advance by way of the collection of merit and advance by way of the collection of wisdom, and they also ripen their continuums, which were not [previously] ripened."[17]

This passage presents an appeal to tradition and to the authority of Buddha and is apparently meant to convince people who might doubt the veracity of the teachings presented in the sūtra. Those Buddhists who are convinced that the teachings of the *Saṃdhinirmocana* are indeed spoken by Buddha will have strong reasons for accepting them as authoritative. A traditional Buddhist (or a traditionalist of any religion) will tend to accept even very questionable doctrines as being highly probable if they are supported by the evidence of the authority of the founder of the tradition. Based on such authority, Buddhists can accept Buddha's teachings as being highly probable even if they see no way that they can be true and even if they appear to contradict other teachings. Thus, a traditional Buddhist can accept as true such apparently contradictory proposi-

---

16 Stog p. 57.5; D p. 39.7.

17 Stog p. 58.1; D p. 40.6.

tions as: (1) Buddha is omniscient; (2) Buddha's teachings express the truth; and (3) Buddha's teachings often contradict each other.

As the sūtra indicates, recognition of doctrinal conflict does not necessarily lead to rejecting of tradition. As John Skorupski states,

> The traditional thinker is, precisely, traditional: this is not directly a matter of being unwilling to reject one's own theories, but of unwillingness to reject traditionally handed-down ones—of piety for what actually, allegedly, or presumably has always existed.[18]

Thus, given a basic presupposition of the authoritativeness of Buddha's teachings, a traditional Buddhist who hears the teachings of the sūtra would be very reasonable in accepting its doctrines as definitive. Especially if he/she belongs to an interpretive community that accepts the sūtra as normative, this is the most reasonable conclusion that a traditional thinker could draw. The traditional Buddhist (and traditionalists of all types) accepts cognitive principles that in effect limit the range of possible criticism of apparently contradictory doctrines. In order legitimately to accept or reject particular teachings attributed to a Buddha, one would presumably need to have actualized for oneself the state of a Buddha. Until this point, the most reasonable response is that of those beings who accept what Buddha says because he says it.[19] They can reasonably accept his statements on his authority, even though they might not be able to articulate how apparent conflicts that arise from his teachings might be reconciled. For the audience of the *Sūtra Explaining the Thought*, the question of whether or not the doctrines presented by Buddha in this sūtra really represent his final thought would seem to be irrelevant given the context: since Buddhists believe that Buddha adapts himself to each audience and only tells them what will be most beneficial to them, the members of the au-

---

[18] John Skorupski, *Symbol and Theory* (Cambridge: Cambridge University Press, 1976), p. 204.

[19] This has been noted by Paul J. Griffiths (*On Being Mindless*; La Salle: Open Court, 1986, p. 77), who writes of the *Saṃdhinirmocana-sūtra*, "Texts of this kind do not provide analytical philosophical discussion since they are intended to present the word of the Buddha to his faithful hearers."

dience should reasonably conclude that what they are hearing is the ideal teaching for them.[20]

This should not, however, be taken as indicating that I think that Buddhist traditionalists are irrational or anti-rational. On the contrary, I would contend that, given the cultural and religious assumptions under which they operate, they are being very reasonable in accepting Buddha's teachings on his authority. In a similar fashion, when a research chemist describes the intricacies of chemical reactions I accept his/her authority on such matters simply because I have good reasons to believe that a highly trained chemist has an understanding of chemistry surpassing my own, and not because I can personally explain how he/she is right. I assume that a chemist's opinions will be based on experimental evidence, but I have no means of either proving or falsifying the chemist's assertions. In a similar manner, Buddha's assertions are convincing and authoritative for Buddhists because of the total cognitive and hermeneutical matrix within which they operate. It should be noted, however, that accepting Buddha as an authority does not preclude innovation, but rather sets the standards in terms of which innovation takes place, and within the limits and norms of their traditions Buddhist scholars will attempt to "posit the thought" of Buddha in ways that both remain faithful to the tradition and accord with reason and empirical evidence. As Richard Bernstein, quoting Alasdair MacIntyre, states,

> It is a false dichotomy to oppose tradition and reason, or even tradition and revolution, for 'it is traditions which are the bearers of reason, and traditions at certain periods actually require and need revolutions for their continuance.'[21]

In other words, traditions are not to be viewed as ossified and rigid systems that are resistant to change and innovations, but rather as

---

[20] It is worth noting that this distinction between different types of followers corresponds at least partially the the distinction drawn by Nathan Katz between "text-based" and "adept-based" hermeneutical schemas (see "Prasaṅga and Deconstruction: Tibetan Buddhist Hermeneutics and the Yāna Controversy", *PEW*, #34.4, 1984, pp. 185-6).

[21] Richard J. Bernstein, *Beyond Objectivism and Relativism: Science, Hermeneutics, and Praxis* (Philadelphia: University of Pennsylvania Press, 1983), p. 77. The passage from MacIntyre is in his "Epistemological Crises, Dramatic Narrative and the Philosophy of Science", in *Monist* #60 (1977), p. 461.

continually changing organisms that require innovations in doctrine and practice to retain their vitality. Doctrines are modified, interpreted, or discarded to the extent that they contradict compelling evidence or prove unfruitful for new or different questions that come to interest members of the tradition, and this process of innovation and reinterpretation is a sign that the tradition remains vital and relevant for its adherents. Throughout this process of change and adaptation, however, they seek to retain a sense of continuity with the foundational principles of the tradition, despite the fact that these principles may be interpreted and applied in very different ways by various interpretive communities and at different times.

LAMOTTE AND RUEGG ON BUDDHIST HERMENEUTICS

The process outlined above is at odds with the presentations of Buddhist hermeneutics of Étienne Lamotte and David S. Ruegg, both of whom posit very different procedures for Buddhist thinkers seeking to understand their textual tradition. Lamotte stresses the importance of reasoning for Buddhist thinkers seeking to decide what can legitimately be considered the "word of the Buddha". Lamotte pays little attention to the role of tradition, custom, and Buddhist notions of authority in this process.

> [i]n order that a text be accepted as the "word of the Buddha" it is not sufficient to call upon the authority of the Buddha himself, upon a religious community (*saṃgha*) which has been formally established, or upon one of several particularly learned elders; the text in question must also be found in the sūtra (*sūtra 'vatarati*), appear in the vinaya (*vinaye saṃdṛśyate*), and not contradict the nature of things (*dharmatāṃ ca na vilomayati*). In other words, adherence to the doctrine cannot be dependent on human authority, however respectable, since experience shows that human evidence is contradictory and changeable; adherence should be based on personal reasoning (*yukti*), on what one has oneself known (*jñāta*), seen (*dṛṣṭa*), and grasped (*vidita*).[22]

In the section following this, Lamotte notes that faith in a master's word may be necessary for beginners, but he stresses that ultimately one must use one's own reasoning in order to arrive at the truth. Despite this qualification, Lamotte's statement appears to be at vari-

[22] Étienne Lamotte, "The Assessment of Textual Interpretation in Buddhism", p. 13.

ance with the thought of the *Saṃdhinirmocana*, which places a high value on faith and praises those who accept its teachings on the basis of Buddha's authority. In addition, as we have noted, although it presents itself as a sūtra of definitive meaning and indicates that the audience for whom it was taught consists of advanced practitioners, it contains no instructions to seek the truth through individual reasoning; rather, Buddha spells out the definitive teaching, not as a subject for open debate, but as a final statement for his audience to follow. The sūtra does attempt to convince its audience through the presentation of persuasive analogies, arguments, and vocabulary innovations that reconcile conflicts in Buddha's earlier teachings, but at no point does it advise them to question or debate its presentation.

Nor does Buddha advise his audience to look to other texts, such as *vinaya* texts, to corroborate his teachings in the *Saṃdhinirmocana*; rather, the sūtra indicates in a number of ways that its presentations are sufficient as guides for interpretation of Buddhist doctrine. Other texts are only mentioned obliquely, and even then only as parts of a hierarchical schema the internal logic and relations of which are determined by the presentations of the *Saṃdhinirmocana*. Moreover, the sūtra indicates at the end of the last four chapters that people in the audience attained advanced states of spiritual realization as a result of hearing its teachings, which implies that those following the definitive statements of the *Saṃdhinirmocana* can achieve their spiritual goals through practicing its teachings. Most importantly for our present argument, at no point does Buddha urge his audience to use independent reasoning and analysis to examine the veracity or effectiveness of his teachings. The text assumes that the personal authority of the Buddha is sufficient to establish its truth claims.

It should be noted that Lamotte's analysis does accord with statements found in a number of Buddhist texts that stress the importance of reasoning, but his article is an example of a type of Buddhology that views Buddhism in one-sidedly rationalistic terms. It is true that there are many Buddhist admonitions to seek the truth through reasoning, but there are at least as many that praise faith or that are based on traditional Buddhist notions of tradition and authority. Nor are these considerations mutually exclusive: in many Buddhist texts they are found together and no attempt is made to reconcile them. An example is Tsong kha pa's *Essence of the Good Explanations*, a text which from the beginning stresses the importance of reasoning and which states that Buddha's words must be examined by "stainless reasoning".

In the opening section, Tsong kha pa advises Buddhists to seek Buddha's thought through reasoning and to follow the interpretations of the great "openers of the chariot ways" (*shing rta srol 'byed*) Nāgārjuna and Asaṅga. Buddhists ought to rely on them because they used stainless reasoning to settle the difficult points of Buddha's words and because they were predicted by Buddha. In other words, despite the rationalistic bias found in Tsong kha pa's work, part of his argument is based on Buddhist notions of tradition and authority. Tsong kha pa's argument is based *both* on the contention that Asaṅga and Nāgārjuna used stainless reasoning *and* the idea that because they were prophesied by Buddha their analyses are trustworthy. It is also important to note that for Tsong kha pa there is no conflict between these two aspects of his argument, since for him it is obviously reasonable to accept the validity of the interpretations of the openers of the chariot ways precisely because Buddha, the supreme authority, predicted that they would correctly interpret his words.

In the traditional context in which Tsong kha pa wrote and thought, appeal to the authority of Buddha and Buddhist luminaries is not seen as being in conflict with reasoning; in fact, it appears that Tsong kha pa (and other traditional Buddhist thinkers) considered such appeals to be very much in accord with reasoning and rationality. Reasoning takes place within a context, and all traditions (including contemporary science, humanities, etc.) reason within implicit or explicit rules, guidelines, and paradigms. This is also the case with Buddhist reasoning, which operates within frameworks generally accepted by its adherents.

In my opinion, too much of Buddhist studies has focused solely on the rationalism found in Buddhist philosophy, and in order to gain a more balanced view of Buddhist thought it is important to look at the role that tradition played (and continues to play) in the philosophy of Buddhist thinkers. Buddhist rationalism (and probably any sort of rationalism) functions within particular traditional contexts and utilizes the rules of particular traditions. Moreover, Buddhist exegetes generally rely on the texts accepted by their respective traditions and defend their analyses through arguments that rely on Buddhist notions of tradition and authority. Divorcing them from the cultural and religious contexts in which they lived necessarily gives a one-sided view of people who were situated in traditional Buddhist societies, working with Buddhist texts, who implicitly accepted the authority of the Buddha (and important figures in their respective traditions), and who were consciously attempting to present accurate renderings of Buddha's thought, rather than innovative statements of their own individual reasoning processes.

Another sort of rationalistic bias is evident in David S. Ruegg's generally excellent "Purport, Implicature, and Presupposition",[1] which presents a detailed analysis of the terms *dgongs pa* (which he translates as "intention, intended meaning, purport") and *dgongs gzhi* (which he translates as "intentional ground") in relation to Buddhist hermeneutics. While most of this article contains an insightful analysis of these terms, it also contains some statements that overemphasize the role of individual reasoning and analysis and overlook the powerful role of tradition and authority in Buddhist hermeneutics. On page 311, for example, he indicates that Buddhist exegetes search for "the real purport of Buddha's teaching" by searching through and analyzing "the whole of the Buddha's Word (*buddhavacana*), i.e., the entire canonical corpus". On page 313 he returns to this topic and states that the specific trainees

[1] David Seyfort Ruegg, "Purport, Implicature, and Presupposition: Sanskrit *Abhiprāya* and Tibetan *Dgons gźi* as Hermeneutical Concepts", *JIP* #13, 1985, pp. 309-325.

of particular texts are not expected to be able to grasp Buddha's hidden meaning but that

> the competent exegete, who has at his disposal the corpus of the Buddha's teachings (together, eventually, with the oral and/or written commentarial tradition), is able to discover—to 'calculate' as it were—the *dgoṅs gźi* by means of the systematical interpretation of the corpus.[2]

This implies that people of lesser capacity, who rely on the literal reading of Buddha's teachings, only follow the teachings that were taught for them, but "competent exegetes" search through the canon, analyze the teachings of sūtras and commentaries, consider oral explanations, and then come to personal understanding of Buddha's intention as a result of this process of reasoning and analysis. While this is a plausible and reasonable scenario, when one looks at the history of Buddhist exegesis it is difficult to find any Buddhist scholar whose interpretational method exactly matches Ruegg's model. The reason for this is that Ruegg downplays the role of tradition and notions of authority in Buddhist hermeneutics. The vast majority of Buddhist thinkers have been (and still are) self-consciously members of traditions and have to a greater or lesser extent followed the exegetical paradigms of their respective traditions, and even those who created new schools or devised new hermeneutical strategies generally did so on the basis of a particular text (or sometimes a small group of texts), and not through a comprehensive analysis of the entire Buddhist canon.

To fully develop this topic would require a separate (and rather lengthy) study, but a few examples should suffice for our present purposes. The exegetes of the Yogācāra school, beginning with Asaṅga and Vasubandhu, explicated and argued for an understanding of Buddha's final teaching that was based on their readings of the *Saṃdhinirmocana-sūtra*, certain statements in Perfection of Wisdom Sūtras, and passages in other texts that appeared to support their views, but none of these philosophers meticulously searched through the entire Buddhist canon, uncommitted to the textual and

---

[2] See also his "Allusiveness and Obliqueness in Buddhist Texts", p. 300, which contains a similar statement.

oral traditions that had been handed down to them, and devised a system of exegesis based solely on independent reasoning. It is even difficult to imagine the interpretations of such a person being accepted as valid by other Buddhists, since Buddhist scholars are required to justify themselves by demonstrating a concordance between their systems and Buddhist texts and doctrines that are accepted as normative by the audiences for whom they write.

Even Tsong kha pa, a scholar whose knowledge of Indian and Tibetan literature was vast, indicates throughout his works the particular texts on which he is relying in a given context. His *Essence of the Good Explanations*, for example, is divided into two parts (one of which is concerned with the Mind-Only system, and the other with Madhyamaka), and at the very beginning of the text he indicates that his analysis (and those of the two systems he proposes to study) is based on a study of the texts mainly relied on by the adherents of the respective schools studied in the two sections.

Other examples of Buddhist exegetes relying on particular texts can be found throughout Buddhist literature, perhaps most strikingly in several East Asian classification schemes (e.g., those of the Pure Land, T'ien-t'ai, Shingon, and Nichiren traditions), each of which relies on a particular text (or a group of related texts) that enabled exegetes in their respective traditions to make sense of the confusion of the Buddhist canon and to create a coherent system of exegesis.[3] A classic example of this approach is Chih-i's decision to rely on the *Lotus Sūtra* (*Saddharma-puṇḍarīka-sūtra*) after having a dream in which he was in a huge library filled with Buddhist texts. He had been given the task of sorting through these texts and classifying them, but due to the overwhelming profusion of Buddhist literature he was unable to do so until he came across a copy of the *Lotus Sūtra*, which enabled him to understand the rest of the Buddhist canon through relying on its teachings. Other prominent East Asian examples would include Nichiren's classification of Buddhist

---

[3] Descriptions of such systems can be found in the articles of David W. Chappell, Peter N. Gregory, Robert E. Buswell, Thomas Kasulis, and Roger T. Corless in *Buddhist Hermeneutics*.

teachings on the basis of the *Lotus Sūtra* and Hua-yen's classification scheme, which was based on its reading of the *Avataṃsaka-sūtra*.

Many similar examples could be presented, and there might be some counter-examples of independent Buddhist thinkers who demonstrably created new systems without relying on textual, oral, or exegetical traditions (although I am not aware of any), but the main point for our present purposes is that Buddhist thinkers (including the founders of important philosophical schools and scholars renowned in Buddhist literature as great philosophers and meditators) generally follow traditional norms, interpretations, values, etc. (even while putting their distinctive stamp on them and often modifying them or challenging entrenched interpretations). This is not to say that I disagree with Lamotte and Ruegg in emphasizing the significance of reasoning in Buddhist philosophy: on the contrary, they are quite correct in emphasizing its importance for Buddhists, but it is also important to understand that this reasoning functioned within, and was strongly influenced by, Buddhist traditions. As noted in the quote cited earlier by Skorupski, their reasoning is governed by the rules accepted as normative by their traditions, and their arguments would not be perceived as valid if they did not so conform. Any analysis of Buddhist thought that overlooks or downplays this important factor misses an important part of the equation in Buddhist hermeneutics.

PARAMĀRTHASAMUDGATA'S ANALOGIES

During an extensive monologue in which he presents his understanding of Buddha's instructions for Buddha's approval, Paramārthasamudgata offers a series of analogies to help the audience of the *Saṃdhinirmocana* understand the relation between teachings of definitive meaning and those of interpretable meaning. In presenting the first analogy, he states,

> Bhagavan, it is like this: For example, dried ginger is placed in all medicinal powder preparations and all medicinal elixir preparations. Similarly, this teaching of definitive meaning, stemming from non-entitynesses of

> phenomena, and stemming from the non-production, non-cessation, quiescence from the start, and being by nature in a state of nirvāṇa of phenomena, is placed in all sūtras which are of interpretable meaning by the Bhagavan.[4]

Wonch'uk comments that "this is because when dried ginger is put in medicinal powders, they become potent....If one puts these words of non-entityness and so forth in all sūtras of interpretable meaning, then one will understand the thoughts of those sūtras."[5] This appears to mean that teachings of definitive meaning are placed within discourses mainly containing interpretable teachings and that the presence of the definitive teachings enhances these discourses and makes them more potent. It also seems to imply that Buddha slips in definitive teachings when presenting interpretable doctrines because this enhances the effectiveness of his discourses.

The second analogy presents an alternative way of looking at the relation between interpretable and definitive teachings, according to which the latter are present in all sūtras of interpretable meaning, but since Buddha wishes the special trainees of these sūtras to understand them according to their interpretable meaning he teaches in such a way that they will not even notice the definitive teachings that form the backdrop of interpretable statements.

> Bhagavan, it is like this: For example, the basis for the drawing of a picture [e.g., the canvas] is of one flavor in all of the picture, whether [its features] are blue, yellow, red, or white. It brings out whatever is drawn in the picture. Similarly, this teaching of definitive meaning by the Tathāgata, stemming from non-entitynesses of phenomena through to [phenomena being] by nature in a state of nirvāṇa, is of one taste in all sūtras of interpretable meaning. It brings out [whatever is taught in] those [sūtras] of interpretable meaning.[6]

Wonch'uk comments: "For example, the basis on which the painting is drawn—the blue, yellow, etc.—completely pervades all the work of the various aspects of the picture and is of one taste in terms of the sameness of the blue, yellow, etc."[7] In other words, the

---

[4] Stog p. 67.4; D p. 47.3.
[5] Wonch'uk vol. *thi* (119), p. 107.5.
[6] Stog p. 67.6; D p. 47.4.
[7] Wonch'uk vol. *thi* (119), p. 108.2.

color of the backdrop of a picture (whether this is a canvas, a wall, a pot, etc.) permeates the whole picture. What this example seems to indicate is that Buddha's definitive teachings are the basis of his interpretable teachings and permeate them, even if they are not noticed. Without the definitive teachings, however, the interpretable teachings (which Buddha gives for the benefit of those beings who are not ready for the definitive teachings) would have no basis, just as a painting needs a canvas, a wall, etc. upon which an artist sketches the details of the painting and then colors them in. Similarly, Buddha's definitive teachings pervade all sūtras of interpretable meaning and are of one taste in all such sūtras in that they are effectively invisible to those who merely look at the surface features of the teachings. Those who look beyond the surface, however, understand that all of the interpretable teachings are based on definitive teachings and that without the latter the former would be unsupportable.

In the next analogy, Paramārthasamudgata likens definitive teachings to an ingredient added to a recipe that enhances its flavor.

> Bhagavan, it is like this: For example, adding butter to various types of cooked meat and various types of cooked grain is very satisfying. Similarly, when this teaching of definitive meaning by the Tathāgata, stemming from non-entitynesses of phenomena through to [phenomena being] by nature in a state of nirvāṇa, is added to all types of sūtras of interpretable meaning, it is very satisfying and supremely satisfying.[8]

In the fourth and final analogy, Paramārthasamudgata compares definitive teachings to space (*nam mkha'*, *ākāśa*), which is omnipresent and omnipervasive.

> Bhagavan, it is like this: For example, space is everywhere of one taste and also does not obstruct any activities. Similarly, this definitive teaching by the Tathāgata, stemming from non-entitynesses of phenomena through to [phenomena being] by nature in a state of nirvāṇa, is of one taste in all sūtras of interpretable meaning. It also does not obstruct any effort with regard to the Hearer vehicle, the Solitary Realizer vehicle, or the Great vehicle.[9]

---

8 Stog p. 68.2; D p. 47.6.

9 Stog p. 68.5; D p. 48.1.

The upshot of this seems to be that definitive teachings pervade discourses in which interpretable teachings are taught. The comparison with space is interesting: in Buddhist philosophy, space is defined as being a mere absence of obstructive contact, that is, it is a quality of phenomena that is characterized by absence. Definitive teachings, however, are presumably not characterized by their absence, but rather by their subtlety. The analogy implies that they are present in all of Buddha's teachings, but are overlooked by people whose limited spiritual development causes them to focus only on interpretable teachings. Wonch'uk adds that the purport of the analogy is that Buddha's definitive teachings are found in sūtras of interpretable meaning and are of one taste in them. They are so subtly woven into the fabric of these sūtras that they are indistinguishable from the interpretable teachings except to those of advanced insight.[10] He adds that they pervade all sūtras of interpretable meaning, have the one taste which is non-entityness, and they do not obstruct any seeking in the three vehicles.[11] This refers to a subsequent statement by Paramārthasamudgata that the sūtra's teachings are beneficial and appropriate for all types of Buddhist practitioners because in the *Saṃdhinirmocana* "the Bhagavan turned a third wheel of doctrine for those who are engaged in all vehicles".[12]

In these examples, Paramārthasamudgata has offered Buddha four different ways of looking at the relation between what Buddha said on the literal level in his interpretable teachings and the defini-

---

[10] Wonch'uk vol. *thi* (119), p. 109.2. Compare this with Wittgenstein's statement (*Philosophical Investigations*, tr. G.E.M. Anscombe; New York: Macmillan, 1953, part I, p. 129) that "the aspects of things that are most important for us are hidden because of their simplicity and familiarity. (One is unable to notice something because it is always before one's eyes.) The real foundations of his inquiry do not strike a man at all."

[11] See also the discussion of these examples in the commentary attributed to Byang chub rdzu 'phrul, vol. *cho* (205), pp. 262-4. These examples are also mentioned briefly in the *Ārya-saṃdhinirmocana-bhāṣya*, attributed to Asaṅga, who states that Paramārthasamudgata's presentation of these analogies indicates his advanced spiritual attainment (Sde dge edition, p. 15.4).

[12] Stog p. 70.2; D p. 49.3. According to Dpal 'byor lhun grub (p. 30.3), this means that this wheel is taught "for the sake of taking care of trainees of the three lineages" (Hearers, Solitary Realizers, and Bodhisattvas). In other words, third wheel teachings are appropriate and beneficial for all types of Buddhists.

tive teachings that were his actual thought. In the first instance, the definitive teaching is compared to an essential ingredient in a medicinal preparation, without which the whole preparation will lack efficacy. In the second example, the definitive teaching is compared to the basis of a picture, which may not even be noticed by people looking at the picture, but which is essential as the background upon which the lines and colors of the painting are placed. In the third example, the definitive teaching is compared to an important ingredient that is added to a recipe and enhances it. In the final example, the definitive teaching is compared to space, which is all-pervasive and which is subtle, imperceptible, and generally not even noticed, but is essential for the movement of physical bodies. In the same way, the definitive teaching is said to be subtle, difficult to perceive, and so forth, but it is the essence of the explanations given by Buddha in the first two wheels, even when this was not noticed by his audience. Presumably the definitive teachings to which Paramārthasamudgata refers are those found in the *Saṃdhinirmocana-sūtra* or doctrines that are compatible with those of the sūtra.

The logic of Paramārthasamudgata's comments leads to this conclusion, because the sūtra is presented as an explication of Buddha's final thought and as a delineation of rules for distinguishing interpretable from definitive teachings. Thus, the sūtra's teachings (particularly those in the seventh chapter relating to differentiation of interpretable and definitive teachings) become the yardstick by which other types of Buddhist teachings are to be evaluated. Those which accord with the doctrines of the third wheel as presented in the *Saṃdhinirmocana* presumably should be considered to be definitive, while those which are either classified as belonging to the first two wheels or that are antithetical to the thought of the sūtra are of interpretable meaning and are only appropriate to certain trainees less advanced than those of the *Saṃdhinirmocana*. These require explanation and interpretation in order to reconcile them with Buddha's final thought.

WHAT ARE THIRD WHEEL TEACHINGS?

The three wheels schema shows the interrelationship between continuity and change in the thought of the sūtra. It indicates that although Buddha taught doctrines that were contradictory on the literal level there was an underlying thought behind them in terms of which they can be reconciled. Thus, although the sūtra is reinterpreting Buddha's teachings in terms of new vocabulary and doctrines, it is also concerned to show how these are in accord with Buddhist tradition. It indicates that there is an underlying interrelationship between the wheels, in that second wheel teachings refer to and contradict first wheel teachings, and third wheel teachings specify what Buddha was thinking of when he taught the second wheel.

In the third wheel, according to Wonch'uk, Buddha thoroughly explains the thought behind his earlier teachings of entityness and non-entityness, and "because of thoroughly indicating entityness and non-entityness, this is a turning of the wheel of correct doctrine through such thorough differentiation."[13] Dpal 'byor lhun grub expresses a similar thought when he says:

> The Teacher—at the third time, in Vaiśālī, for the sake of taking care of those having all three lineages, the special trainees of [this wheel], stemming from the subject matter of non-entityness and so forth—differentiated well the particulars of true establishment and non-true establishment with respect to the three, imputations, other-dependent phenomena, and thoroughly established phenomena in the third [wheel of doctrine], the wheel of doctrine of good differentiation.[14]

In a discussion of this passage of Dpal 'byor lhun grub's text, Geshe Palden Dragpa (oral commentary) stated:

> Although Paramārthasamudgata asks Buddha explicitly about the thought behind his teaching of the middle wheel, this carries over to the thought behind his teaching of the first wheel. Therefore, Paramārthasamudgata is implicitly asking about Buddha's thought in his teaching of the first wheel.

---

[13] Wonch'uk, vol. *thi* (119), p. 137.1.

[14] Dpal 'byor lhun grub, p. 30.3.

In other words, in the third wheel Buddha's purpose is to clarify the thought behind his earlier statements and to present an exegetical framework that will allow his followers to categorize certain of his teachings. The model that he presents is a contextually based interpretational scheme. According to this model, the teachings he gave to Hearers that were mainly concerned with the four noble truths were valid and beneficial for that audience, but were not of definitive meaning and did not represent his final thought. The teachings that he gave to Mahāyānists in which he made blanket statements that "all phenomena lack entityness" etc. were also of interpretable meaning. The explanations of the *Sūtra Explaining the Thought* indicate how to reconcile them with his final thought on the literal level. The teachings of the third wheel have the same subject matter as those of the second wheel (non-entityness, non-production, etc.), but they are definitive, because they do not require interpretation in order to reconcile them with Buddha's thought. The sūtra's statement that these teachings are unsurpassable, do not provide an opportunity for refutation, are of definitive meaning, and that they do not serve as a basis for dispute indicates that according to the system of the *Sūtra Explaining the Thought* those doctrines that are correct as they stand are definitive, while those that require interpretation are interpretable This is the conclusion reached by Tsong kha pa, who indicates that he thinks that the internal logic of the sūtra suggests that teachings which are literally acceptable are definitive, while those that are not are interpretable. Stated as a general principle, this entails that

> the differentiation of interpretable and definitive scriptures that are set forth stemming from the ultimate derives from whether there is or is not damage by reasoning to the literal reading.[15]

This principle was further developed and refined by Tsong kha pa's followers. As Dkon mchog 'jigs med dbang po expresses it:

> [Proponents of this system] designate a scripture whose explicit teachings cannot be accepted literally as a sūtra requiring interpretation. They des-

---

[15] *Legs bshad snying po*, Sarnath ed., p. 86.18.

> ignate any scripture whose explicit teaching can be accepted literally as definitive.[38]

Following Tsong kha pa's analysis in his *Essence of the Good Explanations*, Dge lugs pa scholars assert that the division of the three wheels of doctrine is made according to subject matter and that the determining factor is how selflessness is presented in each of the wheels. As Jeffrey Hopkins expresses this principle,

> The first turning is comprised of doctrines that set forth the selflessness of persons but do not refute that phenomena are established by way of their own character as bases of names and conceptions. The second is comprised of those that on the literal level set forth the non-true existence of all phenomena, without distinguishing that some do and others do not truly exist. The third is comprised of those that clearly discriminate the true existence of emptinesss and impermanent phenomena and the non-true existence of imaginary phenomena.[39]

In the first six chapters, the sūtra presents a particular worldview based on its presentation of selflessness that is correlated with a particular way of orienting oneself cognitively. This provides the basis for the innovations of vocabulary and doctrine in the seventh chapter. The presentation of the worldview in the seventh chapter is informed by and based on the discussions of the previous six chapters. The doctrines of the three characters and three non-entitynesses, for example, are informed by the discussion of the ultimate in the first four chapters and the discussion of the three characters in the sixth chapter. The discussion of how sentient beings are to transform their cognitions of reality presupposes the presentation of consciousness in the fifth chapter, in which the basis-consciousness (*kun gzhi rnam par shes pa, ālaya-vijñāna*) is described as "flowing like a river" that is constantly changing due to the presence of new predispositions that result from particular cognitive behaviors. The sūtra's delineation of how consciousness is to be transformed in

---

[38] Geshe Lhundup Sopa and Jeffrey Hopkins, *Practice and Theory of Tibetan Buddhism* (New York: Grove Press, 1976), p. 121.

[39] *Meditation on Emptiness* (London: Wisdom, 1983), p. 426. For a discussion of the dangers of focusing only on the literal reading of Buddha's words, see Étienne Lamotte, "The Assessment of Textual Interpretation in Buddhism", p. 22, where he states that in Buddhism grasping texts literally does not lead to comprehension of the *dharma* and is equal to scorning of the *dharma*.

light of the worldview presented in the seventh chapter presupposes the idea of a constantly changing continuum of consciousness that is altered in accordance with the cognitive seeds deposited in it.[18]

The worldview also presupposes and incorporates the presentation of the ultimate that was discussed in the previous chapter. When, for instance, Paramārthasamudgata states that the thoroughly established character is the ultimate, an object of observation for purification, and the selflessness of phenomena, he is fully in accord with the descriptions of the ultimate in the first four chapters. Moreover, these descriptions constitute the basis upon which the worldview is outlined in the seventh chapter, and this in turn is the foundation of the discussion of interpretable and definitive scriptures. This is indicated by the concluding colophon of the seventh chapter, which characterizes the preceding discussion as "this teaching of the ultimate, the definitive meaning". Although the sūtra does not explicitly make this connection, I think that it implies that third

---

[18] As mentioned near the beginning of this study, Étienne Lamotte thnks that the *Saṃdhinirmocana-sūtra* as it exists today is a composite work that is made up of various different texts from different times. He bases his theory on the stylistic differences between the chapters, such as the fact that the first four chapters are considerably shorter than the last four and the fact that each chapter discusses a distinct theme and/or set of doctrines. I think, however, that the sūtra nevertheless has an internal coherence in its thought, and it seems to me that if key doctrinal points were repeated throughout the text this would be evidence of poor writing and editing rather than an argument for the idea that it is a unitary work. Moreover, the minor stylistic differences that the text exhibits are, in my opinion, much less striking than the underlying coherence of thought, and I think that if one views the sūtra as a whole and as a philosophical work which attempts to present a coherent worldview based on the presentation of the ultimate, a picture of strong underlying unity emerges. The text first describes the setting of the discourse, then lays out the foundations of the later discussion through its delineation of the nature of the ultimate and similes illustrating its nature, then it describes the nature of consciousness, which is significant for its later discussion in that it provides a basis for understanding how the mind may be reoriented in terms of the new worldview presented in the sūtra. The sixth chapter lays the groundwork for the discussions of the seventh chapter by describing the three characters. Building upon this, the seventh chapter lays out a worldview based on the discussion of the ultimate, the three characters, the three non-entitynesses, and the three wheels. The eighth and ninth chapters draw out the implications of this discussion in terms of how it is to be applied in the context of meditative practice, and finally the tenth chapter outlines the nature of Buddhahood, which appears to be the result of successfully following the path outlined in the *Saṃdhinirmocana*. This internal coherence does not, however, disprove the possibility that the sūtra might have been composed in stages. I wish merely to point out that Lamotte's evidence does not establish his case and that his argument for its gradual formation is not proven on the basis of the inconsistencies that he sees in the internal structure of the text.

wheel teachings are the doctrines and vocabulary innovations of the *Saṃdhinirmocana* that differentiate Buddha's interpretable and definitive teachings and that accord with the worldview of the sūtra's presentation of selflessness. This worldview is presented to a particular audience that perceives Buddha's teachings concerning non-entityness and so forth as contradicting his first wheel teachings.

The *Saṃdhinirmocana* outlines a worldview that allows the members of the audience to reconcile the cognitive conflicts of the first two wheels, and the worldview provides guidelines for textual analysis that both show how what is taught in the first two wheels is not literally acceptable and how to posit the thought behind those teachings. The worldview incorporates and builds upon the discussions of the ultimate, the analysis of consciousness, and the delineation of the three characters in the first six chapters. The presentation of selflessness in the seventh chapter—which shows both the problems with the first two wheels and how to posit Buddha's thought—serves as the basis for the hermeneutical method of the sūtra. According to this method of differentiating the wheels, they are distinguished by the presentations of selflessness implied by each, and not by other criteria, such as the time or place at which they were presented.

Robert Thurman, however, contends that the division of Buddha's teachings into the three wheels is a chronological one and that the three wheels refer to periods in Buddha's life. According to Thurman, "...this scheme of the *Saṃdhinirmocana*...is both historical (as relating to Buddha's biography) and philosophical, as relating to the content of the teaching."[19] This is a plausible conclusion, since some of the language used in the sūtra and the commentaries might suggest this (for example, the fact that the discussion of the first wheel is introduced with the words, "initially, in the area of Vārānasī..." and the second wheel is introduced with the words,

---

[19] Robert Thurman, "Buddhist Hermeneutics", *JAAR*, 1978, p. 28. Donald Lopez ("On the Interpretation of the Mahāyāna Sūtras", in *Buddhist Hermeneutics*, p. 57) expresses the same idea when he writes, "Paramārthasamudgata offers a chronology of the Buddha's teaching".

"during the second period..."), but I think that the internal logic of the sūtra indicates that Thurman's statement is problematic, since no Mahāyāna text that I have seen suggests that Buddha taught Hīnayāna doctrines for a certain period and then switched to teaching exclusively Mahāyāna doctrines. Rather, Buddhist texts generally contend that he adapted his teachings to each individual and group he encountered, giving each what would be most beneficial. In Mahāyāna literature, Buddha is portrayed as a skillful teacher who encountered different types of students during his life and was able to present each student or group of students the teachings that would be most helpful. As Nāgārjuna's *Ratnāvalī* explains this,

> Just as grammarians
> Begin with reading the alphabet
> So the Buddha teaches doctrines
> That students can bear.
> To some, he teaches doctrines
> For reversal of sins.
> To some, for the sake of achieving of merit;
> To some, doctrines based on duality;
> To some, [he teaches doctrines] based on non-duality.
> To some, the profound, frightening to the fearful,
> Having an essence of emptiness and compassion,
> The means of achieving enlightenment.[20]

In the *Sūtra Explaining the Thought*, the same principle applies, and Buddha indicates that for those who will benefit from first wheel teachings he teaches the four truths and related doctrines, while for those who would most benefit from second wheel teachings he teaches that all phenomena lack entityness, etc. For those who require the explanations of the third wheel, he differentiates his interpretable and definitive teachings with reference to the previous two wheels. To say that the three wheels refer to periods of Buddha's life does not appear to accord with the thought of the sūtra, since there is no indication in the *Sūtra Explaining the Thought* that Buddha only encountered first wheel trainees during the first part of his teaching career, second wheel trainees during the second part, and

---

20 *Ratnāvalī*, chapter four, verses 94-97, ed. Michael Hahn, *Nāgārjuna's Ratnāvalī* (Bonn, 1982), pp. 129-131.

third wheel trainees during the third part. Tsong kha pa rejects the idea that the division of the three wheels is based on chronology when he contends that

> the three stages of wheels [of doctrine] mentioned in the *Sūtra Explaining the Thought* are posited, not by way of the assemblies of [Buddha's] circle or by way of periods in the teacher's life and so forth, but by way of the subjects of expression.[43]

Mkhas grub elaborates on this by adding,

> Furthermore, those are in terms of the mode of settling the meaning of selflessness—an explanation that mostly does not refute true existence, an explanation that all phenomena are without true existence, and a good differentiation of true existence with respect to the three natures. [The differentiation of] three wheels is done in terms of the fact that they respectively teach such.[44]

According to Tsong kha pa and Mkhas grub, it is incorrect to say that the division of the three wheels is based either on periods of Buddha's life or on which persons were present in the audience of particular teachings. Rather, the basis for the division is how the meaning of selflessness is settled in each of the wheels. According to Tsong kha pa, in the first wheel Buddha implicitly spoke of the selflessness of persons, but the teachings of this wheel gave his audience the impression that the aggregates and so forth were ultimately truly established. In the second wheel, he refuted this idea and declared that all phenomena without qualification lack such true establishment. In the third wheel, he individually differentiated which phenomena are established by way of their own character and which are not. According to Tsong kha pa,

> Initially, at Vārāṇasī he spoke of the selflessness of persons; [thus] there is one cycle in which the true establishment of the phenomena of the aggregates and so forth, except for a few, is not refuted and true existence is mentioned frequently. Then, there is one cycle in which, without [clearly] making distinctions, true establishment is refuted [on the literal level] with respect to all of the phenomena of the aggregates and so forth. Then there arose one cycle in which, with respect to those, he individually dif-

---

[43] *Legs bshad snying po*, Sarnath ed., p. 87.11.

[44] From Mkhas grub's *Stong thun chen mo*, in *The Collected Works of the Lord Mkhas-grub rje dge legs dpal bzaṅ po*, vol. 1, p. 179; translated by Jeffrey Hopkins, unpublished manuscript, ch. 4, p. 2.

> ferentiated the mode of the first nature [the imputational nature] as being not established by way of its own character and the other two as being established by way of their own character. Therefore, [the wheels of doctrine that are the bases for differentiation of the interpretable and the definitive in the "Questions of Paramārthasamudgata Chapter" and in the texts commenting on its thought] are taken in terms of these [modes of teaching subject matter]; other sūtras that teach in a way other than those modes of teaching are not in any sensible way bases of this [school's] analysis of the interpretable and the definitive.[23]

Tsong kha pa's use of the term "cycles" (*skor*) has important ramifications for my argument. It implies that the three wheels are interrelated sets of doctrines that Buddha *began* teaching at different times. The sūtra's statements that the wheels of doctrine were taught during successive "periods" probably only indicates that he began teaching the second wheel after the first, and later began teaching the third after the second had been articulated. This, I think, is the most reasonable conclusion, since, as stated above, there is no indication in traditional biographies of Buddha or in the *Saṃdhinirmocana* that he only encountered first wheel trainees during the first part of his life, second wheel trainees during the second part, and third wheel trainees during the third part. In addition, the statement that he taught the three wheels during successive periods is probably based on the fact that each of the three wheels refers to and requires the previous wheel(s) in order to be intelligible.

Thus, the discussion of the three wheels of doctrine in the seventh chapter of the sūtra is based on the presentation of the previous two wheels, the description of the ultimate in the first four chapters, and on the statements concerning the three characters in the sixth chapter. The teachings of the third wheel should be viewed as the result of a dialectical process. The teachings of the first wheel present an implicit thesis, which is opposed by the anti-thesis of the second wheel. The third wheel is a new thesis that attempts to reconcile the apparent conflicts between the first two wheels, but it could not have intelligibly been formulated without them.

---

[23] *Legs bshad snying po*, Sarnath ed., p. 87.15.

The meaning of third wheel doctrines is highly contextual. Taken alone, they are unspecifiable, and they depend upon the perspectives of the first two wheels for self-definition. In this sense, the doctrines of the three wheels are internally related and mutually constitutive, rather than disjunctively opposed. Moreover, the meanings of third wheel doctrines are constituted by the contextual matrix in which they occur. An attempt to separate them from their context would result in unintelligibility. The dialectical relationships between the three wheels determine the meaning and extension of the third wheel: it comes into being as a result of a dialectical process in which second wheel teachings oppose the implicit assumptions insinuated by the first wheel, resulting in cognitive conflicts that the third wheel attempts to overcome through its new synthesis, a worldview that incorporates the sūtra's presentation of the ultimate, the doctrines of the three characters, the three non-entitynesses, and the three wheels. These new doctrines, in conjunction with its presentation of the ultimate, are intended to reconcile the cognitive conflicts between the first two wheels and to outline a schema through which their harmony with Buddha's thought can be seen, but the meanings of third wheel teachings are constituted through a dialectical interrelationship in which the doctrines of the three wheels mutually constitute each other. The meaning of the third wheel teachings is a function of the correlation of the elements of the dialectical and contextual field of which they are integral members.

Furthermore, the identities of the wheels are mutually established: first and second wheel teachings acquire new identities through the articulation of the third wheel. Before the formulation of the three wheels schema in the *Sūtra Explaining the Thought*, they are simply teachings of Buddha among others, but when the sūtra singles out certain sets of teachings and identifies them as belonging to a specific "wheel of doctrine" they appear in a new light. Similarly, the second wheel and third wheel only achieve their identities through their dialectical relationship to the other wheels. The conclusion of this argument is that the three wheels are taught in successive "cycles" in the sense that the second is formulated in opposition to the implicit assumptions fostered by the first, and the third is taught in order to reconcile the conceptual difficulties that the second wheel caused for some Buddhists.

Underlying the sūtra's discussion of how to differentiate interpretable and definitive teachings is a set of implied foundationalist principles, for example, the assumption that behind the contradictions there is a "thought" that can and should be recognized and articulated. Buddha presents each of his teachings for a particular purpose, and the task of Buddhist exegetes is to uncover it and to represent it accurately. Thus, when the sūtra claims that Buddha had a "thought" behind his earlier contradictory teachings, that he presented them for a particular "purpose", and when he agrees to explain "of what he was thinking" when he taught the first two wheels, the implication is that the meaning of Buddha's teachings is determined by and founded upon his thought. The sūtra provides guidelines that will allow his followers to understand what this thought is.

Its assumptions that Buddha's thought determines what his teachings mean and that explicating this thought is essential to correct understanding accords with E.D. Hirsch's statement that "all valid interpretation...is founded on the re-cognition of what an author meant."[24] Of course, both Hirsch and Buddhist exegetes are aware that differences of opinion occur among qualified interpreters, but this does not mean that the re-cognition of the author's meaning is impossible, although it is sometimes very difficult.[25] The sūtra attempts to overcome the difficulties presented by conflicting teachings by outlining interpretive models that will allow exegetes who base themselves on the *Sūtra Explaining the Thought* to locate the underlying purpose behind the teachings.

Tsong kha pa develops this point in the introduction to his *Essence of the Good Explanations*. He states that Buddha presents

---

[24] E.D. Hirsch, *Validity in Interpretation* (New Haven: Yale University Press, 1967), p. 126.

[25] This idea is discussed by Hirsch in *Validity in Interpretation*, pp. 75-76.

many different teachings and reasonings that enable trainees to understand suchness, but, since these are sometimes in conflict, people must learn to differentiate which scriptures are interpretable and which are definitive. Unless one successfully differentiates the interpretable and the definitive, one will be unable to attain liberation. However, one cannot simply rely on Buddha's statements concerning which teachings are interpretable and which are definitive, because Buddha has given different groups of trainees conflicting guidelines for differentiation. The conclusion Tsong kha pa draws is that

> one must seek [Buddha's] thought, following the [two] great openers of the chariot-ways [Nāgārjuna and Asaṅga], who were prophesied as differentiating the interpretable and the definitive in [Buddha's] scriptures and who commented on the thought of the interpretable and the definitive and, moreover, settled it well through reasoning....[26]

The bases for interpretation, according to Tsong kha pa, are both tradition and reasoning. If one belongs to an interpretive community that accepts the *Saṃdhinirmocana* and the system of Asaṅga, then one should have confidence both in the authoritativeness of the *Saṃdhinirmocana* and in the reasonings set forth by Asaṅga that draw out its meaning. According to Tsong kha pa, this confidence is justified on the basis of tradition, which holds that Buddha prophesied Asaṅga's birth and declared that he would validly interpret and present his thought. The final authority for Tsong kha pa, however, is reasoning, and he states that

> in the end, the differentiation [between the interpretable and the definitive] must be made just by stainless reasoning, because if a speaker asserts a tenet contradicting reason, [that person] is not suitable to be a valid being and because the suchness of things also has reasoned proofs which are establishments by way of [logical] correctness.[27]

This statement, in my opinion, accords with the overall thrust of the discussion of interpretable and definitive scriptures in the *Saṃdhinirmocana*. Although, as stated earlier, throughout the sūtra Buddha simply declares how the audience should understand and interpret

[26] *Legs bshad snying po*, Sarnath ed., p. 3.5.
[27] Ibid., p. 3.10.

his teachings, there is also an implicit appeal to reason, and the text indicates that the audience should find the vocabulary innovations, new doctrines, and analogies of the sūtra persuasive. Moreover, since these principles are apparently meant to be applied to future exegetical situations, they imply a set of principles that can function as models and paradigms in terms of which one can formulate reasonings that will allow one to make distinctions between interpretable and definitive scriptures. In the final analysis, then, the appeal of the sūtra is multi-faceted: the text implies that its teachings should be accepted on the basis of the authority of the Buddha, the authority of tradition, and the persuasiveness of its presentation.

This probably does not mean, however, that every Buddhist is expected to differentiate interpretable and definitive scriptures individually. In Buddhism, this differentiation is done primarily in reliance upon scriptures accepted as authoritative by one's tradition and upon great exegetes whose interpretations are accepted by the tradition as normative, such as Nāgārjuna and Asaṅga. The interpretive community to which one belongs will determine one's hermeneutical orientation to a large extent. Tradition determines the scriptures and exegetes an individual will follow, and until one directly cognizes emptiness for oneself it is generally assumed that one will defer to such authorities. The point of differentiating the interpretable and definitive in texts like the *Sūtra Explaining the Thought* seems to be that such differentiation provides a guide for people to follow until they are able to understand the ultimate themselves and then to formulate informed interpretations.

This is not, however, a rejection of critical thought, but rather is based upon a recognition that others have greater expertise in these matters and should be deferred to. As mentioned earlier, this is similar to the attitude most people without specialized knowledge in chemistry exhibit toward those who are accomplished in that field. Just as I will defer to the opinions expressed by a highly trained chemist with regard to his/her field of expertise, Buddhists who have not directly cognized emptiness would be expected by the tradition to defer to authorities such as Buddha and the great Buddhist exegetes. It should also be noted that although the texts and scholars that one uses as bases for interpretation are those that happen to be normative for the tradition to which one belongs, still most exegetes formulate reasonings based on their normative sources that attempt to demonstrate that their particular tradition's vision is superior to others and is the most persuasive for interpretation. In conclusion, then, the presentation of hermeneutical models in the *Sūtra Explaining the Thought* and their elaboration by later exegetes exhibit a number of interrelated perspectives that appeal to authority, tradition, reasoning, and persuasion, and in order to understand the hermeneutical system of the sūtra these must all be taken into account.

CHAPTER SIX

INTENTION AND MOTIVATION

In the previous sections we have seen a number of discussions of Buddha's thought in relation to his literal teachings. In addition, we have also considered a number of strategies that have been proposed by the sūtra and by Buddhist exegetes to provide models and rules in terms of which this thought may be discovered and explicated. Such ideas undoubtedly set off alarm bells for many people familiar with important trends in contemporary hermeneutics which hold that the author's intention is forever unknown and in principle unknowable (or more extreme formulations of this idea which propose to do away completely with the institution of the author). Since the time of Heidegger, the idea that the author is remote in time, language, worldview, horizon, etc. has been an important factor in discussions of hermeneutics, and any attempt to study Buddhist hermeneutics ought to consider this in relation to Buddhism.

Gadamer, a student of Heidegger whose classic *Truth and Method* revolutionized attitudes about the role of the author, contends that readers who are separated from an author by temporal, cultural, personal, and linguistic differences can never experience the world as the author did and that a written text assumes a separate identity from its author and ought to be encountered through an open dialogue, rather than through the lens of preconceived and distorting methodologies. The use of a method pre-structures interpretation, since the method one uses determines what one will find. Gadamer contends that anyone seeking to understand a text must perform an act of "projecting" in which he/she initially posits an idea of the text's meaning, which is then confronted with the text itself, and the new understanding that emerges is again subjected to conversation, in an ongoing process of dialogue.

> A person who is trying to understand a text is always performing an act of projecting. He projects before himself a meaning for the text as a whole as soon as some initial meaning emerges in the text. Again, the latter emerges only because he is reading the text with particular expectations in regard to a certain meaning. The working out of this fore-project, which is constantly revised in terms of what emerges as he penetrates into the meaning, is understanding what is there.[1]

As Gadamer describes it, the process of understanding is always dialectical and involves a conversation between an interpreter and the object of interpretation (whether this be a text, work of art, or verbal utterance) which begins with a set of pre-judgments (*voruteile*) on the part of the interpreter (including pre-judgments that are cultural, linguistic, philosophical, or methodological) that influence all stages of interpretation. Moreover, in confronting the object to be interpreted, these pre-judgments are tested, modified, and transformed through the process of dialogue.

Thus, according to Gadamer, there is no such thing as "presuppositionless" interpretation; the interpreter is always already involved in the hermeneutical process and can never step outside of his/her horizon of understanding and encounter a text from an objectively neutral standpoint. One's own present standpoint is already a factor in any process of understanding. For Gadamer, speaking of an "objectively valid interpretation" is naive, because it assumes the possibility of finding a standpoint outside history from which an interpreter can examine a text apart from his/her pre-understandings. This idea is mistaken, according to Gadamer, because every interpreter is profoundly influenced by the attitudes of his/her time, culture, language, etc. There is no presuppositionless interpretation, because although an interpreter may become aware of particular biases and pre-judgments, he/she can never become free from his/her own facticity, from the ontological condition of having a

---

1 Hans-Georg Gadamer, *Truth and Method* (London: Sheed and Ward, 1973), p. 236.

finite temporal horizon within which whatever he/she understands assumes meaning.

Just as there is no presuppositionless interpretation, there is no non-positional subject, and so there is no such thing as a non-positional understanding. All understanding is always already positional. Meaning is thus a matter of relationship and context. It is not fixed and determinate, but rather is always related to a perspective and is open to future re-understanding.

For Gadamer, interpretation requires that one move beyond the text in order to draw out what it did not and could not say. It is not necessary that one understand an author better than he/she understood himself/herself (as Schleiermacher contends), but it is necessary that one understand differently than the author understood. A text is presented to us in a fixed form, but the interpreter's task is to bring it out of this form, to allow it to speak to the present age, and to engage in a conversation with it. Gadamer sees all texts as incomplete statements that are open toward the future. Their meanings change over time. In speaking of scriptural interpretation, he assumes that all understanding is finite and historically conditioned and that linguistic expressions always fall short of what they awaken in and communicate to their interpreters.

> If by the meaning of a text we understand the *mens auctoris*, that is, the 'actual' horizon of understanding of the original Christian writers, then we do the New Testament authors a false honor. Their honor should be precisely in the fact that they proclaim something that surpasses their own horizon of understanding.... Nowhere does understanding mean the mere recovery of what the author 'meant'....The *mens auctoris* does not limit the horizon of understanding in which the interpreter has to move, indeed, in which he is necessarily moved, if, instead of merely repeating, he really wants to understand.[2]

The task of the interpreter, then, is not faithfully and accurately to reconstruct the thought processes and intentions of an author, but

---

2 Hans-Georg Gadamer, *Philosophical Hermeneutics*, p. 210. See also Richard Palmer, *Hermeneutics*, p. 185, who states that, "only with the passage of time can we grasp 'what it is that the text says'; only gradually does its true historical significance emerge and begin to address us in the present." Hermeneutics involves an attempt to span the distance between a text from the past and one's present situation. Thus, it is not enough to show what it meant in its own context: if it means anything at all, it must mean something in one's present context.

rather to enter into an open dialogue with a text and foster an encounter between his/her horizon and the horizon of meaning opened up by the text. This merging of horizons (*horizontverschmelzung*) is the primary hermeneutical activity. It involves remaining open to new possibilities of meaning that may be revealed by the text, since the meaning of a text is never fixed or settled, but remains open for re-interpretation by other people. Gadamer states that the meaning of a text is only revealed over time, and there is never a point where one can confidently state that the meaning of a text has been fully understood and explicated.

> Every time will have to understand a text handed down to it in its own way, for it is subject to the whole of the tradition in which it has a material interest and in which it seeks to understand itself. The real meaning of a text as it addresses the interpreter does not just depend on the occasional factors which characterize the author and his original public. For it is also always co-determined by the historical situation of the interpreter and thus by the whole of the objective course of history....The meaning of a text surpasses its author not occasionally, but always. Thus understanding is not a reproductive procedure, but rather always also a productive one....It suffices to say that one understands differently when one understands at all.[3]

A text does not simply set forth a fixed statement of meaning for all time, but rather is open to new forms of disclosure of meaning at different times and places and "gives ever new answers to the person who questions it and poses ever new questions to him who answers it."[4] One does not simply explicate a determinate meaning in a static text; rather, the act of understanding leads one to greater self-understanding through the process of dialogue, and this in turn opens up new horizons of meaning. In this process, one does not seek to just understand what the text actually said, but rather to reformulate the existential questions with which the text is concerned in terms of their present relevance.

This formulation of the hermeneutical process has had a profound effect on Western understandings of hermeneutics, but, as we have seen, is foreign to Buddhist hermeneutics, which is founded on

---

3 *Wahrheit und Methode*, p. 280; quoted in *Philosophical Hermeneutics*, p. xxv.

4 *Philosophical Hermeneutics*, p. 57.

the assumption that the author of a scriptural text like the *Sūtra Explaining the Thought* had an intention (or set of intentions) that can in principle be realized and explicated by competent exegetes.[5] This assumption, which Gadamer labeled the "romantic endeavor", is central to Buddhist commentarial literature, and it is also clearly found in scriptures like the *Sūtra Explaining the Thought*, which assumes throughout that Buddha had a hidden intention when he made conflicting statements and that this intention can (and indeed must) be discovered by his followers, even those who are separated from him in time, language, etc. It is of crucial importance for Buddhists to discover this thought, since Buddha's words were all spoken with a particular intention, and his followers believe that they too can approach the truth through personally understanding his thought.

This intention also has a soteriological dimension, since Buddhists believe that Buddha teaches each person or group whatever will be most beneficial, and he does so with the intention of bringing his followers progressively closer to a state of enlightenment. Since there is a difference in understanding between Buddha and his followers, he uses various devices and strategies to lead them toward direct understanding of reality. In the *Sūtra Explaining the Thought*, for example, he presents philosophical arguments, innovations in vocabulary, and analogies to lead his followers toward a conceptual understanding, and eventually this should result in a direct, intuitive experience of truth. An underlying premise of Buddhist philosophy and meditation theory is that Buddha has actualized a potential that is present in all sentient beings, and all beings (particularly human beings) share the capacity to progress in understanding and eventually attain the state of Buddhahood. Understanding can occur because there is some correspondence between our

---

[5] This has been noted by a number of people who have written on Buddhist hermeneutics, for instance Michael Broido ("Killing, Lying, Stealing, and Adultery: A Problem of Interpretation in the Tantras", in *Buddhist Hermeneutics*, p. 87), who notes that Buddhist hermeneutics is based on the idea that one can in fact explicate an author's intention.

own inner experience and the experience and teaching of Buddha. As Donald Lopez expresses this,

> If the goal of Mahāyāna philosophy is to bring oneself and others to the experience of enlightenment, which is nothing more or less than a repetition of the experience of the Buddha, then the attempt to establish the intent of the author, the goal of what Gadamer terms the romantic endeavor, has strong soteriological overtones for the Buddhist.[6]

As Lopez notes, the methodology of Buddhist exegetes has been (and continues to be) much closer to that of Schleiermacher than Gadamer. Like Schleiermacher, Buddhist exegetes have traditionally believed that despite the gulf between themselves and Buddha, his enlightenment experiences are always present possibilities for anyone who follows the path he explicated. Like Schleiermacher, Buddhist philosophers and mystics (the two groups are not, of course, mutually exclusive) proposed to understand a text by understanding the mental processes of the author. In Buddhist hermeneutics, one re-experiences to some degree the thought processes of the author through the medium of the text and through oral and written commentarial traditions. The intuitive understanding of emptiness, for example (or the attainment of complete enlightenment), is not dependent on, or conditioned by, a particular place, time, language, etc. Buddha has perceived ultimate truth, this truth is the same at all times and for all beings, and so despite the historical gulf separating Buddha and the present time, his contemporary followers believe that they can in all relevant respects come to the same direct experience of reality that he attained 2,500 years ago.

This does not mean, however, that I accept the notion that Buddhism is ahistorical or that, because of its emphasis on the timelessness of truth, Buddhism ignores history. On the contrary, as has been noted by Maraldo, Buddhist texts often demonstrate an acute awareness of history and of historical processes, although this historical consciousness sometimes differs from some contemporary notions of history.[7] The *Saṃdhinirmocana-sūtra*, for example, is a

6 Donald S. Lopez, "Introduction", in *Buddhist Hermeneutics*, p. 7.

7 John Maraldo, "Hermeneutics and Historicity", pp. 29-30.

text that is clearly conscious of history and that sees itself as not only situated historically but as potentially influencing the future course of Buddhist discourse. The three wheels schema reflects an understanding of historical development in Buddhist doctrine and, as we have seen, could not intelligibly have been formulated prior to the discourses in which the first two wheels of doctrine were taught.

The *Sūtra Explaining the Thought* implicitly contains an understanding of the history of Buddhist doctrine in which its new statements are presented as being part of a dialectical process and as influencing the course of future developments. Even though its statements are presented as coming from the timeless perspective of a fully enlightened being, they are clearly expected to have an impact on the history of those who receive them. Those belonging to traditions that accepted the sūtra as normative are to understand the teaching of this text as a part of a historical process that began with the pronouncements identified in the sūtra as belonging to the "first wheel". These are challenged and undermined by the subsequent statements of the "second wheel". The third wheel projects toward the future in its resolution of the conflicts.

The sūtra implies a process in which Buddha first taught a set of doctrines (which are now being identified as constituting a related group of teachings). Later, in a new cycle of teachings, he began to undermine and challenge the implicit assumptions that some of his followers had developed. Now in the *Saṃdhinirmocana* he is setting in motion another cycle of teachings that clarify the intended meaning of his previous utterances, and these are intended to alter the subsequent history of interpretation. Thus, for Buddhist exegetes the gulf that Gadamer sees between an author from the distant past and an interpreter of a later time is not felt. Rather, the goal of Buddhist hermeneuticians is closer to Hirsch's contention that "the interpreter's aim is to posit the author's horizon and carefully exclude his own accidental associations".[8] The interpretations, attitudes, and

---

[8] E.D. Hirsch, *Validity in Interpretation*, p. 222.

pre-understandings of Buddhist exegetes may (and do) reflect differences of history, language, culture, etc., but Buddhist hermeneutics presents this as a difficulty requiring caution on the part of the interpreter and not as an insuperable barrier that makes re-cognition of Buddha's thought impossible. Finding Buddha's meaning is difficult, and the gulf in understanding between Buddha and an unenlightened exegete makes it necessary that he/she initially identify and then rely on sūtras of definitive meaning, but it is assumed that through this process one may in fact bridge the temporal distance separating Buddha from one's own time, culture, etc. A good description of this attitude can be found in Hirsch's statement that

> the root problem of interpretation is always the same—to guess what the author meant. Even though we can never be certain that our interpretative guesses are correct, we know that they *can* be correct and that the goal of interpretation as a discipline is constantly to increase the probability that they are correct.[9]

Buddhist thinkers, of course, believe that at advanced stages of spiritual development a person does know Buddha's thought with certainty. In the context of the level of experience of ordinary beings, however, Buddhist thought in general is aware of the historical distance between the Buddha and a given time period or culture, but this is not seen as a reason to think that one can never find Buddha's final thought. It is seen as constituting a good reason to exercise caution with respect to which authorities one will follow and to constantly examine one's conclusions through reasoning in accordance with one's tradition. Buddhists who lived after the time of Buddha understood that there were differences between the time of Buddha and their own times (as is evidenced by various formulations of the idea that the doctrine has undergone a continual process of degeneration since his death), but there is always a sense that the distance can be bridged by relying on sūtras of definitive meaning and engaging in meditative training in accordance with their teachings.

---

9 Ibid., p. 206.

Gadamer contends that "every encounter with tradition that takes place within historical consciousness involves the experience of the tension between the text and the present",[10] which accurately reflects a concern of Buddhist hermeneutics. Unlike Gadamer, however, Buddhist exegetes think that this gap is not an unbridgeable one and that through following proper exegetical principles (that is, the principles accepted by their respective traditions) and through practicing meditation in accordance with Buddha's instructions they can re-cognize Buddha's meaning and re-create in their own minds his understanding of reality. In order to do this, as we have seen, it is of crucial importance initially to identify which of Buddha's teachings are definitive and to use these as a guide in understanding the thought behind his interpretable teachings. Through this process one's understanding deepens to the point where one is able to move beyond the mere verbal meaning of Buddhas's utterances and progressively penetrate their deeper purport. This process, if successful, eventually enables one personally and intuitively to re-create the enlightenment experience of Buddha through a profound existential transformation.

It should be stressed that although Buddhist hermeneutics is closer to the thought of Schleiermacher than that of Gadamer, it is difficult to imagine a Buddhist embracing the idea advanced by Schleiermacher that the task of the interpreter is "to understand the text as well as and then even better than its author".[11] Since Buddhists believe that a Buddha has reached the pinnacle of understanding and enlightenment, the goal of his followers is faithfully to recreate in their own consciousnesses his enlightened perception of reality, not to surpass him in terms of understanding the import of his teachings. Buddha is thought to be omniscient and prescient, and he is not bound by history or time. His words express his understanding as well as the limitations of language allow, and they serve

---

[10] *Truth and Method*, p. 236.

[11] See the edition of Schleiermacher's hermeneutical writings translated by James Duke and Jack Forstman in F.D.E. Schleiermacher, *Hermeneutics: The Handwritten Manuscripts* (Missoula, MT: Scholars Press, 1977), p. 150.

as guides for others to follow in their quest for enlightenment. Since enlightenment is timeless, these teachings are relevant for anyone at any time, and the state of Buddhahood for Buddhists is not a unique and unrepeatable event that occurred thousands of years ago, but rather an enduring possibility in the contemporary world.

POLITICAL DIMENSIONS

Our study thus far has been mainly descriptive: the primary concern has been to look at the hermeneutical theories of the sūtra and to speculate on how these are linked with, and influenced by, Buddhist notions of tradition and authority. In the present section, I propose to step back from the text a bit to look at the political intentions behind the vocabulary innovations of the *Saṃdhinirmocana*. The focus of this analysis is to examine the possible intended consequences of the sūtra's doctrines and the motivations of the persons who formulated and explicated these vocabulary innovations, i.e., what sort of practical results they were trying to achieve. It is also concerned with the context in which the text was produced, because this can provide important clues regarding how and why certain doctrines were formulated. As George Bond has noted, "contexts generate texts", and one of the primary concerns for anyone seeking to understand the thought of the *Saṃdhinirmocana* must be the context in which it was written.[12]

---

[12] See George D. Bond, "The Gradual Path as a Hermeneutical Approach to the *Dhamma*", in *Buddhist Hermeneutics*, p. 30. I should mention that although the initial idea of considering the sūtra in terms of functionality and power relations was partially motivated by my reading of Michel Foucault, my analysis is rather different than the ones I have read in Foucault's works. I am primarily concerned with how the doctrines of the sūtra might have affected power relations within Buddhist philosophy, and not with, for example, the effects of power and coercion on individuals who are at a disadvantage in power relations or how social institutions affect the individuals over whom they have power (which are important concerns of Foucault's). My goal is to show how political concerns might have influenced the text and what effects the sūtra had on power relations, and not to analyze Indian Buddhist society, monastic structures, etc. in terms of their power relations. Nor will I be concerned with actual manifestations and excercises of power. The focus of this essay is primarily speculative and theoretical in that it is mainly concerned with trying to understand what sort of practical ends the vocabulary innovations of the sūtra were attempting to bring about.

My analysis is inspired by a recent project which required reading a wide range of contemporary feminist philosophy, particularly philosophy of language. Feminist thinkers have often noted how certain terms reflect power relations and how the development of new termi-

At the outset, it should be noted that a good deal of this analysis is necessarily speculative, since there is much that is unknown about the early formative period of Mahāyāna literature (the period from which I assume the *Saṃdhinirmocana* dates), and most of our information must be drawn from sectarian textual sources. Nevertheless, these provide some interesting clues about reasons behind the formulations of the sūtra's distinctive doctrines, such as the three wheels of doctrine and the three non-entitynesses, and what effect these doctrines had on successive generations of thinkers.

Taking these as our beginning point, it is instructive to consider what sort of political motivations might have prompted the vocabulary innovations of the three wheels and the three non-entitynesses. As we have seen, these doctrines refer to certain types of Buddhist literature, primarily texts that were important to Hīnayāna schools and the Perfection of Wisdom Sūtras (which were central to the Madhyamaka school). The doctrines of the three wheels and three non-entitynesses not only provided a hermeneutical model in terms of which people following the *Saṃdhinirmocana* could reconcile certain of Buddha's teachings that had created cognitive conflicts among his followers, but they also gave certain people (those who belonged to traditions that accepted the *Saṃdhinirmocana* as normative) a measure of control over the texts in which they were propounded. This control had a political dimension, since these were texts that were important to schools that propounded rival doctrines. By creating terminology that influenced other Buddhist thinkers, the author(s) of the sūtra altered the course of future debate on subjects that were central to the school that developed from the *Saṃdhinirmocana-sūtra*, i.e., the Yogācāra, and altered power relations by influencing the terms of understanding of key doctrines in other schools of thought. In other words, the author(s) of the sūtra created new paradigms (concepts, models, terms) that redirected future debate and thought.

---

nology can influence and alter these relations. My contention in the present section is that the vocabulary innovations of the *Saṃdhinirmocana* reflect a concern with these facts and are an attempt to alter power relations through the coining of new vocabulary.

Buddhist hermeneutics was never divorced from such political concerns, as is evidenced by Buddhism's extensive polemical and sectarian literature, and part of the work of Buddhist exegetes was (and still is) concerned with who had the authority to influence or legislate how a text (or group of texts) should be interpreted. In order to determine this, Buddhist thinkers resorted to arguments based on reasoning, tradition, authority, and scripture, and their work often resulted in shifting power relations between schools, individuals, and texts. The more successfully a Buddhist thinker argued a particular position within the rules, confines, and contexts of traditional Buddhism, the more authority he and his followers gained, and one result of this was often a greater control over the interpretation of rivals' texts and doctrines. Furthermore, the fact that certain authors and texts are studied by successive generations and by contemporary scholars reflects the fact that some thinkers are better at influencing power relationships than others.[13] Those who are studied by later generations are those who formulate compelling new paradigms and vocabulary and who write at a time in which these influence others. Buddhist literature is full of texts by authors whose writings never had a major influence, and Buddhist history is undoubtedly peopled with many great mystics and philosophers who either never wrote or whose writings never had an impact and were lost or forgotten.

Within the society of monastic Buddhism in India, power resided with those who were accepted as having authority, those who were in control of dominant and persuasive ideologies, and those who were at the forefront of important movements. The primary authority was of course the Buddha, but by the time of the *Saṃdhinirmocana* Buddha was mainly a symbol that was appropriated for sectarian purposes and interpreted according to the interests, concerns, and goals of individual groups. Those groups who were in dominant positions sought to defend their authority by demonstrating their affinity with Buddha and his teachings, and

---

[13] I owe this particular thought to Professor Deane Curtin, Dept. of Philosophy, Gustavus Adolphus College, who was kind enough to help me talk out some of these ideas.

groups attempting to create a shift in the power balance had to demonstrate (within the accepted rules of discourse) that their doctrines were closer to the thought of the founder than those of their rivals.

The *Saṃdhinirmocana* is an example of a successful attempt to alter power relations. (The Buddhist canon is full of unsuccessful attempts: texts that proposed new doctrines and vocabulary, but never succeeded in gaining a following or having a major influence.) Its new doctrines and vocabulary had an important impact on future discussions of Buddhist philosophy and forced members of rival schools to respond to its evaluations of the relative positions of their respective doctrines and texts.

In addition, because the *Saṃdhinirmocana* had the authority of a sūtra, later schools had to deal with the hierarchical model that it propounded, which placed key Hīnayāna doctrines at the bottom of Buddhist teaching, placed key passages of the Perfection of Wisdom Sūtras above those, and placed the third wheel (as represented by the *Saṃdhinirmocana* and as inherited by its followers) at the top. The three non-entitynesses provided an exegetical model through which one could reconcile conflicting statements attributed to the Buddha by positing the intentions behind his statements, and this in turn allowed the traditions following the sūtra to influence the interpretation of certain texts. Thus, the doctrine of the three wheels at least partially had the effect of placing the teachings of the sūtra and the tradition following from it at the top of the hierarchy and, more importantly, forced rival schools to debate on its terms and in terms of its vocabulary in order to defend their doctrinal positions.

The same could of course be said of most, if not all, Buddhist texts (and is probably true of many or most originators of paradigm shifts and vocabulary innovations). In attempting to formulate more consistent, persuasive, or popular doctrines, the authors of texts are trying to convince people of the superiority of their views and doctrines, and in so doing they gain power due to increases in numbers of followers, recognition by other scholars and philosophers, diffusion of their ideas and doctrines, and enhanced status and prestige within Buddhist monastic society.[14] In some cases, there would also be more material rewards, such as royal favor, fame, and increased patronage. These are important motivators that are generally overlooked in contemporary Buddhist studies, which often implicitly assume that the authors of Buddhist texts were austere, other-worldly scholar-monks ensconced in their monasteries and aloof from worldly concerns and politics.

In fact, even a cursory study of Buddhist literature reveals that many Buddhist thinkers were very involved in politics, both within the monasteries and in the larger society, and that Buddhist texts are often written in order to alter power relations within the Buddhist community. For example, as Graeme MacQueen has pointed out, many early Mahāyāna texts contain strongly sectarian statements that were obviously designed to establish the validity of their doctrines against the opposition of Hīnayāna opponents.[15] (Indeed, the coining of the names "Mahāyāna" and "Hīnayāna" is clearly an attempt to alter power relations within Buddhism by characterizing one's own group as superior to a rival group.) A similar concern can be seen in the vocabulary innovations of the *Saṃdhinirmocana*, which place the texts and doctrines of competing schools of thought in a hierarchical relationship. In such relationships, one's own texts and doctrines serve as the standards by which others' texts and doctrines are to be evaluated.

It is important to note that words are not only tools that are used to express thoughts, develop arguments, and persuade others; they

---

[14] The same is of course true within contemporary interpretive communities, such as the community of academics, which holds shared notions of rationality, rules of debate, and power relations between groups. These power relations are influenced by the development of powerful new models, vocabularies, and methodologies, and much of contemporary academic activity could be analyzed in terms of various attempts to influence power relations. A good example would be the growing influence of "political correctness", a movement which regularly gives rise to new vocabulary that challenges (and that seeks to undermine) existing power relationships and structures that its adherents view as oppressive. Its adherents also often use their vocabulary innovations as weapons to be wielded against people who oppose their ideas and agendas.

[15] See Graeme MacQueen, "Inspired Speech in Early Mahāyāna Buddhism", *Religion* #11, 1981, pp. 303-19 and #12, 1982, pp. 49-65.

can also function as weapons to undermine the positions of others, to force them to debate on one's own terms, and in some cases to force one's opponents into silence. This is true both in ancient India and in contemporary Western society. Groups with particular aims and agendas often use new terminology to defeat opponents, to alter power relations in their favor, or to force others to debate on their terms.

Power relations within the Buddhist community were influenced by success in debate, by numbers of followers, the personal fame of great teachers, and a number of other factors. A text like the *Saṃdhinirmocana* that successfully developed and explicated doctrinal innovations like the three wheels and the three non-entity-nesses altered the political landscape by calling into question the value of the doctrines, texts, practices, and teachers of other schools.

This is not to say that Buddhist scholars were cynical, power-hungry politicians; on the contrary, most probably saw their thought and writing as being concerned with truth and as aiming at the benefit of other sentient beings. In addition, most probably sincerely thought that their respective positions *were* superior to those of rival schools and sought to defend them for these reasons, but they also were not immune to political realities, and they often used political maneuvers in their thought in order to establish their positions. In addition, Buddhist history contains numerous examples of Buddhist monks using political and military force to suppress rival schools and their doctrines.[16]

---

[16] Fully developing this idea would require a separate study, but an excellent example would be the suppression of the Jo nang pa school in Tibet by the Dge lugs pa sect, which took over the main monastary of the Jo nang pas, had their texts destroyed, and forced Jo nang monks to convert to Dge lugs pa. Some striking examples can be found in Japan, where monasteries often had soldier-monks whose duty was to defend the monastery against attacks, and sometimes to attack and conquer the monasteries of rival schools. One could also point to the history of the Nichiren school, which, beginning with its founder, has been very concerned with gaining political power. Nichiren himself wrote several letters to people in power (including the Emperor) urging them to suppress other schools (particularly Pure Land schools) with military force and to make his own sect the only school of Buddhism in Japan.

I want to stress, however, that the presence of rivalries between schools and attempts to alter power relations through the creation of new terminology are often not negative phenomena. On the contrary, such tensions and rivalries often spur creativity and innovation, breathing new vitality into traditions that have become complacent. The creation of a powerful new model often causes those whose models it attempts to displace to reformulate their ideas and remake their respective traditions in ways that make them more resistant to the new criticisms and that also indicate new directions for growth. The positive effects of rivalry and opposition are often overlooked by contemporary philosophers, many of whom view them as wholly destructive.

This is true, for example, of Michel Foucault, particularly in his earlier writings. As Kyle Pasewark has noted, Foucault tends to view power conflicts in terms of a "zero-sum game" in which one side wins everything and the other loses and is dominated.[17] In fact, the situation is far more nuanced than this, and such conflicts are often signs of vitality, change, and innovation. Pasewark also notes that in his later writings Foucault came to realize that power can also have a productive dimension, and I think that this is particularly true of cases where rival groups are not trying to conquer each other through force of arms but rather to restructure the balance of power in their favor through written and oral debate. This can be seen both in the language of the terminological innovations of the *Sūtra Explaining the Thought* and in the answers put forward by other groups whose positions were challenged by them.

In religious groups, competition is often a sign of vitality, while absence of competition can be a sign of complacency, rather than a sign of ecumenical good will. It often motivates great thinkers to produce some of their most notable works, and religious texts are

---

[17] Pasewark develops this idea in an insightful analysis of the importance of Foucault's ideas for theology, entitled *A Theology of Power* (Ph.D. dissertation, University of Chicago, 1991; this has been published by Fortress Press under the title *A Theology of Power: Being beyond Domination* (Minneapolis, MN: Augsburg Fortress, 1992). Professor Pasewark was kind enough to lend me a draft copy of his book, which was very helpful in this study, particularly in terms of understanding the differences between Foucault's concerns and my own.

often written in order to argue in favor of the doctrines and practices of particular groups and against the doctrines and practices of competitors. As Jay Newman notes, when competition

> promotes fanaticism, animosity, persecution, and painful division, it is plainly disastrous for a denomination. But if carried on in the spirit of tolerance, it can be a boon to a denomination, preventing the communal faith from becoming stagnant, reviving the religious spirit of the weary, and giving the disaffected a new tie to the community of believers. The fact is that no religious denomination can survive, grow, and spiritually prosper if it is wholly incapable of accommodating some degree of theological diversity; it will be forever losing its members to sects, new denominations, and older and livelier denominations, and it will become increasingly irrelevant to a world that refuses to stand still. And where there is theological diversity, there will eventually be theological competition, for no individual or group is willing to be wise all alone.[18]

Religious thinkers who are convinced of the correctness of their doctrines and those of their own groups are seldom willing to remain silent in this belief. The motives for this can be political and self-serving, altruistic, or a combination of both. If one is convinced that the beliefs and practices of rival groups are mistaken and dangerous, one will likely feel compelled to oppose them, since if one is successful this will be beneficial for those who are rescued from the wrong ideas and for one's own group, which promotes and upholds what is most correct and most beneficial for religious practitioners. Such competition can have positive effects on one's rivals, also, since it can spur them to develop innovative and compelling vocabulary to combat the threat. It also might inspire them to reform their conduct in order to demonstrate the superiority of their group. In the same way that high-level competition often brings out the best in athletes, religious competition (when it avoids degenerating to the use of force) can lead to innovation, doctrinal development, religious reforms, and changes that allow religious traditions to adapt themselves to changing social and religious circumstances.

An example of such development is the model of the three wheels, which provided a paradigm in terms of which Buddhists

---

[18] Jay Newman, *Competition in Religious Life* (Waterloo, Ontario: Wilfrid Laurier University Press, 1989, p. 166.

could reconcile conflicts in Buddha's teachings. By indicating doctrinal conflicts in terms of a hierarchical schema that placed tenets of rival schools in inferior positions, it made explicit a set of conflicts that were present in teachings attributed to Buddha and posited a model in terms of which they might be reconciled. Some members of other groups, particularly people later labeled Mādhyamikas, perceived this as containing an implicit threat to their own interpretations and traditions, and so they answered with counter-attacks that often adopted the new vocabulary but reinterpreted it. This process of debate and the often ingenious ways that people of various groups attempted to restructure power relationships by formulating new doctrines (within the confines of generally accepted notions of authority and tradition) indicated that these traditions remained vital and relevant to their adherents. It is important to remember that the political dimensions of their doctrinal innovations did not necessarily indicate a degeneration into internecine warfare.

The doctrines of the three wheels and the three non-entitynesses are good examples of ideas with political overtones. The three wheels doctrine clearly implies that other Buddhist texts should be read in light of the *Saṃdhinirmocana*. The sūtra established a new range of possibilities for discourse, debate, and exegesis that either operated within the rules it explicated or that were at least compelled to take them into account. By placing itself in the position of doctrinal yardstick, the text forced later thinkers who were opposed to its formulations to use its vocabulary while presenting rival viewpoints. A good example can be found in Tsong kha pa's *Essence of the Good Explanations*, which holds that the supreme Buddhist philosophical system is Prāsaṅgika-Madhyamaka, but which attempts to use the vocabulary and doctrines of the *Saṃdhinirmocana* against themselves.

Tsong kha pa concedes that the sūtra states that the third wheel (as represented by the *Saṃdhinirmocana*) is said by Buddha to be of definitive meaning, unsurpassable, etc., and that the other wheels are placed below the third wheel, but he tries to argue for the supremacy of the second wheel by making a distinction between types of trainees. He states that the intended audience of the second wheel takes the doctrines of the Perfection of Wisdom Sūtras concerning non-entityness etc. literally (as Buddha indicates in the *Saṃdhinirmocana*),[19] but Tsong kha pa argues that there are other trainees, who he calls the "special trainees" (*ched du bya ba'i gdul bya*), who hear Buddha's second wheel teachings and understand the thought behind them without needing to have him spell it out for them. Dpal 'byor lhun grub comments that this indicates that

> the special trainees of this middle [wheel], without depending on commentaries on the thought of these sūtras of the middle wheel—such as that of, for instance, the *Sūtra Explaining the Thought*—realize completely the thought of the sūtras of the middle wheel and do not conceive them to be literal, and so the trainees of this middle [wheel] have greatly sharper faculties than the trainees of the *Sūtra Explaining the Thought.*[20]

The trainees of the third wheel, Tsong kha pa and Dpal 'byor lhun grub argue, are not as advanced as these special second wheel trainees (who are characterized by Dpal 'byor lhun grub as being Bodhisattvas of sharp faculties: *byang chub sems dpa' dbang po rnon po*), since the latter do not require the explicit distinctions of the sūtra. Thus, according to Tsong kha pa and Dpal 'byor lhun grub, the trainees of the third wheel operate only on a verbal level and need to have Buddha's doctrines and intentions spelled out for them, whereas the "special trainees" of the second wheel are able to grasp Buddha's thought immediately without needing such special help. Tsong kha pa and Dpal 'byor lhun grub conclude from this that the second wheel is actually superior to the third, since it is really aimed at superior practitioners. They cleverly use the terminology and internal logic of the sūtra against themselves in order to argue for a rival position, but the significant thing for our present discussion is that they were forced to use the terminology and distinctive doctrines of the *Saṃdhinirmocana* in order to advance a system

---

[19] *Legs bshad snying po*, Sarnath ed., p. 85.1.

[20] Dpal 'byor lhun grub, p. 30.1.

(i.e., Prāsaṅgika-Madhyamaka) that they saw as being superior to the system of the sūtra and in opposition to its pronouncements.

Similar presentations can be seen in a number of post-*Saṃdhinirmocana* Madhyamaka thinkers, such as Candrakīrti and Bhavya, who argued against Yogācāra doctrines and figures but, because of the prestige of the sūtra and the continuing vitality of its vocabulary innovations and seminal doctrines, were often forced to argue on terms set by the sūtra and its exponents by using the terminology and language of their opponents. This fact is mentioned by Luis Gómez in his discussion of Buddhist hermeneutics in the *Encyclopedia of Religions*, in which he notes that there were alternative formulations of the three wheels that were at variance with the presentation of the *Saṃdhinirmocana*, but that "the scriptural weight of the *Saṃdhinirmocana* was such that the scholastics could not ignore its clear statement".[21] He mentions Tsong kha pa as an example of a scholar who puts forth doctrines that are at variance with the sūtra and who "goes through the most subtle arguments to show that the *sūtra*'s ordering of the turnings does not imply a privileged position for the doctrine of mind-only".[22] Even though Tsong kha pa saw Madhyamaka doctrines as being superior to those presented in the *Saṃdhinirmocana*, he was not able to ignore the sūtra and felt compelled to argue on its terms and using its vocabulary in order to justify his own position.[23]

How did the author(s) of the sūtra accomplish this? A number of factors contributed to the philosophical and political success of

---

[21] Luis O. Gómez, "Exegesis and Hermeneutics", in *Encyclopedia of Religion*, ed. Mircea Eliade (New York: Macmillan, 1987), p. 537. For examples of alternative restatements of the three wheels, see Kennard Lipman, "Nītārtha, Neyārtha, and Tathāgatagarbha in Tibet", *JIP* #8, 1980, pp. 87-8 and Ian Charles Harris, *The Continuity of Madhyamaka and Yogācāra in Mahāyāna Buddhism* (Leiden: E.J. Brill, 1991), p. 70.

[22] Gómez, p. 538.

[23] In the *Essence of the Good Explanations*, he also has a section devoted to Madhyamaka hermeneutics, which is based on the *Akṣayamati-nirdeśa-sūtra*, but the significant point for our present discussion is the fact that he devotes half of his study of Buddhist hermeneutics to a discussion of the Mind-Only system. Apparently the sūtra's doctrines were influential enough that he felt compelled to explain away the problem of Buddha telling the audience of the *Saṃdhinirmocana* that second wheel doctrines (which are the basis of Madhyamaka) are of provisional meaning.

the sūtra and its doctrinal innovations: firstly, the fact that it was written as a sūtra ensured that the text and its doctrines would be immune to fundamental criticisms to the extent that the *Saṃdhinirmocana* was accepted as the word of Buddha. Any teaching that is widely accepted as originating from Buddha assumes a measure of authority due to this association. An example of this authority is the *vinaya* literature, the coercive force of which derives from Buddha. It tells Buddhist monks how to live, where to live, what company they can keep, what to eat, etc., and in traditional Buddhist monastic society the *vinaya* has provided the primary body of rules that regulate power relations and everyday life. Since Buddhists traditionally view Buddha as an "authoritative being" (*pramāṇa-bhuta*), any statement he made (or that some people think he made) assumes a potent prescriptive and coercive power.[24]

Since Buddha is the supreme authority for Buddhists, all of his teachings are proper for their respective audiences and beneficial to sentient beings, and so no teaching of Buddha can be conclusively rejected. There are a number of Buddhist texts, such as the *Saṃdhinirmocana*, that go so far as to state that people who reject new doctrines and texts that they have not previously heard often do so under the influence of Māra, the Buddhist Satan.[25] Mahāyāna literature in particular contains many such statements, and so Buddhists are cautioned through these to be receptive to new doctrines. Even in the Pāli canon, which is generally more conservative in such mat-

---

[24] A parallel process is outlined by Erich Frauwallner with respect to the development of the Pāli canon (*The Earliest Vinaya and the Beginnings of Buddhist Literature*; Rome: Serie Orientale Roma, vol. VIII, 1956). He contends (p. 63) that the story of a "First Council" in which 500 Arhats gathered to recount their recollections of Buddha's word is a fiction created by some of his followers to give the force of Buddha's authority to a particular edition of the canon. He compares the creation of this story to the attribution of Hindu texts to famous authorities of the past: "When the Upaniṣads place a text in the mouth of a famous teacher, this has the purpose of placing it under his authority". Frauwallner contends that the story of the First Council was created by some Buddhists "in order to place their own holy tradition under a common authority, to which recourse could be made through a list of teachers on the Vedic model". See also Hermann Oldenberg's introduction to the *Vinaya Piṭaka* (London: Luzac & Co., 1964), vol. I, p. xi, which also questions the authenticity of the story of the First Council.

[25] See, for example, Graeme MacQueen, "Inspired Speech in Early Mahāyāna Buddhism", which provides several examples of early Mahāyāna texts that use this argument to undermine the counterattacks of their opponents.

ters, there is a statement in *Aṅguttara-nikāya* IV.163 that "whatever is well spoken is the word of the Buddha",[26] which is often taken to mean that anything not fundamentally at variance with Buddhist doctrine and practice can legitimately be adopted.

Since the *Saṃdhinirmocana* is written as a sūtra and accepted as such by Mahāyāna Buddhists, even those who disagreed with it had to deal with it as a scripture that derived its normative status from the supreme authority for Buddhists. In the Buddhist power hierarchy, the figure of the Buddha resides at the top position, and so by invoking his authority, the author(s) of the sūtra assured that even those who disagreed with its doctrines would be unable simply to reject them as mistaken or as being the product of shoddy thinking. The figure of the Buddha is a powerful shared symbol in the system of discourse in which the sūtra situates itself, and his authority renders the sūtra immune from much of the polemical infighting that developed between rival schools.

In addition, as noted above, the sūtra itself has a number of internal devices that establish its high status: it is set in a celestial palace inhabited by the Buddha and very advanced disciples, and all of the interlocutors of the sūtra (with the exception of Subhūti) are very advanced Bodhisattvas, which implies that their questions reflect their high level of realization. In addition, the sūtra frequently declares that its doctrines are in accord with the perceptions of Superiors (*'phags pa, ārya*) and are not correctly understood by "ordinary beings" (*so so'i skye bo, pṛthag-jana*). This implies that anyone who does not understand and accept the sūtra's statements demonstrates personal deficiencies in terms of understanding and spiritual attainment and not deficiencies on the part of the sūtra or its author. Furthermore, at the end of the last four chapters, the sūtra

---

[26] This passage and its implications for Buddhist exegesis are discussed by George Bond in *The Word of the Buddha* (Columbo: M.D. Gunasena, 1982), p. 30ff. He notes that this idea is not confined to this single instance but is also found in one of Asoka's edicts (see Bond's note 37, which refers to P.H.L. Eggermont and J. Hoftizer eds., *The Moral Edicts of King Asoka*; Leiden: E.J. Brill, 1962, p. 38). For another classical source of this idea, see the *Adhyāśaya-saṃcodana-sūtra*, in which Buddha states, "Maitreya, whatever is well spoken is the word of the Buddha" (*yat kiṃ cin maitreya subhāṣitaṃ tad buddhavacanaṃ*).

declares that it is a teaching of definitive meaning (*nges pa'i don, nītārtha*) and should be accepted as such by those who hear and read it.

When taken together, these features make it difficult for anyone simply to dismiss the text or to characterize it as a teaching for people of dull faculties. The followers of the sūtra were thus able to claim a privileged position for their doctrines and their interpretations of others' texts because of the status of the purported author of the sūtra, the internal logic of its doctrinal statements, and its own statements about its status. In other words, the persuasive doctrinal innovations and internal statements of its advanced status are on some level intended to alter power relationships within Buddhist society by characterizing the doctrines of rival schools as provisional and requiring interpretation on the terms stated in the *Saṃdhinirmocana* and by unequivocally indicating that it is a teaching for advanced practitioners, which ensured that it would have to be confronted directly by opponents rather than being dismissed. This in turn gave followers of the *Saṃdhinirmocana* a measure of control over their opponents' texts and some influence over their interpretation.

CHAPTER SEVEN

CONCLUSION

The previous chapters have attempted to look at the distinctive doctrines and philosophical ramifications of the *Sūtra Explaining the Thought* in terms of a number of perspectives, including textual and philological analysis, consideration of traditional commentaries from India, Tibet, and China, and through the application of some contemporary interpretive models, such as discussions of hermeneutics, cognitive dissonance theory, and an analysis of the political dimension of its doctrines. Each of these is an attempt to understand a facet of the thought and significance of this important text, and each hopefully provides a cogent perspective through which its meaning and significance may be understood.

I view this procedure as a philosophical equivalent of Clifford Geertz' idea of "thick description" in anthropology. Geertz' approach involves providing as much detail and information as possible in order to give a holistic picture of the object of study. My approach is similar: in providing a number of alternative approaches and interpretations, it is hoped that the multifaceted thought of the sūtra will be drawn out and that its ramifications will be opened up to modern readers.

It is important to note that this study is by no means a complete analysis of the doctrines of the *Sūtra Explaining the Thought* or of its impact on Buddhist thought. Our analysis has focused primarily on the first seven chapters, and within that has been mainly concerned with the sūtra's presentation of Buddhist hermeneutics and its influence on Buddhist thought. The seminal statements of idealism in the eighth chapter of the sūtra, its presentations of meditation, the Bodhisattva path, the nature of buddhahood, and the application of reasoning processes (which are important concerns of the last four chapters) have been either barely mentioned or bypassed. These are all important parts of the thought of the sūtra, but all fall outside the scope of the present study. They are another story for another time, and hopefully this story will eventually be told, perhaps in a later work.

I suspect that if there is anything original in this work, it lies in the fact that it has utilized interpretive models not normally found in Buddhist studies, such as cognitive dissonance theory and contemporary studies of the connection between tradition and rationality. It is worthwhile in Buddhist studies to attempt to reconstruct the context in which particular doctrines were formulated, since the context of an utterance or doctrine is of crucial importance in determining its meaning and application. Buddhist doctrines operate within the context of a functioning system of shared symbols and assumptions, and a contemporary interpreter should seek to understand and explicate this context. Buddhist teachings are meaningful to Buddhists primarily insofar as they are perceived as saying something significant about human existence, and this is what Buddhists try to find in them. Buddhist philosophers and meditators are generally not primarily concerned with learning about other topics (e.g., history, geography, etc.) that are not perceived as being relevant to this soteriological orientation. Rather, Buddhist texts are considered to be important insofar as they reveal something about human existence and how human beings can realize their highest potential through attaining the state of Buddhahood.

I have argued that all rationality functions within a tradition of shared assumptions and methods and that Buddhist thought is no exception to this rule. Buddhist thinkers attempted to justify their ideas through recourse to tradition and accepted notions of authority, and their reasoning processes cannot intelligibly be lifted from their context and studied in isolation. It is important to note that the Buddhist thinkers considered in this study were Buddhist monks, people who received initiation into the Buddhist *saṃgha*, who attempted to live according to the rules of the *vinaya*, and whose thought processes were powerfully conditioned by these factors.

Much of contemporary Buddhist studies, it seems to me, implicitly assumes that their philosophies can legitimately be studied apart from the social and cultural context in which they lived and worked. This, I contend, is a fundamentally misguided notion: the robes worn by Buddhist monks are not just fashion statements, nor are their monastic vows simply words uttered in isolation from their lives and philosophies. In order to understand traditional thinkers or texts, it is necessary to attempt to reconstruct as much as possible the rules of thought and discourse in which they operated.

In addition to such considerations, this study has attempted to provide a speculative overview of the way in which the *Saṃdhinirmocana* attempted to influence power relations and some examples of how it succeeded in doing so. This aspect of the study has implications for contemporary philosophical studies as well, since it seems probable that much of the history of philosophy in any culture reflects changing power relations. In contemporary hermeneutics, for example, the "philosophical hermeneutics" of Gadamer can be viewed as a powerful challenge to the tradition of Schleiermacher, whose idea of faithfully reproducing the intention of an author had profoundly influenced interpretation theory and practice. Gadamer's successful formulation of new vocabulary and doctrines changed existing power relations. It put those who followed Schleiermacher on the defensive, and the writings of E.D. Hirsch and others can be seen as attempts to change the balance of power in their direction. These in turn are answered by broadsides from other factions, and the status of a particular person or school within the world of contemporary thought changes as a result of perceptions of the persuasiveness of a particular thinker or text.

Moreover, within contemporary society there are any number of groups (e.g., women's rights groups, advocates of various formulations of civil rights, etc.) who are creating new vocabulary innovations in attempts to alter existing power relations in their favor. These groups implicitly or explicitly realize that language and terminology can be extremely powerful and that changes in vocabulary can both reflect and influence the relative prestige, vitality, and power of individuals or collectives.

Such concerns, of course, are nothing new, and politics and concern with power relations tend to become operative in any group of people, no matter how small. Even in Buddhist monasteries, which are institutions devoted to the pursuit of enlightenment, politics and power are matters of concern, and Buddhist thinkers are often aware of and influenced by such concerns, whether consciously or unconsciously. I wish to stress that I am not attempting to categorize Buddhist philosophers as avaricious and corrupt politicians venally seeking temporal power; rather, my intent is to point out that political concerns can be seen in their thought and that the success or failure of particular texts and schools is connected with historical and political circumstances. A study of Buddhist literature that ignores the political dimension ignores an important factor in the equation, a factor without which the picture becomes incomplete.

The analogy in the seventh chapter in which Paramārthasamudgata compares the relation between Buddha's interpretable and definitive teachings to the relation between a picture and the basis on which it is drawn is appropriate here. The internal logic of influential Buddhist texts like the *Saṃdhinirmocana* often reflects power relations, and a study of a seminal text like this sūtra (which is concerned with influencing and altering power relations) that ignores this dimension is like a painting without a basis. Buddhist thinkers in general undoubtedly do not view themselves as politicians trying to manipulate and alter power relations, but rather as faithful interpreters concerned with explicating the truth contained in Buddha's words. Despite this qualification, however, they do often use political maneuvers to advance their own doctrines and schools. Successful creators of new vocabulary and writers of commentaries are those who know their intended audience and what will have an effect on it. Different interpreters will notice different things, emphasize certain details, and formulate distinctive vocabulary and doctrines. Those who are successful are those who have an impact on subsequent thought and power relations. Their texts restructure the rules of debate for successive generations of thinkers and their traditions are able to influence the interpretation of texts of their own schools and sometimes those of rival factions.

BIBLIOGRAPHY

The Sūtra and Its Commentaries

Saṃdhinirmocana-(mahāyāna-)sūtra (*'Phags pa dgongs pa nges pa 'grel pa (theg pa chen po'i) mdo*).

Editions used in this study: (1) Stog Palace edition (in *The Tog Palace Edition of the Tibetan Kanjur*. Leh: Smanrtsis Shesrig Dpemzod, 1975-1978, vol. 63, pp. 1-160); (2) a photocopy of the Them spangs ma edition brought to Japan by Ekai Kawaguchi, now kept in the Tōyō Bunko Library in Tokyo; (3) Sde dge edition: Delhi Karmapae Choedhey, vol. *mdo sde ca*; Tohoku #106; (4) Peking edition: Tokyo: Tibetan Tripiṭaka Research Institute, Suzuki Research Foundation, vol. 29, #774, 1958; (5) Lhasa edition: microfische distributed by the Institute for Advanced Studies of World Religions, vol. *mdo nga*; (6) Snar thang edition: microfische distributed by the Institute for Advanced Studies of World Religions, vol. 51; (7) Co ne edition: microfilm copy obtained from the Library of Congress in Washington, D.C., Kanjur vol. 5; (8) the *Viniścaya-saṃgrahaṇī* (Peking #5539, vol. 110, p. 233 - vol. 111, p. 121; Tohoku Catalogue #4038, *sems tsam* 8-9); (9) Stein Tib. 194 (a manuscript from Tun-huang containing most of the seventh chapter in the old translation style); (10) Stein Tib. 683 (another manuscript from Tun-huang in the old translation style that contains a portion of the seventh chapter); (11) the Chinese translation of Hsüan-tsang, entitled *Chieh shen mi ching*, 解深密經.

Canonical Commentaries

Asaṅga (Thogs med). *Ārya-saṃdhinirmocana-bhāṣya* (*'Phags pa dgongs pa nges par 'grel pa'i rnam par bshad pa*): (1) Delhi: Delhi Karmapae Choedhey, Gyalwae Sungrab Partun Khang, 1985, Sde dge vol. *ti* (118); Tohoku #3981; (b) Peking #5481, vol. 104, pp. 1-7.

Byang chub rdzu 'phrul. *Ārya-saṃdhinirmocana-sūtrasya-vyākhyāna* (*'Phags pa dgongs 'grel nges par 'grel pa'i mdo'i rnam par bshad pa*): (a) Delhi: Delhi Karmapae Choedhey, 1985, vol. *cho* (205); Tohoku #4358; (b) Peking #5845, vol. 144, p. 191 - vol. 145, p. 89.

Jñānagarbha (Ye shes snying po). *Ārya-saṃdhinirmocana-sūtre-ārya-maitreya-kevala-parivarta-bhāṣya* (*'Phags pa dgongs pa nges par 'grel pa'i mdo las 'phags pa byams pa'i le'u nyi tshe'i bshad pa*): (a) Peking #5535, vol. 109, pp. 196-211; (b) Tohoku #4033, Ōtani University Press, *sems tsam* vol. 2 (*bi*).

Wonch'uk (Tibetan: Wen tshigs; Chinese: Yüan-ts'e). *Ārya-gambhīra-saṃdhinirmocana-sūtra-ṭīkā* (*'Phags pa dgongs pa zab mo nges par 'grel pa'i mdo'i rgya cher 'grel pa*): (a) Delhi: Delhi Karmapae Choedhey, Gyalwae Sungrab Partun Khang, 1985, *mdo 'grel*, vol. *ti* [118]; Tohoku #4016; (b) Peking #5517, vol. 106, pp. 1-345.

Works by Indian Authors

Asaṅga. *Abhidharmasamuccaya* (*Chos mngon pa kun las btus pa*): (1) Peking #5550, vol. 112, pp. 236-272; (2) Tohoku #4049, *sems tsam* 12; (3) ed. Pradhan, Prahlad. *Abhidharmasamuccaya of Asaṅga*. Santiniketan: Viśva-Bhāratī, 1950; (4) ed. Tatia, Nathmal. *Abhidharmasamuccaya-bhāṣyam*. Patna: K.P. Jayaswal Research Institute, 1976 (Tibetan Sanskrit Works Series #17); (5) tr. Rahula, Walpola. *Le Compendium de la Super-Doctrine (Abhidharmasamuccaya) d'Asaṅga*. Paris: l'École d'Extrème-Orient, 1971; reprint 1980.

___. *Bodhisattvabhūmi* (*Byang chub sems pa'i sa*): (1) ed. Wogihara, Unrai. *Bodhisattvabhūmi*. Leipzig: 1908 & Tokyo: Seigo Kenkyūkai, 1936 (Romanized Sanskrit text; 2 vols.).

___. *Mahāyānasaṃgraha* (*Theg pa chen po bsdus ba*): (1) Peking #5549, vol. 112, pp. 215-236; (2) Tohoku #4048, *sems tsam* 12; (3) tr. Lamotte, Étienne. *La Somme du Grand Véhicule d'Asaṅga (Mahāyānasaṃgraha)*, Louvain: Université de Louvain, 1938.

___. *Śrāvakabhūmi* (*Nyan thos kyi sa*): (1) *Yogācārabhūmau Śrāvakabhūmi*, Peking #5537, vol. 110, pp. 35-130; (2) Tohoku #4036, *sems tsam* vol. 6; (3) Shukla, Karunesha. *Śrāvakabhūmi of Ācārya Asaṅga*. Patna: K.P. Jayaswal Research Institute (Tibetan Sanskrit Works Series, #16), 1973.

___. *Viniścayasaṃgrahaṇī* (*Rnam par gtan la dbab pa bsdu ba*; also known as *Nirṇayasaṃgraha*): (1) Peking #5539, vol. 110, p. 233 - vol. 111, p. 121; (2) Tohoku #4038, *sems tsam* 8-9.

Jinaputra (Rgyal ba'i sras). *Abhidharmasamuccaya-bhāṣya* (*Chos mngon pa kun las btus pa'i bshad pa*): (1) Peking #5554, vol. 113, pp. 83-141; (2) Tohoku #4053, *sems tsam* 13.

Sthiramati (Blo gros brtan pa). *Madhyāntavibhāgaṭīkā* (*Dbus dang mtha' rnam par 'byed pa'i 'grel pa*): (1) Peking #5534, vol. 109, pp. 136-196; (2) Tohoku #4032, *sems tsam* vol. 2; (3) ed. Yamaguchi, Susumu. *Madhyānta-vibhaṅga*. Nagoya: Hajinkaku, 1934 and 1939; reprint, Tokyo: Suzuki Research Foundation, 1966.

Vasubandhu (Dbyig gnyen). *Madhyāntavibhāga-bhāṣya* (*Dbus cing 'brel bar 'byung ba dang po dang rnam par dbye pa bshad pa*): (1) Peking #5528, vol. 112, pp. 121-33; (2) Tohoku #4027, *sems tsam* vol. 2; (3) ed. Nagao, Gadjin. *Madhyānta-vibhāga-bhāṣya*. Tokyo: Suzuki Research Foundation, 1964.

___. *Mahāyānasaṃgraha-bhāṣya* (*Theg pa chen po bsdus pa'i 'grel pa*): (1) Peking #5551, vol. 112, pp. 272-307; (2) Tohoku #4050, *sems tsam* 12.

___. *Triṃśikā-kārikā* (*Sum cu pa'i tshig le'ur byas pa*): (1) Peking #5556, vol. 113, pp. 231-33; (2) Tohoku #4055, *sems tsam* 14.

___. *Trisvabhāvanirdeśa* (*Rang bzhin gsum nges par bstan pa*): (1) Peking #5559, vol. 113, pp. 236-237; (2) Tohoku #4058, *sems tsam* 14; (3) ed. and English tr. Anacker, Stefan. *Seven Works of Vasubandhu*. Delhi: Motilal Banarsidass, 1984, pp. 464-466 and 287-298.

___. *Vādavidhi*: (1) ed. Frauwallner, Erich. "Vasubandhu's *Vādavidhi*". *WZKSOA*, #1, 1957, pp. 104-134; (2) tr. Anacker, Stefan. *Vasubandhu: Three Aspects* (Ph.D. dissertation, University of Wisconsin, 1969), pp. 87-98.

___. *Viṃśatikā-kārikā* and *Viṃśatikā-vṛtti* (*Nyi shu pa'i tshig le'ur byas pa* and *Nyi shu pa'i 'grel pa*): (1) Peking #5557, vol. 113, pp. 233-34; (2) Tohoku #4056, *sems tsam* 14; (3) ed. and English tr. Anacker, Stefan. *Seven Works of Vasubandhu*. Delhi: Motilal Banarsidass, 1984, pp. 413-422 and 157-180.

Works by Tibetan Authors

Gung thang dkon mchog bstan pa'i sgron me (1762-1823). *Bstan bcos legs bshad snying po las sems tsam skor gyi mchan 'grel rtsom 'phro rnam rig gzhung brgya'i snang ba*: (1) *Collected Works*. New Delhi: Ngawang Gelek Demo, 1975, vol. 1, pp. 725-876.

___. *Drang nges rnam 'byed kyi dka' 'grel rtsom 'phro legs bshad snying po'i yang snying*: (1) Sarnath: Guru Deva, 1965.

Tāranātha. (Tā ra nā tha, born 1575). *Dpal gyi byung gnas dam pa'i chos rin po che 'phags pa'i yul du ji ltar dar ba'i tshul gsal bar ston pa dgos 'dod kun 'byung*, also called *Rgya gar chos 'byung*: (1) ed. Schiefner, Anton. *Tāranātha's Rgya gar chos 'byung* (Tibetan text with German tr.). St. Petersburg, 1868; (2) tr. Lama Chimpa and Alaka Chattopadhyaya. *History of Buddhism*. Simla: Indian Institute of Advanced Studies, 1970; reprint Calcutta: K.P. Bagchi and Co., 1980.

Blo bzang phun tshogs, Ser shul dge bshes. *Drang nges rnam 'byed kyi zin bris zab don gsal ba'i sgron me*: (1) Mysore: Sera Byes Monastery, n.d.; Library of Congress #75-906392.

Dbus pa blo gsal (14th century). *Grub pa'i mtha' rnam par bshad pa'i mdzod*: (1) ed. & tr. Mimaki, Katsumi. *Blo gsal grub mtha'*. Kyoto: Zinbun Kogaku Kenkyūshō, 1982.

Tsong kha pa blo bzang grags pa (1357-1419). *Drang ba dang nges pa'i don rnam par phye ba'i bstan bcos legs bshad snying po*: (1) Sarnath: Pleasure of Elegant Sayings Printing Press, 1979.

___. *Yid dang kun gzhi'i dka' gnas rgya cher 'grel pa legs par bshad pa'i rgya mtsho*: (1) Sarnath: Gelugpa Students' Welfare Committee, Central Institute of Higher Tibetan Studies, 1984.

Rabten, Geshe (Tre hor dge bshes rta mgrin rab brtan, 20th century). *Drang nges rnam 'byed legs bshad snying po dka' gnad rnams mchan bur bkod pa gzur gnas blo dga' ston*: (1) Delhi: Lhun-grub-chos-grags, 1978; LC #78-904230.

Bsod nams grags pa, Paṇ chen (1478-1554). *Legs bshad snying po'i dka' gnad dogs gcod*: (1) Indian blockprint, n.d.

Works on Buddhism by Contemporary Scholars

Anacker, Stefan. *Seven Works of Vasubandhu.* Delhi: Motilal Banarsidass, 1984.

____. *Vasubandhu: Three Aspects* (Ph.D. dissertation, University of Wisconsin). Ann Arbor: University Microfilms, 1969.

Bond, George. *The Word of the Buddha.* Columbo: M.D. Gunasena, 1982.

Davidson, Ronald Mark. *Buddhist Systems of Transformation* (Ph.D. dissertation, University of California, Berkeley, 1986.

de la Vallée Poussin, Louis. "Notes Bouddhiques: XX. Les Trois 'Caractères' et les trois 'Absences de Nature Propre' dans le *Saṃdhinirmocana*, Chapitres VI et VII". *BCLS*, 5th series, 1934-35, pp. 284-303.

____. "Le Petit Traité de Vasubandhu-Nāgārjuna sur les trois natures" (*Trisvabhāvanirdeśa*). *MCB*, #2, 1933, pp. 147-161.

____. "Vasubandhu l'Ancien". *BCLS*, #16, 1930, pp. 15-39.

____. *Vijñāptimātratāsiddhi: La Siddhi de Hiuan-tsang traduité et annoté*. Paris: Paul Geuthner, 1928 (2 vols.).

Demiéville, Paul. "Le Chapitre de la *Bodhisattvabhūmi* sur la Perfection du Dhyāna". *Rocznik Orientalistyczny*, #21, 1957, pp. 109-128; *Choix d'Études Bouddhiques*, 1929-1970. Leiden: E.J. Brill, 1973, pp. 300-319.

____. "Review of Étienne Lamotte, *Saṃdhinirmocana-sūtra*". *JA*, #228, 1936, pp. 645-656.

____. "*Saṃdhinirmocanasūtra*". *Bulletin de l'École Française des Études Orientales*, #24.1, p. 53.

Eckel, Malcolm. *Jñānagarbha's Commentary on the Distinction Between the Two Truths*. Albany: SUNY Press, 1987.

Frauwallner, Erich. *On the Date of the Buddhist Master of the Law Vasubandhu.* Rome: IsMeo (Serie Orientale Roma), 1951.

____. "Landmarks in the History of Indian Logic". *WZKSOA*, #5, 1961, pp. 129-132.

Fukaura, Masafumi. *Kokuyaku Issaikyō*, Kyōshū-bū, vol. 3 (Japanese translation of Hsüan-tsang's Chinese version of the *Saṃdhinirmocana-sūtra*).

Gómez, Luis O. "Exegesis and Hermeneutics". in *Encyclopedia of Religion*, ed. Mircea Eliade. New York: Macmillan, 1987.

Guenther, Herbert. *Philosophy and Psychology of the Abhidharma*. Delhi: Motilal Banarsidass, 1978.

Hakamaya, Noriaki. "A Consideration of the *Byams shus kyi le'u*, from the historical point of view". *IBK*, #14.1, Dec. 1975, pp. 20-30.

____. "Mirokushōmonshō wayaku" (Japanese translation of the Maitreya chapter (ch. 8) of the *Saṃdhinirmocana-sūtra*). *KDBR*, #6, 1975, pp. 210-190.

___. "The Old and New Translations of the *Saṃdhinirmocana-sūtra*: Some Notes on the History of the Early Tibetan Translations". *KDBK*, #42, 1984, pp. 1-17.

Harada, Satoru. "Analysis of the Tun-huang Manuscripts of the sGom rim dang po". *Report of the Japanese Association for Tibetan Studies*, #28, 1982, pp. 4-8.

Harris, Ian Charles. *The Continuity of Madhyamaka and Yogācāra in Indian Mahāyāna Buddhism*. Leiden: E.J. Brill, 1991.

Honda, Megumu and Rahder, Johannes. *Annotated Translation of the Daśabhūmika-sūtra*. New Delhi: International Academy of Indian Culture, 1968 (Śata-piṭaka Series, #74).

Hopkins, Jeffrey. *Meditation on Emptiness*. London: Wisdom Publications, 1983.

Hotori, Rishō. *Saṃdhinirmocana-sūtra* ch. I and *Bodhisattvabhūmi*. *Shūkyō Kenkyū*, #56.4, 1983, pp. 633ff.

Iida, Shotaro. *The Great Silla Monks of Korea*. Soeul: Yemun Ch'ulp'ansa, 1988.

___. "The Three Stūpas of Ch'ang An". *Papers of the First International Conference on Korean Studies*. Soeul: The Academy of Korean Studies, 1980, pp. 484-497.

___. "Who Can Best *Re-turn* the Dharma-cakra: A Controversy Between Wonch'uk (623-696) and K'uei-chi (632-682)". *IBK*, #34.2, 1986, pp. 948-951.

Inaba, Shōju. *Enjiki Gejinmikkyōsho Sanitsububan no kanbunyaku*. Kyoto: Hōzōkan, 1949.

___. "Enjiki *Gejinmikkyōsho* no Sanitsuban no Kanbunyaku". *Ōtani Gakuhō*, #24, 1971.

___. "On Chos-grub's Translation of the *Chieh-shen-mi-ching-shu*". Kawamura, Leslie and Scott, Keith, eds. *Buddhist Thought and Asian Civilization* (Festschrift H.V. Guenther). Emeryville, CA: Dharma Press, 1977, pp. 105-113.

___. *Restoration of Yüan-tse's Chieh-shen-mi-ching-shu Through Its Tibetan Counterpart*. Kyoto: Hierakuji, 1972.

___. "Saimyōji Enjikikei Yuishikigaku no ruden" (The Transmission of the Vijñānavādin Wonch'uk of Hsi-ming Temple). Nogami, Shunjō, ed. *Ōtani Daigaku shozō Tonkō Koshakyō* (Ancient Copies of Buddhist Scriptures Discovered in the Tun-Huang Caves, Now Preserved in Ōtani University), Seminar of Oriental Studies in Ōtani University, vol. II. Kyoto: 1972, pp. 113-119 (First vol. 1965).

___. *Yuishiki Gakujutsu-go Sakuin* (Index of Technical Terms of the Vijñaptimātratā School). Kyoto: Ōtani University, 1952.

Itō, Hidenori. "A Study on 'Miyi' in the *Saṃdhinirmocana-sūtra* Translated into Chinese by Xuán-zàng". *IBK*, #22.1, 1973, pp. 134-35.

___. "Xuán-zàng's and Bodhiruchi's Views on 'Pratītyasamutpāda' in the *Saṃdhinirmocana-sūtra*" (in Japanese). *IBK*, #23.1, 1974, pp. 398-401.

Jaini, Padmanabh S. "On the theory of the two Vasubandhus". *BSOAS*, #21, 1958, pp. 48-53; summarized in *Proceedings of the International Congress of Orientalists*, #24, Munich, 1957, vol. 1, pp. 552-554.

Kaplan, Stephen. "A Holographic Alternative to a Traditional Yogācāra Simile". *EB*, #23, 1990, pp. 56-78.

Kawasaki, Shinjo. "Analysis of Yoga in the *Saṃdhinirmocana-sūtra*". *Buzan Gakuhō*, #21, 1976, pp. 170-156.

Keenan, John. "Buddhist Yogācāra Philosophy as Ancilla Theologiæ". *Japanese Religions*, #15.5, 1988.

Kiyota, Minoru, ed. *Mahāyāna Buddhist Meditation*. Honolulu: University of Hawaii Press, 1978.

Lalou, Marcelle. *Inventaire des Manuscrits Tibétains de Touen-houang conservés à la Bibliotèque Nationale*, I. Paris: 1939.

Lamotte, Étienne. "L'ālayavijñāna (Le Réceptacle) dans le *Mahāyānasaṃgraha*". *MCB*, #3, 1934-35, pp. 169-255.

___. "La Critique d'Interpretation dans le Bouddhisme". *Annuaire de l'Institut de Philologie et d'Histoire Orientales et Slaves*. Bruxelles: Université Libre de Bruxelles, IX, 1949, pp. 341-361; English tr. Boin-Webb, Sara. "The Assessment of Textual Interpretation in Buddhism". in Lopez, Donald S., ed. *Buddhist Hermeneutics*. Honolulu: University of Hawaii Press, 1988, pp. 11-27.

___. *Histoire du Bouddhisme Indien*. Louvain: Université de Louvain, 1958 (English tr. Webb-Boin, Sara. *History of Indian Buddhism*. Louvain-la-Neuve: Université Catholique de Louvain, 1988).

___. *Saṃdhinirmocana-sūtra*. Louvain and Paris: Université de Louvain & Adrien Maisonneuve, 1935.

___. *La Somme du Grand Véhicule d'Asaṅga (Mahāyānasaṃgraha)*. Louvain: Université de Louvain, 1973.

___. "Les Trois Caractères et les Trois Absences de Nature-propre dans le *Saṃdhinirmocana-sūtra*, Chapitre 6". *BCLS*, 1935, pp. 289-303.

Lancaster, Lewis "The Oldest Mahāyāna Sūtra". *EB*, vol. 8 #1, 1975, pp. 30-41.

___. *Prajñāpāramitā and Related Systems*. Berkeley: Berkeley Buddhist Studies Series, 1977.

Lin, Chen-kuo. *The Saṃdhinirmocana-sūtra: A Liberative Hermeneutic*. Ph.D. dissertation, Temple University, 1991.

Lipman, Kennard. "Nītārtha, Neyārtha, and Tathāgatagarbha in Tibet". *JIP* #8, 1980.

Lopez, Donald S., ed. *Buddhist Hermeneutics*. Honolulu: University of Hawaii Press, 1988.

MacQueen, Graeme. "Inspired Speech in Early Mahāyāna Buddhism". *Religion* #11, 1981, pp. 303-19 and #12, 1982, pp. 49-65.

Maraldo, John C. "Hermeneutics and Historicity in the Study of Buddhism". *EB* #19.1, 1986.

Mejor, Marek. "A Contribution to the Biography of Vasubandhu from Tibetan Sources". *TBS*, #2, 1984, pp. 159-174.

Murti, T.R.V. *The Central Philosophy of Buddhism*. London: 1955.

Nagao, Gadjin. "The Buddhist World-View as Elucidated in the Three-Nature Theory and its Similes". *EB*, #16, 1983, pp. 1-18.

___. "The Logic of Convertibility". In *Mādhyamika and Yogācāra*. Albany: SUNY Press, 1991.

___. *Madhyamaka and Yogācāra* (English translation of *Chūkan to Yuishiki*). tr. Kawamura, Leslie S. Albany: SUNY Press, 1989.

___. *Madhyānta-vibhāga-bhāṣya*. Tokyo: Suzuki Research Foundation, 1964.

___. "Vasubandhu" (in Mircea Eliade, ed., *Encyclopedia of Religions*; New York: Macmillan, 1987), pp. 191ff.

___. "What Remains in Śūnyatā: A Yogācāra Interpretation of Emptiness". Kiyota, Minoru, ed. *Mahāyāna Buddhist Meditation*. Honolulu: University of Hawaii Press, 1978, pp. 66-82.

Nagasawa, Jitsudō. "On the First Chapter, '*Gambhīrārtha-saṃdhinirmocana-parivarta*', of the *Saṃdhinirmocana-sūtra*". *IBK*, #6.1, 1958, pp. 209-212.

___. "A Problem Concerning the Mirror Simile Found in the *Saṃdhinirmocana-sūtra*". *IBK*, #7.2, 1959, pp. 647-50.

Nagayama, Shūichi. *Study of the Saṃdhinirmocana-sūtra*. Kyoto: Nagata Bushōdō, 1975.

Nakamura, Hajime. *Indian Buddhism: A Survey with Bibliographical Notes*. Hirakata: Kufs Publications, 1980.

Nishioka, Soshu. "*Putun bukkyōshi*". in *Tōkyō Daigaku Bungakubu Bunka Koryū Kenkyū shisetsu Kenkyū Kiyō* #4 (1980), pp. 61-92; #5 (1981), pp. 43-94; #6 (1983), pp. 47-201.

Nozawa, Jōshō. *Daijō-Bukkyō Yuga-gyō no kenkyū* (*Studies in the Yogācāra School of Mahāyāna Buddhism*). Kyoto: Hōzōkan, 1957.

Ohasaki, Akiko. "On the Citta, Manas, and Vijñāna in the *Saṃdhinirmocana-sūtra*". *IBK*, #24.1, 1975, pp. 200-203 (in Japanese).

Péri, Nöel. "À Propos de la date de Vasubandhu". *BEFEO*, #11, 1911, pp. 339-390.

Powers, John. "Accidental Immortality: How Wonch'uk Became the Author of the *Great Chinese Commentary*", *JIABS* #15.1, 1992, pp. 95-103.

___. "The Tibetan Translations of the *Saṃdhinirmocana-sūtra* and *Bka' 'gyur* Research". *Central Asiatic Journal*, 1993.

___. *The Yogācāra School of Buddhism: A Bibliography*. Metuchen, NJ: Scarecrow Press, 1991.

Pradhan, Prahlad. *Abhidharmakośa*. Patna: K.P. Jayaswal Research Institute, 1967; revised second ed. Patna: 1975.

___. *Abhidharmasamuccaya of Asaṅga*. Santiniketan: Viśva-Bhāratī Studies, #12, 1950.

Rahder, Johannes. "*Daśabhūmikasūtra*". *Le Muséon*, #39, 1926, pp. 125-252.

___. *Daśabhūmikasūtra et Bodhisattvabhūmi: Chapitres Vihāra et Bhūmi*. Paris: Paul Geuthner, 1926.

___. "*Daśabhūmika-sūtra*, Seventh Stage—Sanskrit Text Including Translation of Vasubandhu's Commentary". *Acta Orientalia*, #4, 1925, pp. 214-256.

Rahula, Walpola. "Ālayavijñāna". *Mahabodhi*, #72, 1964, pp. 130-133.

___. "Asaṅga". *Encyclopedia of Buddhism*. ed. Malalasekhara, G.P. Columbo: 1961, #2.1, 1966, pp. 133-146.

___. *Le Compendium de la Super-Doctrine d'Asaṅga (Abhidharma-samuccaya)*. Paris: Publications de l'École Française d'Extrème-Orient, LXXVIII, 1971; reprint 1980.

Ruegg, David S. "Allusiveness and obliqueness in Buddhist texts". Caillat, Collette, ed. *Dialectes dans les Littératures Indo-Aryennes*. Paris: Institut de Civilisation Indienne, 1989.

___. "An Indian Source for the Tibetan Hermeneutical Term *Dgoṅs Gźi* 'Intentional Ground'". *JIP*, #16, 1988, pp. 1-4.

___. "On the Knowability and Expressibility of Absolute Reality in Buddhism". *IBK*, #20.1, 1971, pp. 1-7.

___. "Purport, Implicature, and Presupposition: Sanskrit *Abhiprāya* and Tibetan *Dgoṅs pa/Dgons gźi* as Hermeneutical Concepts". *JIP*, #13, 1985, pp. 309-325.

___. *La Théorie du Tathāgatagarbha et du Gotra*. Paris: Publications de l'École Française d'Extrème-Orient, LXX, 1969.

Ryōtai, Hatani. "Yuishiki-shū no lha" (A Different Branch of Vijñānavāda; discusses Wonch'uk's commentary on the *Saṃdhinirmocana-sūtra*). *Shūkyō Kenkyū*, #1.1, 1916, pp. 65-84; #3, pp. 505-547; #4, pp. 705-744.

Schiefner, Anton. *Tāranātha's Rgya gar chos 'byung*. St. Petersburg, 1868.

Schmithausen, Lambert. *Ālayavijñāna*. Tokyo: The International Institute for Buddhist Studies, 1987.

___. "Der Nirvāṇa-Abschnitt in der *Viniścayasaṃgrahaṇī* der *Yogācārabhūmiḥ*". Wien: Veröffentlichungen der Komission für Sprachen und Kulturen Süd- und Ostasiens, Heft 8, 1969.

___. "On the Problem of the Relation of Spiritual Practice and Philosophical Theory in Buddhism". *German Scholars on India*, vol. 2. Bombay: Nachiketa Publications, 1976.

___. "On the Vijñaptimātra Passage in *Saṃdhinirmocana-sūtra* VIII.7". *Acta Indologica*, vol. VI, 1984, pp. 433-455.

Shukla, Karunesha. "Asaṅga in Buddhist Literature". *Journal of the Ganganatha Jha Research Institute*, #27.1-2, 1971, pp. 17-22.

___. *Śrāvakabhūmi of Ācārya Asaṅga*. Patna: K.P. Jayaswal Research Institute, 1973 (Tibetan Sanskrit Works Series, #14).

Sopa, Geshe Lhundup and Hopkins, Jeffrey. *Practice and Theory of Tibetan Buddhism*. New York: Grove Press, 1976.

Sponberg, Alan. "Dynamic Liberation in Yogācāra Buddhism". *JIABS*, #2.1, 1979, pp. 44-64.

___. "The Trisvabhāva Doctrine in India and China". *Bukkyō Bunka Kenkyū-jo Kiyō*, #21, 1982, pp. 97-119.

Steinkellner, Ernst. "Remarks on Tantristic Hermeneutics". L. Ligetti, ed. *Proceedings of the 1976 Csoma de Körös Symposium*. Budapest, 1978 (Biblioteca Orientalia Hungarica #23), pp. 445-458.

___. "Who Is Byaṅ chub rdzu 'phrul?". *Berliner Indologische Studien*, 1989, pp. 229-51.

Takakusu, Junjiro. "The Date of Vasubandhu". *Indian Studies in Honor of Charles Lanman*. Cambridge, MA: 1929, pp. 78-83.

___. "The Life of Vasu-bandhu by Paramārtha". *T'oung Pao*, ser. II, #5, pp. 269-296; reprint Leiden: E.J. Brill, 1904.

___. *Records of the Buddhist Religion by I-tsing*. Oxford: Clarendon Press, 1896.

___. "A Study of Paramārtha's Life of Vasubandhu and the Date of Vasubandhu". *JRAS*, 1905, pp. 33-53.

Takasaki, Jikidō. "The Date of Vasubandhu the Great Buddhist Philosopher". *Indian Studies in Honor of Charles Lanman*. Cambridge, MA: 1929, pp. 79-88.

Takeuchi, Shōkō. "Phenomena and Reality in Vijñaptimātratā Thought". Kawamura, Leslie S. and Scott, Keith, eds. *Buddhist Thought and Asian Civilization*. Emeryville, CA: Dharma Publishing, 1977.

Tatia, Nathmal. *Abhidharmasamuccaya-bhāṣyam*. Patna: K.P. Jayaswal Research Institute, 1976 (Tibetan Sanskrit Works Series, #17).

Thurman, Robert. "Buddhist Hermeneutics". *JAAR*, #46.1, 1978.

Tola, Fernando, and Dragonetti, Carmen. "The *Trisvabhāva-kārikā* of Vasubandhu". *JIP*, #11, 1983, pp. 225-266.

Tucci, Giuseppe. "Idealistic School of Buddhism". *Dacca University Bulletin*, #12, 1926, pp. 1-16.

____. *Pre-Dignāga Buddhist Texts on Logic From Chinese Sources*. Baroda: Gaekwad Oriental Series, #49, 1929.

____. *On Some Aspects of the Doctrines of Maitreyanātha and Asaṅga*. Calcutta, 1930.

____. "*Vādavidhi*". *IHQ*, #4, 1928, pp. 630-636; reprint in *Opera Minore*, pp. 163-168.

Ueda, Yoshifumi. "Two Main Streams of Thought in Yogācāra Philosophy". *PEW*, #17, 1967, pp. 155-165.

____. "Two Views on Vijñāna—The View that Vijñāna Develops and the View that Vijñāna Knows". *Yūki kyōju shōju kinen bukkyō shisōshi ronshū* (*Essays on the History of Buddhist Thought Presented to Professor Reimon Yūki*). Tokyo: Daizō Shuppan, 1964, pp. 211-222.

Ueyama, Daishun. "Daibankoku Daitoku Sanzōhosshi Shamon Hōjō no Kenkyū". *Tōhō Gakuhō*, #38, pp. 133-198; and #39, 1968, pp. 119-222.

____. "On the Tibetan Translation of the *Saṃdhinirmocana-sūtra*". *Bukkyō Bunken no Kenkyū*. Kyoto: 1968, pp. 191-209.

____. "A Study of the Tibetan Translations of the *Saṃdhinirmocana-sūtra*". *Zenbunka Kenkyosho Kiyō*, #8, 1976, pp. 33-103.

Ui, Hakuju, et al. *A Complete Catalogue of the Tibetan Buddhist Canon*. Tokyo, 1934.

Warder, A.K. *Indian Buddhism*. Delhi: Motilal Banarsidass, 1970.

Wayman, Alex. *Analysis of the Śrāvakabhūmi Manuscript*. Berkeley: University of California Publications in Classical Philology (#7), 1961.

____. "Nescience and Insight According to Asaṅga's *Yogācārabhūmi*". Balasooriya, S., ed. *Festschrift for Walpola Rahula*, 1980, pp. 251-266.

____. "The Rules of Debate According to Asaṅga". *JAOS*, #78, Jan.-March, 1958.

____. "Yogācāra and the Buddhist Logicians". *JIABS*, #2.1, 1979, pp. 65-78.

Wei tat. *Ch'eng wei shih lun*. Hong Kong: Dai Nippon Printing Co., 1973.

Weinstein, Stanley. "The Ālayavijñāna in Early Yogācāra Buddhism: A Comparison of its Meaning in the *Saṃdhinirmocana-sūtra* and the *Vijñaptimātratāsiddhi* of Dharmapāla". *Kokusai Tōhō Gakusha Kaigikiyō*, #3, 1959, pp. 46-58.

___. "The Concept of Ālaya-vijñāna in pre-T'ang Chinese Buddhism". *Yūki kyōju shōju kinen bukkyō shisōshi ronshū*, (*Essays on the History of Buddhist Thought Presented to Professor Reimon Yūki*). Tokyo: Daizō Shuppan, 1964, pp. 38-51.

Willis, Janice Dean. *On Knowing Reality*. New York: Columbia University Press, 1979; reprint Delhi: Motilal Banarsidass, 1982.

Wilson, Joe B. *The Meaning of Mind in the Mahāyāna Buddhist Philosophy of Mind Only* (Ph.D. dissertation, University of Virginia). Ann Arbor: University Microfilms, 1984.

Wogihara, Unrai. *Bodhisattvabhūmi*. Leipzig, 1908; and Tokyo: Seigo Kenkyūkai, 1936.

Wood, Thomas E. *Mind Only: A Philosophical and Doctrinal Analysis of the Vijñānavāda*. Honolulu: University of Hawaii Press, 1991.

Yamaguchi, Susumu. *Madhyāntavibhāgaṭīkā*. Nagoya: Librairie Hajinkaku, 1934 (3 vols.); reprint Tokyo: Suzuki Research Foundation, 1966.

Yoshimura, Shyūki. *Comparative Study of the Chinese and Tibetan Texts of the Yoga-vibhāga-parivarta in the Saṃdhinirmocana* (in Japanese). Kyoto: 1959.

Works on Western Philosophy and Theology

Barthes, Roland. "From Work to Text". *Textual Strategies: Perspectives in Post-Structuralist Criticism*. Harari, J.V., ed. Ithaca: Cornell University Press, 1979.

Bernstein, Richard J. *Beyond Objectivism and Relativism: Science, Hermeneutics, and Praxis*. Philadelphia: University of Pennsylvania Press, 1983.

Bleicher, Josef. *Contemporary Hermeneutics*. London: Routledge & Kegan Paul, 1980.

Booth, Wayne C. *Critical Understanding*. Chicago: University of Chicago Press, 1979.

Carroll, Robert P. *When Prophecy Failed*. New York: Seabury, 1979.

Coats, George W., ed. *Canon and Authority*. Philadelphia: Fortress Press, 1971.

Dreyfus, Hubert L. and Rabinow, Paul. *Michel Foucault: Beyond Structuralism and Hermeneutics*. Chicago: University of Chicago Press, 1982.

Fish, Stanley. *Is There a Text in This Class?* Cambridge, MA: Harvard University Press, 1980.

Foucault, Michel. *The History of Sexuality, Volume I: An Introduction*. tr. Hurley, Robert. New York: Random House, 1980.

____. *The Order of Things: An Archeology of the Human Sciences*. tr. Sheridan-Smith, Alan. New York: Random House, 1973.

Frei, Hans. *The Eclipse of Biblical Narrative*. New Haven: Yale University Press, 1974.

Funk, Robert W. *Language, Hermeneutics, and the Word of God*. New York: Harper & Row, 1966.

Gadamer, Hans-Georg. *Philosophical Hermeneutics*. tr. David E. Linge. Berkeley: University of California Press, 1976.

____. *Truth and Method*. tr. G. Barden and J. Cumming. New York: Seabury Press, 1975.

Geertz, Clifford. "Religion as a Cultural System". D. Cutler, ed. *The Religious Situation*. Boston: Beacon Press, 1968, pp. 639-88.

Goldingay, John. *Approaches to Old Testament Interpretation*. Downers Grove, IL: Inter-Varsity Press, 1990.

Heidegger, Martin. *Being and Time*. tr. John Macquarrie and Edward Robinson. New York: Harper & Row, 1962.

____. *Poetry, Language, Thought*. tr. Hofstader, A. New York: Harper & Row, 1971.

Hirsch, E.D. *The Aims of Interpretation*. Chicago: University of Chicago Press, 1976.

____. *Validity in Interpretation*. New Haven: Yale University Press, 1967.

Hollinger, Robert, ed. *Hermeneutics and Praxis*. Notre Dame: University of Notre Dame Press, 1985.

Kintsch, Walter, ed. *Method and Tactics in Cognitive Science*. New Jersey: Lawrence Erlbaum Associates, 1984.

Lindbeck, George. *The Nature of Doctrine*. Philadelphia: Westminster Press, 1984.

Morgan, Robert. *Biblical Interpretation*. Oxford, 1988.

Palmer, Richard E. *Hermeneutics*. Evanston: Northwestern University Press, 1969.

Rabinow, Paul, ed. *The Foucault Reader*. New York: Pantheon, 1984.

Ricoeur, Paul. *The Conflict of Interpretations*. Ihde, Don, ed. Evanston: Northwestern University Press, 1974.

____. *Essays on Biblical Interpretation*. Mudge, L.S., ed. Philadelphia: Fortress Press, 1980.

____. *Interpretation Theory*. Fort Worth: Texas Christian University Press, 1976.

____. "The Metaphorical Process as Cognition, Imagination, and Feeling". *Critical Inquiry*, #5.1, 1978, pp. 143-59.

Skorupski, John. *Symbol and Theory*. Cambridge: Cambridge University Press, 1976.

Stout, Jeffrey. *The Flight from Authority*. Notre Dame: University of Notre Dame Press, 1981.

Taylor, Mark C. *Deconstructing Theology*. Chico, CA: Scholars Press, 1982.

____. *Erring: A Postmodern A/theology*. Chicago: University of Chicago Press, 1984.

Troeltsch, Ernst. "What Does 'Essence of Christianity' Mean?". Morgan, Robert, ed. *Ernst Troeltsch: Writings on Theology and Religion*. Atlanta: John Knox, 1977.

Westermann, Claus. *Essays on Old Testament Hermeneutics*. Richmond, VA: John Knox Press, 1963.

Wicklund Robert A. and Brehm, Jack W. *Perspectives on Cognitive Dissonance*. New Jersey: Lawrence Erlbaum Associates, 1976.

Williams, Michael. *Groundless Belief*. New Haven: Yale University Press, 1977.

INDEX

अनुवादक

हरिवंशराय बच्चन

मोतीलाल बनारसीदास